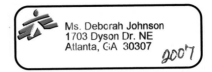
W9-BAA-705

FREEDOM

Georgia's ANTISLAVERY Heritage
1733–1865

MICHAEL THURMOND

LONGSTREET PRESS

Atlanta

Published by
LONGSTREET PRESS, INC.
2974 Hardman Court
Atlanta, GA 30305

Printed in the United States of America

1st printing 2003

Library of Congress Catalog Card Number: 2003100233

ISBN: 1-56352-687-5

Front cover photograph of Susie King Taylor

Jacket and book design by Burtch Hunter Design LLC

Dedicated to those Georgians who lived,
fought, and died for freedom.

FOREWORD

Over the last few years, controversies have raged in several Southern states around the Confederate flag, a symbol of the rebellion known as the Civil War. In South Carolina and Alabama, people have debated whether this flag should fly over their state capitols. And in Georgia and Mississippi, decisions over whether the Confederate flag should make up a substantial part of the modern-day state flags have dominated political discussions. Why do events that ended more than 137 years ago still grip so tightly the hearts and minds of the modern South with its tall buildings and high-tech companies? This mystery has puzzled authors for years. A popular recent book by Tony Horwitz, *Confederates in the Attic: Dispatches from the Unfinished Civil War*, makes the argument that, in spite of the facts, the romanticized view of Southern history found in *Gone with the Wind* has become the accepted and approved version, and the Confederacy is now an American institution much like baseball and apple pie. Astounding but true.

To this debate Michael Thurmond brings his powerful book *Freedom*, which traces the interrelationship of Georgia's white and black populations from the time of the colony's founding through the end of the Civil War. Although Georgia may be renowned for its red clay, readers will find that the hues that have determined her history are black and white. Thurmond demonstrates that, contrary to the romanticized story of slavery where servants sang in the fields and were content with their condition, Georgia's black slave population was eager to drink of the fountain of emancipation. They were always ready to fight and die for whichever governing power offered them freedom at the time, be it the British, Spanish, Native Americans, or Americans.

To understand the unique nature of Georgia's race relations, Michael Thurmond focuses on the colony's founding and the influence of religion in the early debate over slavery. He points out, for example, that it was an abolitionist opposed to slavery on moral and practical grounds, James Edward Oglethorpe, who founded Georgia. Yet almost from the beginning, agitators began to challenge the ban on slavery Oglethorpe and his supporters imposed. In this struggle, the religion espoused by the foremost evangelist of the day, George Whitefield, was on the side of slavery, in order to "Christianize" a heathen people. But Oglethorpe and John Wesley, who later founded the Methodist church, as well as the Lutheran Salzburgers and Calvinist Scots who settled parts of Georgia, strenuously advocated maintaining the ban and saw slavery for what it was: a debasing institution bereft of any moral foundation. Oglethorpe and his group eventually lost the battle—but how Georgia's (and the nation's) history might have been different if they had prevailed!

The analysis *Freedom* provides is long overdue. It shatters, with carefully documented facts, the long-held myth that black subservience was the desired condition of the subservient. It also comes at an opportune time to help explain why symbols of long ago are still so treasured and controversial today. These symbols hearken back to an era considered by many to represent a "simpler" time, when all were content with their station in life. But Thurmond's book reveals that such an idealized "old South" never existed. The truth is that all of mankind yearns to be free, and African Americans were, and are, no different. *Freedom* proves this yearning is the one constant that has pervaded the interaction of black and white in Georgia.

Roy E. Barnes
Governor of Georgia
September 2002

Contents

FREEDOM

"Not only is Georgia thus the geographical focus of our Negro population, but in many other respects, both now and yesterday, the Negro problems have seemed to be centered in this State."

W.E.B. DuBois
The Souls of Black Folk, 1903

INTRODUCTION

———

During the spring of 1993, I salved the wounds of a failed congressional campaign by rereading several American literary classics. One of my selections was W. E. B. Du Bois's *The Souls of Black Folk*, published in 1903 at the dawn of the twentieth century. The former Atlanta University professor observed that "Not only is Georgia thus the geographical focus of our Negro population, but in many other respects, both now and yesterday, the Negro problems have seemed to be centered in this State." This intriguing statement captured my imagination. What was the historical rationale for Du Bois's bold assertion that Georgia was the epicenter of America's long-festering racial problems? My desire to answer this question became a minor obsession and the catalyst that fueled ten years of research and introspection. Ultimately, the Du Boisian analysis proved to be correct, profound, and even prophetic.

Decades before Dr. Martin Luther King Jr., a native Georgian, gained international prominence as the leader of the modern Civil Rights Movement, generations of enslaved blacks waged a historic struggle to overcome slavery in Georgia. In many ways Georgia's past became America's prologue. The Civil Rights Movement of the 1960s was not an isolated historical event, but the continuation of a protracted struggle that spanned more than twelve generations. More significantly, my research revealed that the origins of black America's fight for freedom and justice are firmly rooted in Georgia's red-clay soil.

Throughout the slavery era, black Georgians broke the shackles of bondage through escape, armed confrontation, organized resistance, and individual acts of defiance. Fugitive Georgia slaves preserved their freedom by helping the Spanish repel British invaders from Florida during the colonial era. The Revolutionary War provided black Georgians with the opportunity to earn their freedom by serving the British as soldiers, spies, guides, orderlies, and laborers. Following the occupation of Cumberland Island by the British during the War of 1812, hundreds of coastal Georgia slaves answered the English call to arms and emancipation. And early in the nineteenth century, fugitive Georgia slaves formed a powerful biracial coalition with Seminole Indians, stymieing American expansion into Florida for three decades.

Yet escape and armed struggle were not the only strategies utilized by black slaves to secure the precious commodity called freedom. So-called "loyal" slaves shed blood by the side of white slave owners when freedom was offered as compensation for military service. Following the completion of their masters' work, some enterprising blacks were allowed to "hire themselves out," eventually earning enough money to purchase freedom for themselves and their loved ones. My research documents the fact that the magnitude and scope of these events are unique to Georgia history.

The publication of this book will give voice and profile to thousands of nameless, faceless black Georgians who lived, fought, and died for freedom. The colony, and later the state, was located at the strategic center of a politically and militarily unstable region. Georgia slaves shrewdly manipulated this international struggle for control of the southeastern section of North America to their advantage. They formed strategic and shifting alliances with the major contestants: England, Spain, the United States, and Native Americans. In addition, several thousand fugitive Georgia slaves escaped to freedom on the lesser-known "Underground Railroad" that ran south—across the international border between Georgia and Spanish-controlled Florida.

Chronicled herein are the deeds of unsung heroes and heroines who helped shape the history of Georgia, the South, and the United States of America. Hopefully, I have liberated these freedom fighters from the caricature of fawning "loyal slaves" and reintroduced them as rational human beings, capable of influencing the ebb and flow of history. This book will help dispel widely disseminated but distorted depictions of Southern slaves stoically, if not happily, bearing the yoke of slavery. It also rejects, in large part, the equally destructive notion that blacks were hapless victims, unwilling and unable to challenge the institution of slavery.

Black Georgia's fight for freedom is presented in the context of what is generally regarded as the "official" history of the state. Therefore, important historical events have been retold, with emphasis placed on black Georgians and their contributions to the state's growth and development. It is important to note that this black "emphasis" did not equal white "exclusion." The task of weaving a cohesive historical tapestry from disparate spools of white, black, and red yarn did, however, present unique intellectual and ethical challenges. Dr. John Hope Franklin's astute observation that "historical forces are all persuasive and cut through the most rigid barriers of race and caste" was an important source of guidance and direction. In other words, focusing exclusively on black history would have invariably led to the repetition of past sins—the only distinction being that a black hand, rather than a white one, would have wielded the pen of omission. My fondest wish is that future generations of students and historians will find this "contextualized" presentation useful in the research of more racially and culturally inclusive state histories.

The words, deeds, and attitudes of white Georgians provide unvarnished insight into the religious, economic, political, military, and psychological imperatives that undergirded that most "peculiar" of institutions. However, this story would not be complete if it did not include the efforts of a small but determined group of white Georgians who actively opposed slavery. Readers may be surprised to learn that Georgia's most outspoken antislavery advocate during the colonial period was General James Edward Oglethorpe, the colony's founding father. He planted the seeds of abolition in the Deep South and was among the first white men in North America to oppose the institution. Because of his determined resistance, slavery was prohibited in Georgia from 1733 until 1751.

Many people assisted in the research and writing of this book. I am grateful to Dr. F. N. Boney and Dr. Charles Wynds, who volunteered their advice and counsel. I am also indebted to the staffs of the Auburn Avenue Research Library, the University of Georgia Main Library (especially the Hargrett Special Collections), the Richard B. Russell Library, the Athens Regional Library, Clark Atlanta University's Woodruff Library, the British Library, the Georgia Historical Society, the Georgia State Archives, the Carl Vinson Institute of Government, the DeKalb County Libraries, the Paine College Library and the Atlanta Public Libraries for their kind assistance.

I am grateful to my editor, Tysie Whitman at Longstreet Press, for her constructive criticism. Many friends and supporters too numerous to name graciously provided assistance and encouragement along the way. Special thanks go to my sisters, Dr. Vera Thurmond and Barbara T. Archibald, Judge Joseph Gaines, who first introduced me to Austin Dabney, Caesar Williams, Laura Carter, Al and Conoly Hester, Rachel Henderson, Loretta Scott, Carl McCoy, Rev. Thurmond Tillman, Clara B. Jones, and Mathew Ware.

Simple words cannot express my appreciation for the unwavering love and support of my wife, Zola, whose encouragement and administrative assistance proved to be invaluable during the research and writing of this book. Our twelve-year-old daughter, Mikaya, literally grew into adolescence during this period and she is owed a very special debt of gratitude for teaching her "old-school dad" how to use the family computer.

MLT
April 2003

CHAPTER I

———

GEORGIA'S ANTISLAVERY HERITAGE

On November 17, 1732, James Oglethorpe and 120 colonists set sail from Gravesend, England, destined for a new life in the New World wilderness that would be known as Georgia. All but a few were leaving behind lives of poverty and religious persecution. Their spirits were ablaze with the promise of economic opportunity and personal liberty embodied in the Georgia Plan.

This bold and visionary plan would establish Georgia, the youngest of North America's English colonies, as a unique social welfare and economic experiment. The colony was envisioned as an "Asilum of the Unfortunate," a place where England's "worthy poor" could earn a "comfortable subsistence" exporting goods produced on small farms. Most significantly, Georgia would be a sanctuary free from the evils of the international slave trade. The framers of the plan were convinced that widespread economic vitality could not be achieved in a society dominated by slave labor. Oglethorpe, a member of parliament and the father of Georgia, would be among the first white men in North America to advocate against the institution.[1]

The movement that gave birth to the Georgia Plan originated in the British Parliament on February 25, 1729, when the Committee on Jails was charged with the responsibility of investigating the condition of England's debtor prisons. Longstanding legal precedent gave creditors the right, which they frequently exercised, to sue for the imprisonment of debtors unable to satisfy their obligations. Although England enjoyed unparalleled prosperity during the early eighteenth century, economic dislocations and political indifference plunged thousands of citizens into poverty and prison.

During the parliamentary proceedings, committee chairman Oglethorpe became acquainted with Dr. Thomas Bray, an influential minister and humanitarian who advocated resettling impoverished British citizens in the New World. The investigation exposed horrible living conditions at three debtor prisons, uncovered widespread corruption among prison officials, and transformed the thirty-three-year-old Oglethorpe into a national hero. Parliament subsequently passed a statute entitled An Act for the Relief of Debtors, which authorized the release of ten thousand indebted citizens.

The statute eased the overcrowding that plagued the prison system, but at the same time added to the mass of unemployed, homeless beggars who crowded the streets of London and other cities. Undaunted, the ever-resourceful Oglethorpe decided to solve the dilemma of impoverished citizens set adrift on a sea of wealth and prosperity. He marshaled the support of well-known British philanthropists, politicians, and clergymen to assist in establishing a charity colony in America for England's "miserable wretches" and "drones." Prominently represented among the group were several associates of the now-deceased Thomas Bray, ten members of Parliament, and four Anglican ministers. These social reformers gained control of two charitable trusts that were combined and redirected to assist in settling one hundred former debtor prisoners in the New World. As the Georgia Plan evolved, the group decided not to limit the charitable enterprise to debtors, and instead sought to help as many poor people as their funds would allow. [2]

From the outset, Oglethorpe and his colleagues found the idea of slavery inconsistent with the goals of the proposed colony, arguing that it would undermine the labors of hard-working white colonists. They insisted that the importation of Negro slaves be prohibited in Georgia—which would distinguish it as one of the first British settlements in North America to officially do so. Several state historians have concluded that this historic prohibition was the most important element of the Georgia Plan. Decades after the founding of the colony, Oglethorpe contended that he and his "friends" prohibited slavery in Georgia because it was "against the Gospel, as well as the fundamental law of England" and they had absolutely "refused . . . to make a law permitting such a horrid crime." [3]

On the other side of the Atlantic, Carolina colonists supported the settlement of a buffer colony on their southern frontier for economic and military reasons. They were convinced that the establishment of a British colony between the Savannah and Altamaha Rivers would protect them from the Spanish in Florida. For more than sixty years, beginning with the founding of their colony in 1670, the Carolinians had been threatened by Spain, which claimed ownership of land far to the north of Florida.

More importantly, proslavery Carolina officials believed settlement of this strategic territory would stem the tide of fugitive slaves who were fleeing to freedom in Florida. Since 1693, a succession of Spanish governors had offered freedom, land, and religious sanctuary to all British slaves who escaped to St. Augustine and converted to Catholicism. Financial losses associated with the escape of black slaves and their eventual alliance with the Spanish threatened to destabilize the Carolina colony.

The Carolinians were also convinced that a buffer colony would provide additional security from the Indians who literally surrounded them—proud nations of Creeks and Cherokees. Evershifting relations with these tribes, coupled with their ferocity on the battlefield and their skill in the fur trade, challenged the courage and ingenuity of the Carolina colonists.

During the summer of 1730, a petition was presented to King George II requesting a charter to establish the Georgia colony. Two years later, on June 9, 1732, the charter was granted to twenty-one original Trustees. The document contained unique provisions designed to prevent the development of an economy dependent on slave labor. There was, for example, no requirement for the establishment of a colonial legislature. Initially, this insulated the Trustees in London (only Oglethorpe would live extensively in Georgia) from political pressure generated by the proslavery lobby in Georgia. Conflict-of-interest restrictions forbade the Trustees from profiting, directly or indirectly, from investments in the colony. Thus, they were less likely to be influenced by the possibility of personal gain associated with the enslavement of Africans. Their official motto, in fact, was *Non Sibi, Sed Aliis* ("Not for ourselves, but for others").

The charter also stipulated that all but a small percentage of landholdings would be restricted to small tracts. By implementing "Strict Agrarian Law," the Trustees sought to prevent the proliferation of large plantations that they feared would concentrate the colony's wealth in the hands of a few slave owners. Finally, they specified that silk and wine would be the primary staples produced in Georgia—neither of which required the use of slave labor.

Although the Georgia charter did not contain a specific prohibition of slavery, supporting documents submitted by the Trustees provided detailed pragmatic arguments justifying their opposition to the institution. On the military front, they argued that slaves would pose a constant threat to white women and children because of Spanish-inspired rebellions or individual acts of defiance. The Trustees believed that a Negro presence in Georgia would allow Carolina runaways to blend into the black population until they reached Spanish Florida. Turning their attention to economic concerns, they argued that poor white farmers would be enticed into mortgaging their farms to buy slaves, a circumstance guaranteed to keep them in the impoverished condition they were trying to escape. The Trustees also felt that the presence of slaves would encourage laziness and inequality among Georgia's white population, which would ultimately defeat the purpose of their grand experiment.

The Trustees' rationale for a slave-free colony was a frank and unflinching discourse on what they deemed to be the evils of slavery. But the wilderness that greeted Oglethorpe and the original settlers upon their arrival in Georgia abounded with stark realities that would not yield to idealistic ideologies. The southeast region of the New World was a complex mix of competing nations, warring races, and ever-shifting economic objectives. It was rife with political intrigue and violence, a hostile environment that constantly tested the resourcefulness of European colonists. This world was far removed from the stately courts of England, where well-mannered men politely, if often naively, plotted the course of Georgia's development. In the untamed North American wilderness, economic necessities and military imperatives dictated the ebb and flow of events.

Georgia's early history is therefore replete with inconsistency regarding the use of slave labor. Although the importation into the colony of Negroes, slave or free, was prohibited, at least one slave was already in the area when the colonists disembarked at Yamacraw Bluff on February 12, 1733. The black man was owned by Indian traders John and Mary Musgrove, who lived on Pipemakers Creek, near the future site of the Savannah settlement. Ironically, this first black Georgian was a slave named Justice.

Black slaves toiled in Savannah from the settlement's earliest days, despite the prohibition. A Mr. Bryan of the Carolina colony brought four of his slaves to help saw trees and build houses in Savannah during its first weeks. In the winter and spring of 1733, twenty black slaves—their labor donated by William Bull of Carolina—helped Oglethorpe and the colonists clear forty lots for house construction, and they assisted in the delineation of the town squares and streets. One observer wrote: "They [the colonists] worked hard indeed, in building some houses in town, but they labor'd in common, and were likewise assisted by Negroes from Carolina, who did the heaviest work." In this instance, and in numerous others during Georgia's embryonic stages, Oglethorpe conveniently ignored the presence of slave laborers. But his opposition to slavery soon hardened—as did the opposition of his fellow Trustees in England.[4]

During the summer of 1733, Oglethorpe visited Charles Town (later Charleston), where Carolina slave owners tried to persuade him to open Georgia to rum, Negro slavery, and thus the plantation system. The frustrated Carolinians even offered Oglethorpe a bribe in return for his support, but he angrily rebuffed their overtures and departed the colony determined to maintain Georgia's slavery prohibition. What Oglethorpe witnessed on his return to Savannah only served to strengthen his resolve. Entering the settlement, he discovered the colonists had grown "mutinous and impatient of labour and discipline." Oglethorpe blamed their "petulancy" on the presence of black slaves and the widespread consumption of rum. According to him, the settlers had become idle and lazy while slaves worked to build the settlement, so Oglethorpe sent the blacks back to their Carolina owners. He proceeded to destroy every barrel of rum he could find and threatened to withhold provisions from anyone caught distilling or selling spirits. On May 14, 1733, Oglethorpe reported, somewhat prematurely, to his fellow Trustees: "I have brought all our people to desire the prohibition of Negroes and rum, which goes against the grain of the traders in the commodities in this town. But if either of them are allowed our whole design will be ruined."[5]

THE TRIALS OF JOB

🐚

While Oglethorpe was busy establishing his colony in Georgia, an African prince named Job ben Jalla, who had been enslaved in America and would eventually be freed through Oglethorpe's intervention, arrived in London. Job's miraculous deliverance from slavery captured the imagination of British society, and according to Henry Bruce, a nineteenth-century Georgia historian, the travails of the black man had a profound effect on Georgia's founding father. Bruce writes that "Job's history" played a significant role in the continuing development of Oglethorpe's "ideas" on slavery, ideas that ultimately set the stage for a historic debate in Georgia concerning the economic, military, and moral expediency of the institution.[6]

Job, or Ayuba Suleiman Diallo as he was known in his native land, began his amazing journey into and out of bondage in 1730 when he and a servant were captured on the banks of the Gambia River and sold by Mandingo tribesmen to British slavers. They were transported to America and sold to a Maryland tobacco plantation owner who soon realized that Job was "no common slave." Job was a devout Muslim who prayed daily and faithfully practiced rituals of debasement. Following an unsuccessful escape attempt, the enslaved prince was befriended by Reverend Thomas Bluett, a white minister affiliated with the Society for the Propagation of the Gospel. Bluett convinced Job's owner to allow the young black man to write a letter to his father detailing his desperate circumstance. Written in Arabic, the letter passed through the hands of several men until it was placed in the possession of Oglethorpe, who, before founding the Georgia colony, had served briefly as deputy governor of the Royal African Company, an enterprise created for the express purpose of exploiting the West African slave trade. During the summer of 1732, Oglethorpe sent the letter to Oxford University, his alma mater, for translation. The sorrowful details of Job's predicament greatly affected Oglethorpe, who was known throughout England for his "goodness and generosity." He promised, upon Job's arrival in London, to pay forty-five pounds for the purchase of the African's freedom and an additional amount for the cost of his passage to England. Later that year, on December 21, 1732, Oglethorpe sold his stock in the Royal African Company and severed all ties with the British slaving corporation.[7]

Accompanied by Bluett, who tutored Job on the rudiments of the English language during their voyage across the Atlantic, the African prince arrived in London in April 1733. During his twelve-month stay, he received additional instruction and became "a roaring lion" in British society. He helped Sir Hans Sloane, the founder of the British Museum, arrange and interpret a large collection of Arabic manuscripts. Sloane was so impressed by Job's intellect that he orchestrated the induction of the young African into the Gentleman's Society of Spalding. Founded in 1710, the society's membership included some of England's most distinguished scholars, such as Sir Isaac Newton, the founder of the theory of gravity. Job's British hosts also attempted to expose their guest to Christianity by presenting him with a copy of the New Testament. The Society's minute book contained a notation dated June 26, 1733, that a Bible was presented to the "Poor Mahometan Black redeemed by order of Mr. Oglethorpe."[8]

Although he was treated with respect and kindness by his British hosts, Job never lost sight of the fact that he was still a slave. His original benefactor, James Oglethorpe, had promised to purchase his freedom, but Oglethorpe was now in North America, working to establish the fledgling Georgia colony. Oglethorpe's former partners in the Royal African Company decided to purchase the precocious young slave and send him back to Gambia, where he could assist the corporation in securing slaves and other commodities. This particular proposal alarmed Job, who informed Bluett that he feared the slave traders actually intended to sell him to the highest bidder—or that, even if they sent him home, they would force him to pay an unreasonable ransom in exchange for his freedom. Bluett was also concerned that even if the corporation paid Oglethorpe's bond, the transaction would only result in a change in ownership and Job would remain in bondage. He proposed instead that a public subscription be initiated to raise the money needed to purchase Job's freedom. Before this could be accomplished, the Royal African Company purchased Job from a Captain Hunt, who was the bearer of Oglethorpe's bond, for forty-five pounds plus interest.

Bluett obviously did not trust the motives of Job's new owners and he quickly began an effort to raise the money needed to emancipate him. After contributions were received from several of Bluett's influential friends, a "handsomely engrossed" certificate of manumission was presented to the African prince on December 27, 1733. The certificate stated in part that the Royal African Company declared that "Job is a free Man and is at Liberty to take his Passage to Africa . . . in order to return to his Native Country." Although he had regained his freedom, Job did not forget his loyal servant, who was still enslaved in Maryland. He appealed to the Duke of Montagu for help. The duke arranged for the manumission of the slave and paid for the purchase of his freedom. Finally, in July 1734, Job completed his miraculous journey back to Africa. Like his Biblical namesake, he had suffered numerous trials and tribulations, but his sufferings had seemingly been rewarded tenfold. Job returned to Gambia a free man, laden with over five hundred pounds of gifts and treasures from his British admirers.[9]

Unfortunately, Job's generous benefactor, James Oglethorpe, would miss by just months the opportunity to befriend in person the extraordinary African. Oglethorpe himself returned to England that same year to lobby for additional financial and military support for the fledgling Georgia colony, but the paths of the two men did not cross.

A PROHIBITION AGAINST SLAVERY

Despite some criticism from fellow Trustees and waning political support in Parliament, James Oglethorpe was granted the additional financial resources he had requested for the Georgia colony. In December 1734, he led a small flotilla of four ships and approximately six hundred new settlers across the Atlantic. Among the passengers were one hundred rugged Highlanders from Scotland, noted throughout Europe for their skilled use of the broad sword. They, along with the German Salzburgers, an industrious group of religious refugees, would form the core of Oglethorpe's antislavery contingent in Georgia. They would subsequently be joined by John and Charles Wesley, who served as missionaries for the Church of England.

Prior to their arrival in Georgia in March 1735, the Salzburgers spent a brief period in the Carolina colony, recuperating from their voyage to the New World. There they got a first-hand glimpse of Negro slavery and came away shocked by the "irreligious" condition of the slaves. The Germans noted that they were "not faithful" to their masters and were "very malicious." Despite these reservations, the Salzburgers used black slaves to clear land and build the first homes at their village, named Ebenezer. Although they conceded slave labor was "a great convenience," they recognized that these blacks also constituted a clear and present danger.[10]

The Scottish Highlanders eventually settled the seaside town of New Inverness, later renamed Darien. Because of their closeness to the Florida border, the Scots initially objected to slavery primarily for security reasons, although they would later condemn the institution as an affront to humanity and a violation of the will of God. The Scots, themselves victims of oppression in their homeland, maintained that black slaves would escape to Florida and fight with the Spanish, or remain in Georgia, where Spanish instigators would incite them to rise up against their masters. In either scenario, they argued, the importation of slaves would give Georgia's enemies a strategic military advantage. In letters and petitions to the Trustees in England, Oglethorpe, the Darien Scots, and the German Salzburgers expressed agreement on this issue. All parties concluded that the presence of slaves would render the colony vulnerable to attack.

On the economic side, Oglethorpe and others, including John Martin Bolzius, the Salzburger spiritual leader, contended that slavery would take employment away from poor white Georgia colonists who had fled England in search of economic opportunity. Bolzius believed the immigration of additional Salzburgers would help the colony's lagging economy more than the legalization of slave labor would. The Georgia Trustees had originally tried to resolve this severe labor shortage by employing white indentured servants, but they proved to be unreliable and too expensive. The proslavery group, known as the "malcontents," argued that the admission of blacks into the colony would allow Georgia to compete on equal footing with Carolina and other colonies where slaves provided relatively cheap labor.[11]

The religious front also served as a battleground in the struggle between antislavery advocates and their opponents. Two of the most vocal combatants were Bolzius and the Reverend George Whitefield, a popular evangelist who established the Bethesda Orphanage in Savannah. Whitefield arrived in Savannah in 1738 and believed that the importation of black slaves would provide masters with the opportunity to fulfill a divine purpose by Christianizing heathens. His arguments also possessed a strong economic flavor; he maintained that neither the fledging colony nor his Bethesda orphanage could survive without slave labor. He professed that God had created certain hot and distemperate climates, like Georgia's, exclusively for black laborers because white men lacked the physical stamina to perform rigorous work under semitropical conditions. In making that argument, Whitefield expressed a popular eighteenth-century rationale for slavery known as "climatic necessity." This theory was embraced by many slavery advocates, including the malcontents and numerous Carolina merchants. One such merchant, Samuel Eveleigh, warned the Georgia Trustees that the slavery prohibition could destroy the struggling colony.[12]

Bolzius opposed much of Whitefield's argument, but took particular exception to the evangelist's assertions regarding a divine justification for legalizing slavery in Georgia. Bolzius facetiously directed the reverend and others wishing to spread the Gospel among black slaves to work the "Large Field" available in the Carolina colony. Although there was a growing number of neglected and orphaned children in the colony, he concluded it would be better to abandon Whitefield's "Orphan House" in Savannah than allow its use as justification for legalizing slavery.[13]

Another religious voice was added to Georgia's antislavery chorus in the person of the Reverend John Wesley, a young Anglican priest who later founded the Methodist Church. Wesley also challenged those who based their support of slavery on religious arguments. He wrote: "All that might be said about slaves being brought to salvation did not mitigate their being brought also to a condition too similar to that of beasts of burden." Unfortunately, after less than two years of missionary work, Wesley "shook off the dust" of the New World and returned to England. In 1774 he would recall that "Mr. Oglethorpe . . . began settling a colony without negroes, but at length the voice of those villains prevailed who sell their country and their God for gold, who laugh at human nature and compassion, and defy all religion, but that of getting money." [14]

The arguments pro and con were bandied about the colony fervently and tirelessly, but antislavery forces won an important political battle in June 1735, when the Trustees enacted a law entitled "An Act for Rendering the Colony of Georgia More Defensible by Prohibiting the Importation and Use of Black Slaves or Negroes." The law, one of the first statutes to expressly prohibit slavery in a British colony, contained a detailed military rationale for the prohibition.

According to its preamble, black slaves would deter the immigration of English and Christian settlers to Georgia, thereby reducing the number of white men who could be relied on to help defend the colony. The authors of the legislation were convinced that slavery would expose white colonists to the dangers of slave "insurrections, tumults and rebellions," which would undermine internal security, especially during periods of military conflict with foreign nations. The antislavery statute established a maximum fine of fifty pounds for any person convicted of importing, buying, selling, bartering, or utilizing slave labor in Georgia, and it granted local officials the power to seize any Negro (slave or free) found in the colony. It provided that captured slaves would become the property of the Trustees who, with the consent of local officials, could export, sell or dispose of captives in any manner considered in the best interest of the colony. The statute also contained a fugitive slave provision that allowed slave owners from other colonies to reclaim captured slaves after the payment of costs and damages associated with the apprehension.[15]

Passage of the slavery prohibition only served to intensify the debate between Georgia's antislavery minority and the growing proslavery lobby. In 1737 Oglethorpe stood in the courthouse in Savannah and swore that he would completely disassociate himself from the colony if slavery were legalized in Georgia. A series of petitions, counterpetitions, and letters were delivered to the Trustees in London extolling and decrying the advisability of prohibiting slave labor. Matters came to a head in December 1738, when 117 Savannah colonists, including two magistrates, signed a petition that blamed Georgia's deteriorating economic condition on the absence of cheap slave labor. The petitioners assured the Trustees that repeal of the slavery prohibition would avert ruin and guarantee the colony's success. This petition ignited a political firestorm and prompted counterpetitions from the Salzburgers and Darien Scots, and several impassioned letters from Oglethorpe.[16]

Oglethorpe wrote his fellow Trustees in January 1739 and ridiculed the petitioners as men consumed by "idleness" and "luxury" whose ideas could jeopardize the colony's future. His words on the subject anticipated the sentiments of nineteenth-century American abolitionists by proclaiming that legalized slavery in Georgia would "occasion the misery of thousands in Africa . . . and bring into perpetual Slavery the poor people who now live free there." Oglethorpe's expression of concern for the slaves' well-being represented a major shift in the character of the debate in Georgia. It is the first documented occasion in Georgia history where a statement regarding the negative consequences of slavery centered on the suffering of Africans rather than on economic necessity or the security of white settlers.[17]

THE PROPHECY

On January 3, 1739, the Darien Scots wrote and signed an ominous petition addressed to "Governor-General Oglethorpe," urging him not to repeal the 1735 antislavery statute. The document, which some historians claim was actually written by Oglethorpe, laid out specific military and economic objections to slavery, but its strongest arguments were couched in moral and religious terms. The petition branded slavery a sin and prophesied that God would punish slave owners on a day of divine retribution and atonement. "It's shocking to human Nature," the Scots wrote, "that any Race of Mankind and their Posterity, should be sentenced to perpetual Slavery; nor in Justice can we think otherwise of it, than they are thrown among us to be our Scourge one Day or another, for our Sins; and as Freedom to them must be as dear to us, What a Scene of Horror it must bring about! And the longer it is unexecuted, the bloody Scene must be the greater." Despite their ancestors' fervent disapproval of slavery, the slaveholding descendants of these same Darien settlers and their fellow Georgians would eventually face the promised day of retribution. One hundred and twenty-four years later, the Scots' chilling prophecy would be fulfilled with the attack and destruction of Darien by former slaves serving in the Union army.[18]

The proslavery lobby in Savannah charged that the Scots' controversial petition had actually been written by Oglethorpe and that he bribed them into signing the document with an offer of additional livestock and provisions. Oglethorpe certainly exerted a major influence over the Darien Scots, since he had personally secured their migration to the colony, and the general also possessed a lifelong affinity for the Highland Scots and their culture. However, the legitimacy of their opposition to slavery is buttressed by the fact that in 1775 the men of Darien would once again raise their voices in protest of the institution; they would stand alone in Georgia in petitioning the leaders of the American Revolution to abolish slavery because it was "an unnatural practice . . . founded in injustice and cruelty."[19]

In March 1739, two months later, the Salzburgers at Ebenezer endorsed the Darien petition, adding that slavery would undermine Georgia's economy, and urged instead the immigration of additional members of their German clan. The Germans denied that Negroes were essential for the production of rice and corn: "We were told by several People [sic] after our Arrival, that it proves quite impossible and dangerous, for White People to plant and manufacture Rice, being a work for Negroes, not for European People; we laugh at such a Talking." The petitioners implored the Trustees not to legalize the importation of slaves into the colony because experience had shown, they claimed, that houses and gardens would be robbed and the safety of white settlers jeopardized. According to historian Charles Spalding Wylly, these early Georgians "wrote, signed and published . . . the first protest against the use of Africans as slaves, issued in the history of the New World." Another historian, David Brion Davis, suggests the sentiments raised by the Darien petition would eventually reverberate throughout the abolitionist movement and would culminate in President Abraham Lincoln's Second Inaugural Address.[20]

The Trustees in England also responded to Savannah's proslavery petitioners by expressing surprise and indignation toward the local magistrates who had signed the December 9, 1738, petition. They insisted that the proslavery argument was denied because counter-petitions from Darien and Ebenezer were more convincing in revealing the dangers and inconveniences of slavery. The Trustees reiterated that the presence of black slaves would encourage laziness among white Georgians and the colony would become like Carolina, where Negroes greatly outnumbered the whites. In this event, they maintained, the colonists would almost certainly become the victims of servile insurrections and slave-assisted invasions by foreign nations.

Their analysis proved correct. A few months after the Savannah petition was rejected, rebellious Carolina slaves mounted the bloodiest insurrection on the North American continent during the colonial period. The Stono Rebellion dramatically underscored the inherent dangers associated with Negro slavery. Shock waves from the insurrection rippled throughout the British colonies; however, white Georgians were especially agitated, for the insurrectionists had planned to march to St. Augustine, the fugitive slave sanctuary in Florida, by cutting a path of destruction through Georgia.[21]

THE STONO REBELLION

September 9, 1739, dawned peacefully in bucolic Stono, a village located twenty miles west of Charles Town. The colonists casually went about their routines; most, as was their custom, put on their

Sunday best and went to church. The Godfrey family broke from habit and stayed home. The deceptive quietness of the Carolina morning gave no warning that they would soon die in a bloody slave insurrection.

The revolt began when roughly twenty Angolan slaves, executing a well-conceived plan, broke into a public storehouse, beheaded two guards, armed themselves, and set out on a triumphant march toward St. Augustine. Following behind their leader, Jemmy, the insurrectionists hoisted banners in the wind, their cries of "Freedom!" ringing out in a jubilant symphony of rage and exhilaration.[22]

Stepping to the lively beat of two African drums, the rebels planned to cut a bloody swath through Carolina and Georgia on their way to Florida. Gathering supporters along the way, they plundered, killed, and burned as they went, engulfing the countryside in flames. The fugitives came upon the Godfreys, killed them, set their house ablaze, and continued their march toward freedom. Carolina Lieutenant Governor John Bull was returning home from Charles Town when he encountered the heavily armed Negroes. He escaped with "much difficulty" and alerted the congregation at the Wiltown Presbyterian Church. The men left their women and children behind and hurried off to suppress the insurrection.[23]

The rebels, drunk with stolen rum and a premature taste of freedom, halted their ten-mile march in an open field and celebrated by singing, dancing, and yelling. Meanwhile, the whites quietly encircled the celebrants and opened fire. Though some of the black men "behaved boldly," fourteen died in a deadly barrage of hot musket balls. The others ran for their lives into the nearby woods, except for "One Negro fellow" who recognized his former master and advanced on him brandishing a pistol. The slave owner asked the man if he wanted to kill him. The rebellious slave answered by "snapping a pistol" at his master, but it misfired and the white man promptly "shot him thro' the Head." [24]

A few blacks ran back to their plantations, mistakenly believing their absences had not been detected by their masters and overseers. Accounts vary on what happened next. According to historian Kenneth Porter, about fifty Negroes were briefly interrogated and then decapitated by slave owners, who set their severed heads upon every mile post along the road to Stono. Oglethorpe, however, claimed that despite ample provocation, the whites did not torture the blacks but "put them to an easy death." By one account, all told twenty-one whites and forty-four blacks were killed during the bloody rebellion.[25]

Georgia and Carolina officials fixed blame for the carnage on Spanish instigators, contending that they had incited the uprising. The Georgia militia captured two Spaniards and imprisoned them for encouraging the slaves to escape. Fearing some insurrectionists might have avoided capture in Carolina, Oglethorpe issued a proclamation requiring the imprisonment of all Negroes found in Georgia. He also established a reward for the capture of fugitive slaves and dispatched a company of rangers to patrol Georgia's southern frontier with orders to seal off all escape routes to Florida.

Antislavery advocates in Georgia used the uprising to bolster their arguments, and months later Oglethorpe launched a military attack on St. Augustine in an attempt to eliminate it as a haven for fugitive British slaves. But proslavery forces in Georgia were apparently unfazed by the Stono rebellion. Despite the bloodshed in neighboring Carolina—and with cavalier disregard of the prohibition—Georgians persisted in exploiting illegal slave labor throughout the colony. William Stephens, secretary to the Georgia Trustees from 1737 to 1750, recorded numerous instances of violations of the slavery prohibition in his official journal.[26]

Illegal slave labor was especially prevalent in and around the frontier settlement of Augusta, the principal warehousing center for the overland fur trade with the Creek and Cherokee Indians. One contemporary observer noted that the Augustans all but ignored the prohibition, extensively utilizing slave labor in the planting and harvesting of their crops. By 1740, the use of black slaves was so widespread that a complaint filed with Savannah officials alleged that it was almost impossible for white men to find work in Augusta. In 1741 Lord Egmont reported at least eight Negroes were permanently living in the settlement and that many others were serving as guides and laborers in the Indian trade.

That same year, the "malcontents" published a scathing petition entitled "A True and Historical Narrative of the Colony of Georgia in America, 1741," that ridiculed Oglethorpe and the slavery prohibition. The petitioners, now residing in Charles Town, claimed a considerable quantity of corn had been harvested in and around Augusta, in large part with slave laborers. They contended the Augusta settlers owned more than eighty slaves who performed all of the more laborious agriculture tasks. Several Georgia planters, who owned plantations on the Carolina side of the Savannah, easily circumvented the slavery ban by transporting slaves back and forth across the river. The use of illegal slave labor was so pervasive in the area that Augusta was considered by many to be a de facto Carolina city.[27]

Violations of the slavery prohibition were not confined to Augusta, however. Slaves constituted the majority of the boatmen and deck hands involved in the coastal sea trade on the Georgia-Carolina coast, and they were heavily engaged as drovers and herders on the cattle trails between the Edisto and Altamaha Rivers. Planter Paul Amatis avoided the statute by moving from Georgia to Purrysburg, in the Carolina colony, and then transporting his slaves down the river to work on his plantation near Savannah. Another slave owner by the name of Dyson also transported his slaves "to and fro betwixt" Carolina and Georgia.[28]

The most sensational case recorded in Secretary William Stephens's journal involved a Captain Davis, a female slave who was actually his mistress, and an employee named Pope. The very attractive woman cared for her physically disabled owner and managed his lucrative trading business. According to Stephens, the woman not only possessed "an exceedingly fine Shape," but she also possessed "good Knowledge" of the business and had developed expertise in the maintenance of the accounts and ledgers. She apparently enjoyed Davis's full confidence, exercising complete control over all cash receipts and disbursements. All of the businessman's employees and customers were expected to treat the woman with respect. Pope's failure to follow this particular rule was the genesis of a contentious legal battle.[29]

Pope and the "Damsel" became embroiled in a heated argument that ended with the "naturally surly" boat captain striking the woman across the face with a hand fan. Davis subsequently fired Pope, who promptly filed a lawsuit against his former employer, claiming, among other things, that he had been unjustly terminated. Although the presence of the female slave was a clear violation of Georgia's antislavery statute, Stephens's journal is silent on the issue.[30]

A FORTRESS OF FREEDOM

Georgia's tacit approval of slavery came with an exceedingly high price. Black men and women did not submit meekly to perpetual servitude. Slaves in and around the colony regularly ran off from their masters, hiding themselves deep in the swamps of south Georgia and north Florida. From camps and isolated settlements, fugitive slaves known as "Maroons"—a word with Spanish origins meaning wild and unruly—conducted sporadic raids against nearby villages and farms. During these sometimes deadly forays, they would steal provisions and liberate willing slaves. As early as 1734, German settler John Bolzius reported the existence of several such settlements along the Georgia-Florida border. From time to time, Carolina and Georgia militia carried out retaliatory search-and-destroy missions against the Maroons.

The majority of the fugitive slaves headed for St. Augustine, the slave sanctuary in Spanish Florida. This stronghold and principal city of the Spanish colony was a bell that called British slaves to freedom. A handful of Carolina slaves belonging to one Captain James McPherson successfully negotiated the tortuous route to St. Augustine in 1738. The band wounded McPherson's son and killed another man in making their escape. The fugitives slipped through the dense Georgia swamps, passing near the Salzburger village of Ebenezer, where they narrowly avoided capture by local rangers. As they neared the Florida border, one of the blacks was wounded and another killed in a skirmish with hostile Indians. The survivors eventually reached their destination, where Spaniards showered them with "great honors," and their leader was granted a financial commission and a "Coat faced with Velvet." [31]

The Spanish policy of granting sanctuary to fugitive slaves created a growing and menacing security risk for colonists in Carolina and Georgia. Shortly after his arrival in the New World, Oglethorpe realized that St. Augustine was an important military target, the key to preserving security and peace on Georgia's southern frontier. The bloody slave rebellion at Stono, believed by the British to have been instigated by Spanish agents, forced relations between the two colonial powers to a breaking point. But Oglethorpe—aware that additional military support would be needed to launch an attack on St. Augustine—restrained himself and awaited the appropriate opportunity.

In 1739 the War of Jenkins' Ear erupted between England and Spain, the culmination of years of bitter international trade and boundary disputes. The war got its name from an incident in 1731 when Spanish sailors boarded Captain Robert Jenkins's ship, confiscated his cargo, and allegedly cut off one of his ears. Although the incident received little attention at the time, subsequent outrages against British sailors generated anti-Spanish sentiment throughout

Great Britian. Following the official declaration of war, Oglethorpe rushed to invade Florida. In his haste, however, the newly appointed military commander of Georgia and Carolina badly underestimated the strategic significance of Spain's longstanding policy of providing sanctuary to fugitive British slaves.

As he prepared for the invasion, Oglethorpe was probably unaware of the existence of Fort Mose, an enclave garrisoned by one hundred self-emancipated British slaves. Florida Governor Manuel de Montiano had established the fort just north of St. Augustine in 1738, after the arrival of a large group of fugitive slaves. Fort Mose would stand for a quarter century as a "Fortress of Freedom" and the destination of choice for slaves from Carolina and Georgia. According to contemporary reports, the fort was constructed of wood, banked with dirt, and surrounded by a shallow moat. The walls were lined with a prickly foliage and the fortification was equipped with a well house and a lookout tower. The former slaves farmed the fertile land surrounding the fort and fished in the saltwater river that ran through the settlement. They were also organized into a militia unit commanded by Francisco Menendez, an escaped slave from Carolina. On June 10, 1738, the unit had pledged allegiance to Montiano and promised to "always be the most cruel enemies of the English." The men vowed to spill their "last drop of blood" in defense of Spain and the Holy Catholic Faith.[32]

Oglethorpe began his Florida campaign in January 1740 by capturing two Spanish forts west of St. Augustine, buttressing his plans to lay waste to the city. Then, in February, he requested assistance from the Carolina Assembly, which promised to provide money, five hundred militiamen, and seven hundred slave laborers. The assault on Saint Augustine commenced with an invasion force of seven war ships from the Royal Navy and fifteen hundred ground troops composed of Georgia and Carolina militia and a large war party of Creek Indians.

As the British invaders approached St. Augustine, a detail of Spaniards and Negroes was feverishly working to improve fortifications near Fort Mose. Montiano hurriedly ordered the Fort Mose militia and their families to retreat to safety behind the walls of St. Augustine. Following the withdrawal, Oglethorpe directed 140 battle-hardened Scots from Darien to occupy the abandoned fort as a base of operations for the assault on St. Augustine. For several days the British hammered the town with cannon fire, but the continuous bombardment failed to dislodge the Spanish and black defenders from their fortress. Thwarted in his frontal assault, Oglethorpe prepared a land and sea blockade, hoping to starve the enemy into submission.[33]

But the Spanish counterattacked. A detachment of three hundred soldiers, including the Fort Mose militia, launched a surprise attack that literally caught the British sleeping. Acting on Montiano's orders, the black and Spanish soldiers slipped into the fort under cover of night and overwhelmed Captain John McIntosh Mohr and his men. Startled out of their sleep, the Scots fought bravely but were "cut . . . almost entirely to pieces," according to historian Hugh McCall. Sixty-three British soldiers were killed and twenty-six captured during the attack, including Mohr. Ironically, the Darien Scots, vocal supporters of Oglethorpe's slavery prohibition in Georgia, suffered the most casualties in the Battle of Bloody Mose. They had warned fellow Georgia colonists that black slaves would escape to Florida and help the Spanish wage war against their former masters. However, it was the Scots, not their proslavery neighbors, who were forced to drink the bitter brew of slave retribution.[34]

Survivors of the battle limped back to Darien, where they were greeted by the mournful skirl of Scottish bagpipes. So many men had died or been captured at Fort Mose that there was a widespread belief the town was dead and would never recover from the loss of its leading citizens. A somber Georgia colonist observed: "I am sorry that I have no better intelligence from these parts, than that the number of widows are much increased at Darien by their husbands being killed or taken at the late expedition to Saint Augustine." [35]

The humbling defeat completely demoralized Oglethorpe and his men. The Carolinians, "enfeebled by heat, dispirited by sickness, and fatigued by fruitless efforts," simply abandoned the expedition. The ill-fated invasion came to an ignominious end when Spanish reinforcements arrived from Cuba, and the Royal Navy withdrew from the Florida coast. In July 1742 a much-chastened General Oglethorpe withdrew to Fort Frederica in the Georgia colony. Oglethorpe and the Carolinians attributed their defeat to the former slaves who had fought alongside the Spaniards. In a petition to King George II in July 1740, the Carolina Assembly blamed their "ill success" at St. Augustine on "danger from our own Negroes." The following year, in a letter to Sir Robert Warpole, the British prime minister, Oglethorpe attempted to explain his failure by pointing to the superior size of the Spanish force—which, according to him, included 1,515 Spanish troops and 800 Negroes.[36]

Meanwhile in Florida, a triumphant Governor Montiano congratulated his soldiers and wrote a special commendation for Francisco Menendez, captain of the Fort Mose militia. He praised Menendez for his loyal service, specifically noting his courage and valor during the Battle of Bloody Mose. He also acknowledged Menendez for having distinguished himself in the establishment of Fort Mose and encouraging his "subjects" to work hard and develop good customs.[37]

Two years after their victory at Fort Mose, the Spanish launched a major counterattack against the British colonies to the north. Unbeknownst to the Spanish, the campaign would mark the beginning of their end as a colonial power in North America. A Spanish armada appeared off the Georgia coast in late June 1742. The invaders—composed of Spanish troops, the Fort Mose militia, and a regiment of black soldiers from Cuba—eventually landed and occupied an abandoned British fort on St. Simons Island. The black soldiers, according to British sources, enjoyed the respect and camaraderie of their Spanish allies. The black commanders were "clothed in lace, bore the same rank as the white officers, and with equal freedom and familiarity walked and conversed with their comrades and chief." The Negro and Spanish soldiers, acting on orders from Montiano, went about the countryside proclaiming liberty to all British slaves and offering them sanctuary in east Florida.[38]

Oglethorpe sent a message to the Carolinians warning them to guard against possible slave revolts. Then he set off to intercept the Spanish, who were marching up the Georgia coast. Without help from Carolina, the Georgia militia defeated the Spanish in two decisive engagements. The second victory, at the Battle of Bloody Marsh, marked the turning point in the long struggle between England and Spain for control of the southeastern region. Although generally overlooked by state historians, Oglethorpe's insistence on prohibiting the importation of slaves into Georgia directly influenced the outcome of these important battles. If the Spanish had landed in Carolina with its large slave population, instead of Georgia, where relatively few slaves lived, their attempts to incite widespread insurrections probably would have been successful.[39]

Montiano's failed invasion was Spain's last full-scale attempt to dislodge the British from the southern frontier and signaled their demise as a major military influence in the New World. Ironically, Oglethorpe's victory at Bloody Marsh also eliminated what had been his most persuasive argument against legalizing slavery in Georgia. With the erosion of the Spanish military threat, colonists no longer concerned themselves with the possibility of black slaves escaping to Florida and allying themselves with the Spaniards. The elimination of Spain as a colonial power in the New World opened the door for the legalization of slavery.[40]

The following year, on July 22, 1743, Georgia's most ardent defender of the slavery prohibition, James Oglethorpe, departed the colony for the last time. Despite his victory at Bloody Marsh, he sailed to England, toward a future clouded by a pending court martial and the possibility of personal financial ruin. The military proceedings that called him home had been initiated by a disgruntled officer from the St. Augustine invasion, who filed nineteen formal charges against Oglethorpe ranging from treason to larceny. Meanwhile, acting on numerous complaints from proslavery Georgia colonists, British officials refused to reimburse him for substantial expenses he had incurred on behalf of the colony, pending a full accounting. Although he was subsequently vindicated on all charges, Oglethorpe never returned to Georgia. His attendance at Trustee meetings in London declined and eventually ceased after the Trustees voted to abandon the principles that had led to the establishment of the colony. Nonetheless, he maintained a fatherly interest in Georgia, as well as a deep aversion to slavery, for the remainder of his life.

SLAVERY LEGALIZED

Oglethorpe's departure gave proslavery advocates in Georgia the opportunity they had long awaited. Infractions and evasions of the antislavery statute proliferated. By 1748 slave traffickers were landing Africans at the Port of Savannah and openly auctioning them to the highest bidders. In May of that year, Colonel Alexander Heron claimed that everyone in the colony was aware that "Negroes have been in & about Savannah for these several Years" and according to him, local magistrates "knew & wink'd" at blatant violations of Georgia's antislavery statute.[41]

"Negro Fever" had even taken hold in Darien, where a majority of the Scots now supported repeal of the slavery ban. All but forgotten was their 1739 antislavery petition and the prophecy of a day of retribution for slave owners. At Ebenezer, the Reverend Bolzius, a staunch slavery critic, rationalized that religious arguments alone could not stave off the institution, and reluctantly gave his support to the legalization of slavery. Before and during the "Grand Assembly" that convened in mid-1748, he argued that Georgia slaves should be treated as "humanely" as possible and provided with religious instruction. Georgia's political leaders eagerly developed and presented to the Trustees proposed legislation designed to regulate the importation of slaves into the colony. On August 8, 1750, the Trustees adopted the proposal, repealing the prohibition against the institution.[42]

The provisions of the code required slave owners to (1) maintain one white male servant for every four male slaves; (2) treat slaves humanely; (3) register all Negroes born, sold, or imported into Georgia; (4) establish quarantines to prevent the transmission of contagious diseases; (5) provide religious instruction to all slaves and reserve the Sabbath as a day of rest; (6) support the production of silk by maintaining one female slave, skilled in the art of winding silk, for every four male slaves; (7) pay an import duty and a yearly per capita tax on all slaves imported into the colony; and (8) agree not to hire a slave as an apprentice.

The evangelist George Whitefield applauded the action and intimated in a letter to John Wesley that, the cruelties of slavery notwithstanding, Georgia slaves would grow spiritually by virtue of their Christianization. Whitefield failed to consider the far-ranging implications of this spiritual growth. Neither he nor the authors of Georgia's slave code fully comprehended the long-term consequences of exposing African slaves to the Christian concept of "spiritual equality" before God. Belief in "spiritual equality" would ultimately feed the slaves' desire for "corporal equality" under the laws of man, and would help lay the groundwork for the birth of the American abolitionist movement.[43]

The statutory provision requiring slave owners to provide religious instruction to Georgia slaves inadvertently presented the slaves with access to a very powerful weapon in the abolitionist arsenal: the ability to read and write. Many early eighteenth-century Protestant sects believed that Christianization was a tedious and difficult educational experience; it was a process rather than a single act of spiritual conversion. Prior to baptism, black and white worshipers were required to learn a prescribed set of religious tenets, which necessitated the development of basic reading and writing skills. Thus, British missionaries intent on spreading the Gospel throughout the colonies established the first "school" for Georgia slaves in 1750.

Despite some nagging reservations, Georgia leaders aggressively, even recklessly, instituted the enabling mechanisms for legalized slavery. Within sixteen years of legalization, the number of slaves in Georgia grew by nearly 800 percent, from about five hundred in 1750 to more than thirty-five hundred by 1766. Although the provisions of the slave code were executed without significant problems, the requirement of mandatory religious instruction for "heathen" Negroes fueled a bitter debate regarding slave literacy and the insidious threat it posed.

Many Georgia slave owners vehemently opposed teaching slaves how to read and write, contending that learned chattel would engage in dangerous thoughts and dialogue. They believed Christianized slaves who could read and write were "ten times worse than pagans." Others, such as William Knox, supported the effort to Christianize Georgia slaves, but opposed teaching them how to read. He argued that a black man taught "to read one book will of himself read another, and such has been the imprudence of some ill informed writers, that books are not wanting to exhort the Negroes to rebel against their masters." Knox claimed to have developed a catechism that could be learned by memory that, according to him, was better suited to the "capacities and conditions" of slaves.[44]

Henry Melchoir Muhlenberg, a Georgia colonist, recalled an incident involving a young male slave at Ebenezer that typified what he considered to be the danger associated with teaching slaves how to read the Bible. According to Muhlenberg, the literate young slave would spend half the day in the shade studying the Bible. Eventually, he informed the precocious slave that, according to his interpretation of the Scriptures, "One must work if one would eat." With a "wry mouth," the slave told his master this particular brand of Christianity "was not becoming or suitable to him." This incident confirmed Muhlenberg's suspicion that educated slaves were more inclined to rebel against their masters. He wrote: "The knowledge of letters even in the lowest degree, is too often supposed to carry with it a sort of qualification for an easy life, and an exemption from a laborious one and the latter being the Negroes lot, they might perhaps bear it with more unwillingness, or seek some desperate means of ridding themselves of it."[45]

Despite slave owner opposition, in 1750—less than three months after slavery was legalized—the Society for the Propagation of the Gospel, along with the Associates of Dr. Thomas Bray, who were early supporters of the Georgia Plan, provided funds for a schoolmaster to the Negroes of Georgia. The following year, in April, the Trustees passed a resolution instructing the Common Council in the colony to appropriate an additional twenty pounds sterling to supplement the salary. Despite such official support, Joseph Ottolenghe and Bartholomew Zouberbuhler, the first ministers to provide Christian instruction to Georgia slaves, regularly dealt with plantation owners who preferred to keep their slaves in a state of ignorance.

Ottolenghe, a Jew who converted to Christianity, was born in Casale, in Italy's Piedmont region, and in 1761 he was elected to serve in the Georgia General Assembly. His efforts to educate

enslaved black children were plagued by chronic pupil absen-
teeism, primarily the result of lukewarm support from slave
owners. In a letter dated December 20, 1750, Ottolenghe wrote:
"Our school in Savannah at present consists of 41 children and
might increase to many more if masters of slaves would shew a
greater concern to have their young Negroes instructed and
brought up in the knowledge and fear of God." He later complained that the number of pupils in his school fluctuated wildly
between as many as fifty or as few as ten; some would attend for
six months and then disappear for a year or longer. The painstak-
ing educational process prompted the young missionary to conclude that "slavery is certainly a great Depressor of the Mind." [46]

Since many of Ottolenghe's slave pupils were from different
African cultures, the language barrier posed a daunting challenge.
The teacher wrote: "Our Negroes are so ignorant of ye English
language, and none can be found to talk in their own, it is a great
while before you can get them to understand what ye learning of
Words is." The obviously frustrated instructor posed a rhetorical
question: "How can a Proposition be believed, without first being
understood?" Hoping to solve this particular problem, William
Knox suggested that missionaries should limit their instruction to
slaves who had been born in the colonies or those familiar with
the English language. Following a year of study, Ottolenghe filed
a somewhat surprising report regarding the progress of his slave
pupils; they were learning quickly, several were reading "tolerably
well," and the entire class had memorized the catechism. In 1759
his work as schoolmaster to the Negroes of Georgia was terminated by the Society for the Propagation of the Gospel and the
Associates of Dr. Bray because Ottolenghe failed to submit annual progress reports. [47]

The Reverend Zouberbuhler also worked to educate and
spread "The Word" among Georgia's slave population. During
his tenure as rector of Christ Episcopal Church in Savannah,

from 1745 to 1766, he encouraged white members to allow their adult slaves to attend Sunday worship services. On July 7, 1750, Zouberbuhler and his congregation celebrated the opening of Christ Church, as well as the baptism of a Negro woman—the first recorded baptism of a black person in Georgia. Zouberbuhler originally proposed the establishment of a "Public School" for slaves, but slave owner opposition forced him to employ itinerant catechists, who visited the various plantations. When Zouberbuhler died in 1766, he directed through his will that income from one of his plantations, Beth Abrams, be held in trust and used to hire a qualified person to instruct the fifty-two slaves living there in the principles of Christianity. Plantation Trustees were also directed to manumit and ordain all adult male pupils who excelled in their studies.[48]

The Beth Abrams Trustees selected Cornelius Winter, a Methodist minister, to conduct the religious instruction at the plantation. Shortly after Winter's arrival in 1769, Reverend George Whitefield warned him that he would be "whipped off" Beth Abrams by angry colonists if he tried to teach and Christianize black slaves. Winter, who was derisively labeled the "Negro parson," suffered a barrage of threats and other forms of intimidation from Georgia colonists. An attempt was made in the local council to have him officially branded a public nuisance, but the measure failed to receive a majority vote. Winter abruptly left the colony after just twelve months and never returned.[49]

Early in 1770, Reverend John Rennie succeeded Winter as schoolmaster to the slaves at Beth Abrams and pastor of Christ Church in Savannah. But the gathering storm of the American Revolution put an end to his missionary work at the plantation. In September 1777, Rennie was forced to leave the American colonies because of his alleged loyalty to the British. Although the war ended the work of Protestant missionaries among Georgia slaves, the occupation of Savannah by British troops in 1779 would later open a new door to religious freedom for black Georgians. In worn-torn Savannah, three black preachers, George Liele, David George, and Jessie Peter, would convert scores of black worshipers and plant the seeds of an international "independent" black church movement.

ARMING SLAVE SOLDIERS

The debate over the education and Christianization of Georgia slaves—though certainly spirited and contentious—was as the proverbial tempest in a teapot compared to the virulent controversy that swirled around the leading question of the day: Should slave soldiers be enlisted and armed in defense of the colony?

Although Oglethorpe's victory at Bloody Marsh weakened the Spanish as a colonial power in the southeast, the British were still engaged in a long-running dispute with the French and their Indian allies. During the early 1750s, the threat of full-scale war with France reached a fever pitch and Georgia leaders worked desperately to improve the colony's meager defenses. The militia was severely undermanned, primarily because of inadequate funding and a shortage of white adult males available for service. Many eligible slaveowners and overseers simply could not afford to leave their plantations unattended and unguarded, a predicament Oglethorpe had foreseen some twenty years earlier when he was fighting to prohibit slavery in Georgia. Now, the only immediate solution to the colony's problem appeared to be the enlistment of black slaves in the militia. Recognizing that "several Negroes and other slaves have in Time of War behaved themselves with great faithfulness and courage in repelling attacks of his Majesty's Enemies," the General Assembly enacted the Militia Act of 1755.[50]

The new law required slave owners to maintain an accurate

census of all black males between the ages of sixteen and sixty, and promised freedom to slave soldiers who "shall courageously behave . . . in battle so as to kill any one of the enemy or take a prisoner alive," the caveat being that the act of heroism must have been witnessed by a white soldier. Less heroic service by a slave soldier would receive "public notice" and on each anniversary of the slave's act of valor, he was to be exempted from all personal labor and service by his master. According to the statute, each slave soldier would be issued, at the expense of the public treasury, a livery coat, breeches made of "red Negro Cloth turned up with Blue," a black hat, and a pair of black shoes.[51]

A major obstacle to the conscription of black men was opposition by slave owners who were fearful of potential economic losses. The authors of the act addressed these concerns by providing that owners would be paid one shilling per diem during each slave's tour of duty. Slave masters were also entitled to the "full value" of any black soldier killed in the line of duty, as well as reasonable compensation for any slave who was injured or disabled.[52]

On June 17, 1760, the Council of Safety, fearful of slave rebellions, amended the Militia Act by requiring background investigations on all slave recruits to determine their trustworthiness. A list of "qualified" slaves was to be developed, but a second provision prohibited the use of all available slave soldiers in a single military engagement. Only one-third of the qualified slaves could be drafted into the militia at one time, so that the number of black men assigned to active duty would not exceed one-third of the total number of men engaged in combat. The council members were obviously trying to guard against the unwelcome possibility of a majority black militia.[53]

These two provisions were passed to allay the concerns of colonists who believed the Georgia militia would become a refuge for fugitive slaves. Much of the apprehension was fomented by the *Georgia Gazette*, the colony's only newspaper, which published detailed and often gruesome accounts of slave rebellions throughout the British empire. An April 1763 report, for example, told of black rebels on the island of Surinam who, "in the most cruel manner, murdered all the white people they could come at." In that same issue, another article detailed the events surrounding a bloody Jamaican uprising in which a number of Negroes "butchered" their master by cutting off his hands, arms, feet, and legs.[54]

The French and Indian War ended in victory for the British in 1763 and Georgia colonists breathed a collective sigh of relief. Only a few skirmishes had actually been fought in the colony, rendering a full-scale mobilization of slave soldiers unnecessary. Another foreign enemy had been vanquished, setting the stage for a postwar population boom, fueled in part by a highly profitable slave-driven economy. But there were troubling side effects; white Georgians were being forced to confront complex and disturbing issues associated with the growing number of black slaves living in their midst. The colony's dilemma may well have given Oglethorpe a bittersweet taste of vindication as he neared death in England, where he was now a respected elder statesman.

A RACE OF HEROES

In the three decades since General James Oglethorpe had left his colony, slavery had become firmly entrenched and the dire consequences that he predicted would accompany the institution were beginning to materialize. White Georgians were constantly threatened by random acts of slave violence and organized rebellion. The concentration of wealth in the hands of a small number of slave traders and plantation owners was also spawning a growing underclass of poor white Georgians. Oglethorpe must have ruminated over Georgia's plight: his utopian dream of a Zion in the wilderness was being trampled upon by those who profited from the trafficking of human flesh. On the eve of the American Revolution, the now-toothless, eighty-nine-year-old general was still railing against the evils of slavery.

In a letter dated October 13, 1776, Oglethorpe wrote an impassioned letter to Granville Sharp, the famed British abolitionist, explaining why he and the Trustees, some forty years earlier, had prohibited slavery in Georgia. Despite sustained opposition, he claimed that they resolved not "to make a law permitting such a horrid crime." Oglethorpe's anger toward the men who fought for the legalization of slavery in Georgia had intensified over the years, and he lambasted those who had convinced British officials to repeal the charter provision granting the Trustees sole authority over the affairs of the colony.[55]

In that same letter, Oglethorpe took particular exception to an assertion by David Hume, the Scottish philosopher, that dark-skinned people were genetically inferior to white Europeans and incapable of civilized behavior. "What a historian!" he exclaimed. "He must never have heard of Shishak, the great Sesostris, of Hannibal, or of Tirhaka, king of Ethiopia, whose very name frightened the mighty Assyrian monarch." Oglethorpe followed with a rhetorical question: Is it possible Hume never read Herodotus, where the mighty works of the Egyptians who built the ancient pyramids are chronicled? He suggested the Scotsman would have drawn a decidedly different conclusion regarding the capabilities of the Negro if he had taken the time to analyze Leo's geographical description of the African continent. Oglethorpe was certain that if Hume had studied the matter, he would have discovered "that Africa had produced a race of heroes." [56]

The abolitionist Sharp's reply praised the general for having supported and defended the "noble principles" that led to the founding of Georgia. He concluded that Oglethorpe's courageous behavior during the struggle to prohibit slavery in the colony was an "instructive and exemplary piece of history" that would be imitated by future generations. Sharp advised his friend to "enjoy the heartfelt satisfaction" derived from having actually practiced the "disinterested principles and duties" that characterized the abolitionist movement.[57]

It is odd, given Oglethorpe's sustained and fervent opposition to slavery, that numerous state historians and biographers have questioned the legitimacy of his antislavery credentials. Many point to his brief stint from 1731 to 1732 as deputy governor of the Royal African Company, an enterprise that monopolized the West African slave trade, as evidence of his insincerity. This argument is sometimes accompanied by the unsubstantiated charge that Oglethorpe owned or possessed a financial interest in a Carolina plantation that utilized slave labor. Still others have suggested his antislavery zeal lacked substance because it was based solely on a desire to protect the safety and morals of whites, rather than recognition of the humanity of black slaves. These arguments ring hollow in the face of Oglethorpe's well-documented lifelong struggle against slavery. No less an authority than the late Phinizy Spalding, a noted Oglethorpe biographer, concurred that Georgia's founding father was "sincere in his antislavery stance" and honestly sought to limit the proliferation of slavery.[58]

The words and deeds of Oglethorpe foreshadowed by more than 150 years key elements of nineteenth-century abolitionist thought espoused by such leaders as Frederick Douglass and William Lloyd Garrison. When Oglethorpe died on June 30, 1785, a champion of liberty was lost, and a unique chapter in the history of the struggle against slavery ended. He was laid to rest in a vault beneath the floor of the parish Church of All Saints in the English village of Cranham. His widow, Elizabeth, had a large marble plaque carved and mounted on the wall of the church, memorializing the life and contributions of her late husband. Significant among the many platitudes is a notation recognizing and praising

Oglethorpe for setting "the noble example Of Prohibiting the Importation of Slaves" into the Colony of Georgia.

CHAPTER II

———

BLACK GEORGIA DURING
THE REVOLUTIONARY WAR ERA

The Revolutionary War opened an important new chapter in the struggle to restrict or abolish slavery in Georgia. The ideas and theories used to justify the severance of colonial ties to England also energized black slaves as they marched toward freedom. In a very dramatic way, the quest for American independence exposed the political hypocrisy of patriot slave owners. The enslavement of Negroes made a mockery of revolutionary ideology based on the principles of equal justice and human rights. Abigail Adams, a future first lady, stressed this point in a 1774 letter to her husband. "It always appeared a most iniquitous scheme to me," she wrote, "to fight ourselves for what we are daily robbing and plundering from those who have as good a right to freedom as we have." [1]

Several prominent patriot leaders, including Thomas Jefferson and Alexander Hamilton, attempted to resolve this glaring contradiction by arguing, somewhat disingenuously, that the American colonies were unwilling victims of a system designed and perpetuated by England. They contended that King George III's refusal to allow the restriction of the slave trade or the abolition of slavery in some Northern colonies constituted just grounds for rebellion. Both Jefferson and Hamilton believed that prohibiting the slave trade would cripple England's wartime economy and ultimately deal a deathblow to the institution in America.

The revolutionary theories of "personal freedom" and "the rights of man" found a willing audience among black slaves, north and south. Although the authors of the Declaration of Independence decided not to include blacks in the historic phrase "All men are created equal," these words became a clarion call to freedom for America's enslaved black masses. Benjamin Quarles wrote: "The Negro's role in the Revolution can best be understood by realizing that his major loyalty was not to a place nor to a people, but to a principle." This fundamental "principle" was that all men, regardless of color, were endowed with the "inalienable" right to life, liberty, and the pursuit of happiness. Whoever invoked the image of liberty, American or British, could count on a ready response from the slave population. And whenever the opportunity for self-emancipation presented itself amid the political upheaval and wartime disruptions, blacks responded with vigor and determination.[2]

In Georgia, the black man's pursuit of freedom clashed with the equally determined efforts of white men intent on preserving the lucrative slave trade. Colonial leaders refused to acknowledge the political or military imperatives of emancipation and rejected all antislavery arguments, even if it meant continued subjugation to England. By the mid-1700s, Georgia's economy had become almost totally dependent on slave labor, and much of the colony's wealth was invested in it. The depth of its intransigence was revealed when the Continental Congress mounted the first "national" effort to ban the African slave trade: Georgia was the only colony that failed to send a representative to the session, which convened on September 5, 1774. After five weeks of debate and discussion, the delegates resolved not to import or purchase any

British slaves after December 1, 1775. They also pledged not to hire any British ships for the transportation of African slaves or sell commodities or products to those engaged in the trade. The resolution was, in large part, an act of retaliation against the Intolerable Acts that had been imposed on the American colonists by the British Parliament earlier in the year.[3]

The slave-trade prohibition was received without protest in all the American colonies except Georgia, where opposition was "widespread and determined." Proslavery Georgians delayed the ratification meeting for three months in an effort to forestall any interruption and restriction of the slave trade. Once again, an antislavery voice would cry out in the colony to little avail. And once again, it originated from the seaside village of Darien.[4]

On January 1, 1775, the leading men of Darien, full of revolutionary fire, gathered at the town meeting house. Members of the "Darien Committee" chose local delegates to represent the parish at the pending ratification meeting scheduled to convene in Savannah. Not only did the Scots support the slave-trade prohibition, they also called for the complete abolition of slavery. Just as their forebears had done almost four decades earlier, they wrote and adopted a controversial antislavery petition. Declaring their "disapprobation and abhorrence of the unnatural practice of Slavery in America," the Scots pledged to do everything in their power to secure the manumission of all Georgia slaves. Although some of the delegates were slave owners themselves, they acknowledged that the institution encouraged the debasement of other human beings, contributed to the corruption of white morals, and placed America's call for liberty on a foundation of hypocrisy.[5]

The Georgia ratification meeting was finally convened on January 18, 1775, but only five of the twelve parishes sent representatives. Despite their decidedly minority status, the Darien delegates boldly declared their opposition to slavery. But, as one contemporary observer wrote, the powerful slave-trade lobby in

Savannah was "not likely soon to give matters a favorable turn." The majority of the delegates were totally opposed to any interruption in the trade and Georgia slave owners were much divided over the issue. Governor Richard Howley moved quickly to adjourn the assembly, proclaiming it not representative of the colony. Thus, the antislavery efforts of the Darien representatives ended in failure, their deeds having been all but lost to the pages of history.[6]

The colonies that supported the prohibition, including slave-rich South Carolina, responded with a campaign of economic and political pressure against Georgia, eventually forcing their recalcitrant neighbor to accept the provision. On July 4, 1775, the congressional delegates unanimously agreed not to import or purchase any British slave brought into the colonies from Africa or elsewhere. But the lofty pronouncement changed little in Georgia and South Carolina, where a surreptitious slave-trading industry sprang up to meet a demand heightened by the embargo. Thomas Jefferson subsequently charged that Southern officials actively aided and abetted slave smugglers by refusing to enforce the prohibition.[7]

The political debate fueled by Georgia's initial refusal to abide by the slave-trade embargo marked a significant milestone in American history. As the colonies struggled to become a nation, contentious slavery-related issues would be revisited at the framing of two other historic documents, the Declaration of Independence and the United States Constitution. On both occasions, Georgia and South Carolina delegates would bluntly assert that their support was conditioned on the continuation of their unfettered right to buy and own slaves. The outcome of these deliberations changed the course of American history and eventually plunged the nation into bloody civil war.

THE DECLARATION OF INDEPENDENCE

In the original draft of the Declaration of Independence, Thomas Jefferson included a clause accusing the king of England of being the principal culprit in the prosecution of the African slave trade. Jefferson was a Virginia slave owner and the reputed father of several children birthed by Sally Hemings, his slave mistress. He charged that King George had "waged cruel war against human nature itself, violating its most sacred rights of life and liberty in the persons of a distant people who never offended him, capturing and carrying them into slavery in another hemisphere, or to incur miserable death in their transportation hither." Jefferson described the slave trade as "piratical warfare" waged by the "*Christian* king of Great Britain" who was determined to maintain "a market where MEN should be bought and sold." Adding insult to injury, Jefferson charged that the king was now encouraging black slaves to bear arms against their former masters. He wrote: "He is now exciting those very people to rise in arms among us, and to purchase that liberty of which *he* had deprived them, by murdering the people upon whom he also obtruded them: thus paying off former crimes committed against the *liberties* of one people, with crimes which he urges them to commit against the *lives* of another." [8]

This language was totally unacceptable to the Georgia and South Carolina delegates, who realized inclusion of this controversial clause would negate any justification for the continuation of slavery if independence was achieved. A Georgia delegate strongly urged his colleagues not to "meddle" with the institution. "Slavery may be wrong" he argued, "but to prohibit it right now would be extremely unfair to Georgia. In time it will disappear of its own accord. Right now the cultivation of our main crops depends on slave labor: we cannot do without it." The Southern delegates refused to sign the proposed declaration unless the antislavery clause was removed in its entirety. Jefferson later explained that the clause was struck out in order to satisfy South Carolina and Georgia, who were opposed to any restriction of the slave trade. He recalled that some Northern delegates were also troubled by the antislavery language, even though they owned few slaves, because they were "pretty considerable" shippers in the slave trade.[9]

Georgians applauded the removal of the offending clause and heartily endorsed the revised Declaration of Independence. Nonetheless, thinly populated Georgia was woefully unprepared to assist the other American colonies in the Revolutionary War. Early in 1778, a committee of the Georgia House of Assembly, charged with evaluating the strength of the local militia, concluded that the colony was "so weak within and, so exposed without." Its military weakness was primarily attributable to the presence of a large population of black slaves and a shortage of white males available for service in the Continental army. Some twenty years earlier, Georgia leaders had tried to solve this same problem by enacting the Militia Act of 1755.[10]

By 1778 the attitudes of white leaders in Georgia had changed dramatically—slaves now comprised roughly half of the state's total population of only thirty-three thousand people. The ominous presence of "vast numbers of Negroes" had transformed the prospect of arming black men into an even more frightening and unpopular alternative than it had been in 1755. The ever-present threat of slave insurrections also contributed to the disturbing shortage of potential white recruits, for many slave owners declined military service in order to stay home and protect their plantations. Just as General James Oglethorpe had argued years before, slave owners were being forced to choose between guarding their slaves or fighting to defend the colony against foreign invaders.[11]

Although the Northern colonies and the British actively recruited black men into their ranks, patriot leaders in Georgia steadfastly refused to adopt the policy. A few blacks were allowed to join the Southern militias, but the majority pinned their hopes for freedom on the British, not their American masters. According to Joseph T. Wilson, "The love of liberty was no less strong with the Southern than with the Northern colored man. At the North he [the Negro] gained his freedom by entering the American army; at the South, only by entering the British army." This was especially true in Georgia, where some historians estimate that 75 percent of the prewar black population of fifteen thousand flocked to freedom behind the British lines. Georgia's slave exodus distinguishes it as one of the largest mass escapes in the history of American slavery.[12]

IN THE KING'S SERVICE

England's decision to emancipate and enlist American slaves in the British army was born solely out of military necessity. In November 1775 Lord Dunmore, the loyalist governor of Virginia, fearing an American attack, declared martial law and instituted the controversial policy. He issued a proclamation that offered freedom to all indentured servants and black slaves who were willing to bear arms on behalf of the British in the war against the American patriots. Three hundred black men who escaped from their American masters quickly volunteered to serve in the governor's "Ethiopian Regiment."[13]

Although Dunmore had acted without direct authority from the king, British officers throughout the colonies adopted and expanded the policy. Early in 1776, Sir Henry Clinton, commander of British troops in North America, issued the Philipsbury Proclamation, which promised freedom to all American slaves along the Atlantic coast who pledged allegiance to the British. In a significant expansion of Dunmore's proclamation, Clinton's offer of sanctuary was extended to include the wives, children, relatives, and friends of potential recruits. The promise of freedom led to the escape of approximately sixty-five thousand Southern slaves, who found refuge behind the British lines.

In Georgia, the British emancipation policy proved to be an extremely effective recruitment tool. When loyalist Governor James Wright was forced to flee the colony in February 1776, he met with several hundred fugitive slaves outside Savannah, solicited their help, and promised British support and assistance. Scores of fugitive slaves made important contributions to the British war effort in Georgia. So-called "confidential slaves" served as spies and guides, aiding the British with their knowledge of the local terrain. A black man named Sampson guided British ships through the maze of waterways and tributaries along the Georgia coast during the invasion of the colony in December 1778. Another elderly fugitive, Quamino (or Quash) Dolly, led thirty-five hundred British soldiers through secret pathways in the swamps to stage a surprise attack on Savannah, catching the local militia off guard and enabling the invaders to take the city with relative ease. Of the approximately twelve hundred black men working with the British in Savannah in 1779, more than two hundred served as armed soldiers. In 1781 the British garrison at Fort Cornwallis, near Augusta, consisted of four hundred regular soldiers and two hundred black recruits. The Negro soldiers later distinguished themselves at the Battle of Briar Creek, where they helped to rout a regiment of Georgia militiamen commanded by General Samuel Elbert.[14]

Black men were not restricted to land service. In April 1779 fugitive slaves helped solve British Navy Captain Hyde Parker's manpower shortage by manning two boats assigned to patrol the Savannah River. The British captain placed twelve blacks on each boat; he issued orders directing that they be treated as regular seamen in His Majesty's Navy. Fugitive American slaves assisted the

British in various other ways, primarily as cooks, orderlies, and waiters in British regiments. Others, such as slave preacher David George and his wife, labored on the abandoned plantations of Georgia patriots who had fled from the British troops. Hundreds of black men and women were put to work building military fortifications and batteries. Scores of unfortunate souls were claimed by British soldiers and eventually sold back into slavery in the West Indies, but the majority were treated fairly by the British.

A GIFT FOR EXHORTING

The fugitive slaves who descended on Savannah during the British Occupancy of 1778-1783 were presented with a unique opportunity to experience the "freedom of religion." Although Georgia slaves had, to varying degrees, received religious instruction since 1750, their training was primarily designed to ensure obedience and loyalty to their earthly masters. In war-torn Savannah, those who had worshipped under the watchful eyes and attentive ears of slave owners were now free to explore the meaning of a more liberating gospel. This period also witnessed the ascendancy of an enduring African-American tradition—the black preacher as community leader and spokesman. Among the thousands of fugitive slaves who took refuge in the city were three pioneer black preachers, George Liele, David George, and Jesse Peter (Galphin). By marshaling their considerable ministerial skills, this trio helped establish one of the first black churches in North America and subsequently gave birth to a worldwide black church movement.

Prior to their reunion in Savannah, Liele, George, and Peter had worshiped together at the Silver Bluff Baptist Church, a slave church established around 1773 on the Galphin Plantation at Silver

Bluff, South Carolina. Located directly across the Savannah River from Augusta, Georgia, the church's congregation consisted of David George, Jessie Peter, and about thirty other members. The slaves were ministered to by Reverend Waith Palmer, a white evangelist who came south during the first Great Awakening, and his assistant, George Liele, a slave preacher.

Liele was the first black man to be officially ordained as a Baptist minister and he is considered the father of the independent black church movement. Born into slavery around 1750 in Virginia, he moved with his master, Henry Sharp, to Burke County, Georgia, just prior to the beginning of the American Revolution. As was the custom in the colonial South, Liele was allowed to attend services at the local white Baptist church. After six months of Bible study, prayer, and worship, he was baptized and accepted as a member of Sharp's church. According to Liele's personal testimony, he was soon called to preach the Gospel: "Desiring to prove the sense I had of my obligation to God, I endeavored to instruct . . . my own color in the Word of God: the white brethren seeing my endeavors . . . gave me a call at a quarterly meeting to preach before the congregation." Moved by the sincerity of his sermon, church leaders granted Liele a probationary license to preach. He developed an extensive circuit along the Savannah River that included a seventy-five-mile strip of plantations up and down the Georgia-South Carolina border. One of his most frequent stops was at the Silver Bluff Baptist Church, where he first became acquainted with David George and Jessie Peter.[15]

Very little is known about the early life of Peter, but his fellow Silver Bluff worshiper, David George, provided a detailed sketch of the events surrounding his own original enslavement, eventual escape from bondage, capture by Creek Indians, and conversion to Christianity on the Galphin Plantation. He was born on a plantation in Essex County, Virginia, around 1742. George and his family were owned by a brutal slave master who regularly whipped and tortured them. George eventually escaped and sought refuge in Creek Indian territory. After living several months in the wilderness, he was captured by the Creeks, who forced him to become the chattel servant of Chief Blue Salt. The fugitive slave was later sold to George Galphin, the owner of a Plantation and trading post at Silver Bluff, South Carolina. During his stay on the Galphin plantation, George came under the powerful influences of the Christian faith and George Liele.

By his own admission, David George had lived "a bad Life" until his wife gave birth to their first child. Shortly thereafter, a slave named Cyprus convinced him that if he continued to live in sin he would "never see the face of God in glory." After a period of prayer and introspection, George was spiritually touched by a powerful sermon preached by George Liele. The repentant slave recalled, "His sermon was very suitable, come unto me all ye that labor and are heavy laden, and I will give you the rest. When it was ended, I went to him and told him . . . I was weary and heavy laden; and that the grace of God had given me rest." Following his conversion and baptism, George quickly demonstrated "a gift for exhorting" and with his master's permission, Palmer appointed him to the position of elder over the Silver Bluff worshipers.[16]

Palmer and Liele ministered to the fledging congregation until the British marched into the Georgia back country early in January 1779. According to George, local authorities prohibited Palmer and Liele from continuing to preach at Silver Bluff because they feared the ministers would provide the slaves with "too much knowledge." The knowledge he was apparently referring to was the British promise of freedom to Georgia slaves who volunteered to fight against the American colonists. In their absence, David George assumed the responsibility of ministering to the thirty-member congregation.[17]

Liele subsequently purchased his freedom and the freedom of his wife and children and moved from Burke County to Tybee

Island near the city of Savannah. Shortly thereafter his former master, Henry Sharp, who had sided with the British, was killed in the war. Sharp's relatives claimed that Liele's manumission was invalid and attempted to reenslave the black preacher and his family. Although he offered to repurchase his family's freedom, he was arrested and jailed in Savannah. During his incarceration, Liele was befriended by the British commander in Savannah, who arranged for his release from prison.

Prior to or shortly after Liele's release, David George, Jessie Peter, and about ninety other slaves fled the Galphin Plantation and joined the other black fugitives who were crowding into Savannah. George and Peter were soon reunited with Liele, their spiritual mentor. Recognizing that their continued freedom and the freedom of their people was dependent on the British, the three preachers encouraged other blacks to pledge their loyalty to the king. During this period the trio also established what is believed to be the world's first independent black church. The deepening alliance between the British and fugitive Georgia slaves was an indication of the important role blacks were playing in the British war effort and it rekindled a national debate regarding the enlistment of slave soldiers in Southern militias.[18]

SLAVE SOLDIERS IN THE SOUTH

Black men had been among the first to answer the call to arms in America's struggle for independence. They were also among the first to die. On March 5, 1770, Crispus Attucks, a former slave, led a group of angry American colonists—derisively described as "saucy boys, Negro's and mulatto's, Irish Teagues, and outlandish Jack tars"—into a deadly confrontation with British troops in Boston, Massachusetts. The motley group rallied behind Attucks, who shouted, "The way to get rid of these soldiers is to attack the main guard; strike at the root; this is the nest." Possessing "more valor than discretion," the seething mob followed the black man to King Street into a hail of deadly British musket balls. Attucks was the first to fall. Four white colonists were also fatally wounded in what became known as the Boston Massacre. Three days later, hundreds of Bostonians attended a public funeral for the five martyrs, who were buried in a common grave.[19]

Crispus Attucks was the first of thousands of black men, free and slave, who stepped forward to join the American patriots in their struggle for independence. Although patriot leaders eventually prohibited slaves from fighting for a freedom they could not enjoy, by 1778 all the Northern colonies, with the support of General George Washington, were actively recruiting free black men into their militias. More than five thousand black men joined up. Despite Washington's backing, patriot leaders in Georgia and South Carolina stubbornly refused to adopt the policy. The most determined opposition was raised by influential Southerners who believed that slaves were too valuable to emancipate or risk in battle. The Continental Congress, however, was more concerned with the future of the colonies than with the economic interests of a small number of Southern slave owners. Patriot leaders in the North were especially troubled by England's slave-assisted attack and capture of Savannah in December 1778.

Early in 1779, Georgia and South Carolina sent General Isaac Huger to lobby the Continental Congress for additional military support. Huger told the delegates that the Deep South colonies were weakened militarily because the "great proportion of the citizens" were forced to "remain at home to prevent insurrection among the negroes, and to prevent the desertion of them to the enemy." On March 29, 1779, a special congressional committee issued a scathing evaluation of the Southern militias. The panel concluded that regiments in Georgia and South Carolina were not prepared for deployment against loyalist and British troops. These findings came as no surprise to congressional delegates, who were already aware of the "exposed condition" of the two colonies. The committee, which included delegates from Georgia and South Carolina, recommended the enlistment of black slaves, reasoning that they would make good soldiers because they would easily submit to discipline. The delegates also suggested that black enlistment produced the added bonus of reducing the possibility of slave insurrections because the most "vigorous and enterprising" blacks would be occupied with military service.[20]

The Continental Congress passed a resolution requesting that the two Southern colonies begin the immediate recruitment of three thousand able-bodied black soldiers. The resolution stipulated that white officers would command a single battalion in each colony and that slave owners would receive not more than one thousand dollars as compensation for each black enlistee under thirty-five years of age. Black soldiers who faithfully performed their duties and surrendered their weapons after the war would receive fifty dollars and their freedom, according to the legislation.

Acknowledging that the measure might create inconveniences, particularly for slave owners in South Carolina and Georgia, the congress granted the colonies the option of accepting or rejecting the proposal. General Washington dispatched South Carolinian John Laurens to lobby for the measure. Washington hoped to capitalize on the reputation of Laurens's father, Henry, a Carolina slave owner who served as president of the Congress and was a strong supporter of the plan. The elder Laurens had informed General Washington on March 16, 1778, that the British could be driven out of Georgia before the end of July if the American armies could enlist three thousand black soldiers. Four days later, the general wrote his "first crude thoughts" regarding the enlistment of blacks. Washington possessed "not the smallest doubt" that, given the opportunity, black men would step forward and fight alongside white patriots.[21]

Alexander Hamilton stated his unqualified support for the enlistment plan in a letter to John Jay: "Col. Laurens . . . is on his way to South Carolina, on a project which I think . . . is a very good one, and deserves every kind of support and encouragement." However, Hamilton was also aware of the "prejudice and self-interest" that existed throughout the colonies, particularly in the South. He wrote: "The contempt we have . . . for the blacks makes us fancy many things that are founded neither in reason nor experience; and an unwillingness to part with property so valuable . . . will furnish a thousand arguments to show the impracticability or pernicious tendency of a scheme which requires such a sacrifice." [22]

Laurens's father cautioned his son that it would be difficult, if not impossible, to persuade slave owners to part with the basis of their wealth—i.e., slaves—and what they believed to be the source of their happiness. Most delegates, however, were optimistic that Laurens would succeed, because several Southerners, including William Houstoun and Archibald Bulloch of Georgia, had initially raised the idea of slave enlistment. Moreover, General Nathaniel Greene, the patriot commander of the Southern army, enthusiastically supported the plan. He would later assure Southern leaders in 1781 that black slaves would make good soldiers.

But military and political endorsements did not translate into local political support. In May 1779, the plan was placed before a skeptical South Carolina legislature. Laurens made little progress, and his mission was temporarily disrupted by diplomatic concerns that required him to sail for France. He returned in May 1782 and renewed his efforts to raise two battalions of black soldiers in South Carolina and Georgia. Although he discovered that "truth and philosophy had gained some ground," Laurens's efforts were foiled once again by the "triple-headed monster" of prejudice, greed, and cowardliness. After Laurens was angrily rebuffed in South Carolina, Washington correctly predicted that certain failure would follow in Georgia. Despite what Laurens considered to be a promising initial meeting with the governor of Georgia, the legislature delayed voting on the measure until June 1782, when it unanimously rejected the plan. As noted historian U. B. Phillips observed, "Revolutionary liberalism had but the slightest of echoes" in the Georgia colony.[23]

Disappointed and disillusioned, Laurens was consoled by General Washington, who wrote: "That spirit of freedom, which at the commencement of this contest would have gladly sacrificed everything to the attainment of its object, has long since subsided and every selfish passion has taken its place. It is not the public, but private interest, which influences the generality of mankind, nor can the Americans any longer boast an exception. Under these circumstances it would rather have been surprising if you had succeeded."[24]

BLACK GEORGIA PATRIOTS

Despite the legislature's refusal to adopt the congressional resolution, black men and women still contributed to the patriot war effort in Georgia. In October 1779, a French force of thirty-five hundred men joined the Americans at Savannah in an unsuccessful attempt to liberate the city from British control. Fighting with the French was a battalion of 600 black freedmen and slaves from Haiti known as "Frontages Legion," named after their commander, Viscount Francois de Frontages. The Haitians charged into the breach after the French and American soldiers had been completely overwhelmed and turned back by the British, and they saved the Franco-American army from complete humiliation by heroically covering its retreat. Two young Haitian soldiers, Henri Christophe and Toussaint L'Ouverture, returned to their native land and subsequently led the revolutionary movement there that ended decades of French colonial rule.[25]

The most celebrated black Georgia patriot was a mulatto slave named Austin Dabney, who was brought to Georgia from North Carolina by his master, Richard Aycock, shortly after the beginning of the Revolutionary War. Aycock avoided military service by presenting the young slave as his substitute—a practice that Georgia and other colonies permitted. Aycock circumvented the prohibition against slaves bearing arms by swearing that Dabney was a free person of color. Out of necessity or indifference, military leaders apparently ignored Georgia's prohibition against enlisting black men, slave or free, in the militia.

The young recruit served under Colonel Elijah Clarke, and distinguished himself as a brave and loyal patriot. "No soldier under Clarke was braver, or did better service during the revolutionary struggle," wrote an early Georgia historian. In February 1779, Dabney fought in Georgia's bloodiest Revolutionary War battle at Kettle Creek, near the town of Washington in Wilkes County. The Georgia patriots won decisively, but Dabney was shot in the thigh and left seriously wounded on the battlefield.[26]

Giles Harris, a white Wilkes County resident, found Dabney, carried him to his house, and nursed him back to good health. For the rest of his life, Dabney worked to repay Harris for his kindness. To show his gratitude, the war hero became a laborer, friend, and benefactor to the Harris family. Dabney paid Harris's oldest son's tuition at the University of Georgia, and arranged for the young graduate to receive his legal training in the office of a prominent Madison County attorney.[27]

To assure that Dabney would never be forced to bear the yoke of slavery again, the Georgia legislature passed a statue in 1786 officially granting the veteran patriot his freedom. The legislation read as follows:

Whereas Austin a Mulatto man at present the property of the Estate of Richard Aycock, esquire, during the late revolution instead of advantaging himself of the times to withdraw himself from the American lines and enter with the majority of his Color and fellow Slaves in the service of his Brittanick majesty and his officers and Vassals, did voluntarily enroll himself in some one of the Corps under the Command of Col. Elijah Clark, and in the several actions and engagements behaved against the Common Enemy with a bravery and fortitude which would have honored a freeman, and in one of which engagements he was severely wounded, and rendered incapable of hard servitude; and policy as well as gratitude demand a return for such service and behavior from the commonwealth.[28]

The General Assembly accorded the war hero "all the liberties, privileges and immunities of a free citizen . . . so far as free negroes and mulattos are allowed." However, Dabney's military service and free status could not shield him from the pervasive anti-Negro bias that impacted every aspect of Georgia culture. Although his military service qualified him for a land pension, Dabney was denied the opportunity to participate in the 1819 state land lottery because of his race. Two years later, the Georgia Legislature passed a special resolution granting Dabney 112 acres of land for his "bravery and fortitude." Angry white Madison County residents complained that it was an insult to white men for a former slave to be put on equality with them in the land distribution lottery. But Dabney enjoyed the support of several prominent white politicians, including Governor George Gilmer and Stephen Upson of Oglethorpe County, who introduced the legislation. The governor reminded the Madison Countians that Dabney had rendered "courageous service" during the Revolutionary War, and Gilmer chastised them for displaying what he described as "unpatriotic" attitudes.[29]

Dabney's contributions to the war effort were singular, but by no means unique. Several other black men served with distinction as combat troops in the patriot army. Nathan Fry joined Colonel Samuel Elbert's regiment at Savannah in 1775. Monday Floyd secured his freedom in 1782 by an act of the Georgia Assembly, which cited his heroic service during the war and directed the public treasury to pay Floyd's owner one hundred guineas for his manumission.

In addition, Georgia slaves made other important noncombat contributions to the patriot cause. During the fall of 1775, the Georgia Council of Safety impressed scores of slaves in Savannah to help General Charles Lee enclose a military storehouse. In June of the following year, Negro slaves constructed entrenchments around the Sunbury settlement, again under council orders. Much to the chagrin of local slave owners, the council repeatedly used slaves to perform essential noncombat duties. Colonial leaders tried to address their concerns by assuring owners that sick or injured slaves would be provided "sustenance, medicines, and attendance" and by agreeing to compensate owners for slaves killed or permanently injured.[30]

Despite slave owner opposition, slave labor became an increasingly important element in Georgia's military strategy. In 1776, for instance, the Council of Safety ordered that twenty Negroes taken from the plantations of two British loyalists be put to work building a battery on Tybee Island. The following September, the council secured additional black workers by enacting a statute requiring slave owners to maintain a list of male slaves between the ages of sixteen and sixty, one-tenth of whom could be impressed for up to twenty-one days. Slave owners received three shillings a day for each slave approved for service by a panel of four property owners and a government commissioner. The slave-impressment law expired on February 1, 1778, but the war effort in Georgia had become too dependent on slave labor to wean itself from the practice. Patriot leaders authorized Colonel Andrew Williamson to impress Georgia slaves to repair the road between the Ogeechee and Altamaha rivers—with or without slave owner permission.[31]

Captured slaves of British loyalists were also used as bounty to compensate American soldiers and officials. Following the recapture of Savannah, the Safety Council ordered that confiscated loyalist slaves be sold at public auction, and the proceeds divided among American soldiers. In 1782, Georgia Governor John Martin received ten slaves in lieu of salary, and the entire Executive Council was subsequently compensated with captured slaves. In fact, the latter stages of the Revolutionary War in the Southern colonies were largely financed by revenue generated from the sale or confiscation of slaves formerly owned by British loyalists.

EVACUATE TO FREEDOM

In April 1781 Georgia and Carolina patriots began a critical offensive against the British that led to the end of the Revolutionary War in Georgia. Following a two-month patriot siege of Fort Cornwallis near Augusta, British troops surrendered on June 30, 1781. The British eventually surrendered Savannah to the Continental Army in July 1782. Four months later, on November 30, the signing of the Treaty of Paris officially ended hostilities in the American Revolution. One of the key treaty provisions required British troops to withdraw completely from the American colonies and return all confiscated property. The terms of the capitulation were silent, however, regarding fugitive American slaves who tried to escape on board departing British ships.

The pending evacuation of Savannah created a politically sensitive and chaotic situation for fugitive slaves and their British allies. An informal precedent had been established in Boston in 1776 when loyalist blacks were evacuated along with British soldiers. Hundreds of Georgia slaves pleaded to be evacuated on British ships. Georgia slave owners, alarmed by the staggering financial losses a mass black exodus would entail, urgently appealed to the legislature for relief. The lawmakers directed Governor Martin to instruct the British commandant at Savannah not to evacuate fugitive slaves or other American property. The governors of Georgia and South Carolina appointed a special commission to resolve the conflicting claims of American slave masters, white loyalist evacuees, and fugitive slaves. The policy guiding the commission's deliberations was that fugitives claiming protection under the Philipsburg Proclamation, or those who actually served in the British army would remain free.

On July 10 and 11, 1782, British soldiers, white loyalists and their slaves, fugitive slaves, and free blacks began the British evacuation of Savannah. Among the evacuees was Reverend George Liele, who would go on to sow the seeds of the black church throughout the British Empire. Prior to his departure, Liele preached a final sermon in the Yamacraw section of the city and baptized four black worshipers: Andrew Bryan, his wife Hannah, Kate Hogg, and Hagar Simpson. Bryan succeeded Liele as black Savannah's spiritual leader and provided the impetus for the official establishment of the Ethiopian Baptist Church, later renamed the First African Baptist Church.

According to an embarkation record dated August 10, 1782, six ships transported Liele and about 1,500 other blacks to British-controlled Jamaica during the first month of the evacuation. The black preacher worked as an indentured servant for two years, and was subsequently granted his certificate of freedom. Liele resumed his missionary work among the island's slave and free black populations, but was persecuted and tormented by local officials. He and several worshipers were imprisoned and charged with sedition, a capital offense. Liele barely escaped the hangman's noose, while one of the others was found guilty and executed. Undeterred by his close call with death, he went on to establish the Windward Baptist Church in Kingston in 1779—Jamaica's first Baptist church. Carey Robinson, a Jamaican historian, recognizes Liele as a father of the freedom movement that eventually led to the abolition of Jamaican slavery by the Emancipation Act of 1833.

Within a year, an additional 1,956 Negroes, including 107 women and 452 children, left Georgia for British-controlled East Florida. All told, it is estimated that more than 3,500 black men, women and children were eventually evacuated by British vessels from Savannah. This large exodus of Negroes led several slave owners to petition the Georgia Safety Council for permission to travel to east Florida to negotiate the repurchase of fugitive slaves. During the spring of 1783, the governor of east Florida wrote, "There is a considerable influx of transient people from Georgia and South Carolina to recover their property in Negroes." Approximately one thousand slaves were eventually returned to Georgia. By the end of 1783, most of the blacks remaining in east Florida were transported to Nova Scotia, Canada, the Bahamas, Jamaica, and various European ports. David George sailed from Charleston, South Carolina, to Nova Scotia, Canada, where he devoted the next ten years of his life to preaching to black settlers in the Canadian cities of Shelbourne, Brichtown, Ragged Island, and St. Johns, New Brunswick. After establishing a church in Shelbourne, he led a group of disgruntled black settlers back to Freetown, Sierra Leone, on the west coast of Africa, where he established another church in 1792.[32]

England's decision to evacuate former American slaves, and its refusal to compensate their owners, set off a long and bitter diplomatic dispute between the British Empire and her former colonies. In 1783 American diplomats in Europe officially protested the evacuation and repeatedly denounced the British as "slave stealer[s]." Georgia's delegates to the Continental Congress led the fight for the evacuees' return and encouraged General Washington to "get the runaways back." Congress even considered holding British prisoners until the former slaves were returned to American soil. However, England's representatives stubbornly refused the American demands and most of the former Georgia slaves retained their hard-won freedom.[33]

Hundreds more fugitive Georgia slaves, however, were left behind because of insufficient space on evacuation ships or by their own decision. Unlike Liele and George, Jessie Peter was among the blacks who voluntarily chose to remain in Georgia and return to their previous condition of bondage. Peter's new master granted him "uncommon liberties," and encouraged him to expand his ministry to three or four slave congregations, including the remnants of the Silver Bluff Church. Possessing "a grave countenance, charming voice and good delivery," he soon developed a reputation as a powerful preacher who spread the gospel on both sides of the Savannah River. During the mid-1780's, his old friend George Liele wrote that Peter was preaching near Augusta in South Carolina to a congregation of sixty members, and joyfully noted that "a great work is going on there." Peter subsequently moved the Silver Bluff congregation to Augusta, where he founded the historic First African Baptist Church of Augusta, later renamed Springfield Baptist Church. [34]

Many of the black fugitives who remained behind did not voluntarily return to slavery; instead they sought refuge among the Seminoles on Georgia's southern frontier or joined other fugitive slaves in secret maroon camps in the swamps along the Savannah River. Fugitive slaves from Georgia and other Southern states intermarried and assimilated with the Seminoles, eventually developing a unique Negro-Seminole culture. These blacks, or "Estelusti," as they were called in the Muskogee Seminole language, would later play a pivotal role in shaping the history of the southeastern United States.

As early as December 1771, Georgia Governor James Habersham reported "that a great number of fugitive Negroes had committed many Robberies and insults between this town [Savannah] and Ebenezer and that their Numbers were now Considerable [and] might be expected to increase daily." Scores of these self-emancipated blacks and their descendents had managed to preserve their freedom during the Revolutionary War years.

Prior to the British surrender of Fort Cornwallis, more than two hundred former slaves who had helped defend the fort escaped into the swamps along the Savannah River between Augusta and Savannah. These black men formed the nucleus of a guerrilla band that was known as the "King of England's Soldiers." [35]

This legendary band of maroons used military skills learned from the British to make life miserable for their former masters. Described as the "best disciplined band of marauders that ever infested [Georgia] borders," these former slaves plundered at will on both sides of the Savannah River. White Georgians feared the presence of these "freebooters" would instigate widespread insurrections among Georgia slaves, and on several occasions local militia tried unsuccessfully to end the depredations. Finally on May 6, 1786, Georgia and Carolina militia, guided by Catawba Indians, attacked and burned the fugitives' makeshift fortress, which consisted of a rectangular breastwork of logs and cane. All but a few of the King of England's Soldiers were killed or captured in the battle. [36]

The October 1786 edition of the *Massachusetts Gazette* carried a report of approximately one hundred blacks who lived in a secret community on Bellisle Island, about twenty miles north of Savannah. The band conducted numerous raids against white settlements along the Savannah River until the Georgia militia was ordered to locate and destroy the settlement. The fugitives repulsed the Savannah Light Infantry's initial attack, but the next day General James Jackson's troops stormed the camp, burned their houses and huts, and destroyed four acres of green rice. Most of the blacks were killed, wounded, or captured, although a few managed to escape into the nearby swamps and underbrush. Long after the final shots had been fired in the Revolutionary War, Georgia's fugitive slaves continued to struggle for freedom against the Americans. [37]

THE BIRTH OF A NATION

Following their struggle to win independence, American patriots turned their attention to the establishment of a stronger, more centralized national government. George Washington, James Madison, and other Revolutionary War leaders realized that the loose confederation of thirteen "Sovereign" colonies needed to be fused into one united nation. The fifty-five Founding Fathers who gathered in Philadelphia during the summer of 1787 to draft a constitution and give birth to the United States of America were faced with many difficult challenges. The constitutional delegates were painfully aware that the ultimate success of the convention was dependent, in large part, on their ability to resolve differences of opinion between the Southern and Northern colonies. Delegate James Madison astutely observed that the states were divided "principally from the effects of their having or not having slaves." [38]

Although the delegates carefully avoided using the word "slavery" while drafting the historic document, bitter sectional disputes regarding the moral, economic, and political ramifications of the "peculiar institution" threatened to disrupt the constitutional deliberations. On several occasions South Carolina and Georgia delegates declared that they would not support the effort to forge a new nation unless slavery was constitutionally protected. Eleven years earlier, Southern delegates had employed a similar strategy during the deliberations that preceded the signing of the Declaration of Independence. In the original draft of that document, Thomas Jefferson angrily denounced the African slave trade, but the antislavery language was later removed to appease delegates from South Carolina and Georgia. During the constitutional debates, men from the South once again declared that their allegiance and support would be conditioned on the preservation of American slavery.

Georgia was represented at the Constitutional Convention by six men selected by the legislature: William Few, William Pierce, George Walton, William Houstoun, Nathaniel Pendleton, and Abraham Baldwin. Although the Georgia delegation played a relatively minor role during the deliberations, historians credit Baldwin, the first president of the University of Georgia, with being the state's most effective delegate. The soft-spoken Yale graduate and his fellow Georgians routinely allied themselves with the delegates from South and North Carolina. Throughout the convention, the Deep South delegates vigorously defended the institution of slavery against charges that it violated the basic principles of democracy and human dignity. Baldwin later recalled that contentious debates over slavery caused the delegates much "pain and difficulty." [39]

Although slavery was outlawed in Massachusetts prior to 1787, and Pennsylvania, Rhode Island, and Connecticut had all instituted gradual emancipation statutes, no effort to actually abolish slavery was mounted during the convention. The central slavery-related issue was who would have the power to regulate the African slave trade—the federal government or the individual states. However, any mention of the word "slavery" aroused passionate, wide-ranging debates among the delegates as they struggled to fashion political compromise and build consensus. Should slaves, who were legally defined as property, be counted in a census to determine the apportionment of congressional representatives among the various states? If they were to be counted, should they be counted equally with white citizens? Would the federal government be granted the power to prohibit or levy a tax on the importation of African slaves? Would the federal government, if it chose to do so, have the power to legally abolish slavery? Political fault lines opened by these vexing issues eventually forced the convention to the edge of early adjournment and political chaos.

By the late 1700s, more than 755,000 black slaves labored in twelve of the thirteen American colonies. Less than 10 percent of that total lived in the northern colonies of New York, Delaware, New Hampshire, Rhode Island, Pennsylvania, New Jersey, and Connecticut. The use of slaves in the industrialized Northern colonies had steadily declined because slavery had proven to be an unprofitable form of labor in industries that required a more skilled work force. Approximately 400,000 blacks were enslaved in the less industrialized middle colonies of Maryland and Virginia, where the cultivation of tobacco and other staple crops was heavily dependent on slave laborers. In the Deep South the economic realities were very different. Slave labor was absolutely essential for the cultivation of rice and indigo in the semitropical swamps of South Carolina and Georgia. (Cotton was not yet a major crop; Eli Whitney would not invent the cotton gin until 1793.) North and South Carolina held 207,000 blacks in bondage while Georgia, the youngest of the former British colonies, claimed only 29,000, since its slave population had been depleted during the Revolutionary War by the escape of fugitive slaves.

The relatively small number of Georgia slaves was the source of a severe labor shortage and the cause of much concern among Georgians who believed that slave labor was the key to their economic prosperity. The growing demand for black slaves was exacerbated by a postwar influx of settlers from other colonies who rushed to occupy and cultivate cheap land on Georgia's expansive western frontier. Still fresh in the minds of some political leaders was General James Oglethorpe's struggle to prohibit the importation of slaves into Georgia. According to proslavery advocates, the fledgling colony had languished economically and almost perished due to the absence of black slaves. No doubt Georgia's past economic difficulties greatly influenced the actions of her constitutional delegates as they fought to protect and preserve the institution.

The first major debate involving slavery began during the first week of June 1787, when delegate Edmund Randolph presented the Virginia Plan. Randolph proposed that population should be the basis of proportional representation in the upper and lower houses of Congress. The question was immediately raised: Would slaves be counted in determining the number of representatives from each state? A majority of the delegates opposed counting slaves because Southern states would receive a majority of the representatives and a distinct political advantage. For example, if Georgia's 29,000 slaves were not counted, the state would qualify for only one congressman in what would become the House of Representatives. Southern delegates rationalized their support for counting slaves, even though they possessed no legal rights, by arguing that representation in the federal congress should be based on population and wealth. Abraham Baldwin sought to gain additional advantage for the South by proposing that the upper house, or Senate, be apportioned solely on the basis of wealth. (Throughout the constitutional debates, the term "wealth" was often used as a euphemism for Negro slaves.) The benefit to slave owners was obvious—the Southern colonies were wealthier than their Northern neighbors primarily because of the huge sums of money invested in black slaves.[40]

The delegates eventually passed a proposal that became known as the Three-Fifths Compromise. Under this provision, three-fifths, or 60 percent, of a state's slave population would be added to the total free population to determine the number of its representatives in the lower house of Congress. Despite the provision's initial passage, the cumbersome legislative process adopted by the convention required the delegates to revisit the proposal on several different occasions. During the weeks that followed, opposition to counting slaves in the apportionment process coalesced and stiffened. Elbridge Gerry of Massachusetts was the first to object to the plan: "Blacks are property, and are used to the southward as horses and cattle [are used] to the northwards; and why should their representation be increased to the southward on account of the number of slaves, [unless] horses or oxen [are counted] to the north?"

However, Northern opposition was met with the equally determined advocacy of proslavery delegates who insisted on adoption of the controversial three-fifths clause.[41]

By the first week of July 1787, the convention had become paralyzed by the simmering, potentially explosive issue. The majority of delegates now supported the exclusion of slaves from the official census that would be used to apportion seats in Congress—but the Southerners and their allies refused to acquiesce. William Patterson of New Jersey touched off a contentious four-day debate when he voiced his objection to the three-fifths clause. On July 9, Patterson stated that he regarded "negro slaves in no light but as property." He argued that they were not "free agents, have no personal liberty, no faculty of acquiring property, but on the contrary are themselves property, & like other property entirely at the will of the Master." Patterson maintained that allowing blacks to be counted in the census would encourage the continuance of the slave trade and he also noted—with a hint of sarcasm—that Southern states did not count slaves when apportioning their own legislatures.[42]

In the face of growing opposition, the Southern delegates sought to strengthen their precarious political position. It was commonly accepted by delegates from the North and South that, although the Northern colonies were presently more populous, the Southern colonies, with their vast unsettled regions, would eventually overtake them. To ensure that the North would not unfairly maintain its numerical superiority in Congress, Virginian Edmund Randolph proposed that a census be taken on a regular basis in order to "ascertain the alterations in population and wealth," (wealth here was yet another reference to slaves) and that the distribution of congressional representatives be adjusted accordingly. The proposal was adopted with little formal dissent. Ironically, the reapportionment measure, originally proposed to protect the interests of white slave owners, eventually became a key weapon in the fight to extend the voting rights of black Southerners during the latter half of the twentieth century. The willingness of the Northerners to support the reapportionment proposal may have been an attempt to temper Southern anger over what would occur on the following day. On July 11, 1787—voting in a bloc—the Northern delegates passed a provision that not only rejected the three-fifths clause, but also prohibited any inclusion of black slaves in calculations used to apportion congressional representatives.[43]

The proceedings had now reached a critical point. If the majority prevailed and black slaves were not counted either as persons or property, then the Southern delegates would reject the new constitution and refuse to join the union of states. On July 12, 1787, William Davie of North Carolina, who had sat quietly throughout most of the proceedings, rose from his seat and stated that "it was high time to speak out." He was now convinced that some of the delegates were determined to deprive the slaveholding states of any share of representation for their blacks. Davie did not mince his words, asserting that unless the three-fifths clause was reinstated, "the business was at an end." At this point a special committee, consisting of one representative from each state, was selected to resolve the vexing issue of how or if slaves would be counted in the apportionment process. Abraham Baldwin was selected to represent Georgia on what became known as the Committee of Eleven.[44]

The result of the committee's negotiations was the Great Compromise. This compromise between delegates from the large and small states resulted in the creation of a bicameral federal congress and the reinstatement of the three-fifths clause. Representation in the lower house, or House of Representatives, would be based on population, including three-fifths, or 60 percent, of all black slaves. Each state was also granted two votes, regardless of the size of its free or slave population, in the upper house, or Senate. Although the dispute over the counting of slaves in the apportionment process had proven to be a contentious issue, it was only a prelude to the even more divisive debate over the continuance of the African slave trade.

"A PRO-SLAVERY COMPACT"

The constitutional deliberations over the African slave trade began on August 6, 1787, with the presentation of the proposal that forbade the federal government from prohibiting or taxing "the migration or importation of such persons, as the several states shall think proper to admit." The word "migration" referred to free persons while "importation" was another euphemism for black slaves. This ignited a heated debate between Southern delegates and their allies and a vocal group of antislavery delegates who primarily represented the Northern colonies. The resolution would result in a historic "bargain" that ultimately sealed the fate of generations of black slaves.[45]

Gouverneur Morris of Pennsylvania fired the opening salvo in the debate by denouncing slavery as a "nefarious institution, the curse of heaven on the states where it prevailed." Morris declared that he "would sooner submit himself to a tax for paying for all of the negroes in the United States than saddle posterity with a Constitution" that permitted the continuation of the slave trade. He challenged the delegates to compare the prosperity of the free states with their "rich and noble cultivation . . . with the misery and poverty which overspreads the barren wastes of Virginia, Maryland and the other states having slaves. Wretched Africans! The vassalage of the poor has ever been the favorite offspring of aristocracy!"[46]

South Carolinians James Rutledge, Charles Cotesworth Pinckney, and his cousin Charles Pinckney, as well as Abraham

Baldwin of Georgia, rose to defend the institution of slavery. The Southerners raised the political stakes by playing their most effective trump card: Prohibition of the slave trade literally meant that South Carolina and Georgia would not sign the new constitution. On six separate occasions, the Southern delegates reminded their colleagues of their all-or-nothing stance. Rutledge stated that if any of the delegates were under the mistaken impression that South Carolina and Georgia would ever consent to a prohibition of the trade, then that expectation was in vain. The South Carolinian asserted that "Interest alone" should be "the governing principle of nations." He explained with great effect that economic interests, not religion or morality, should control the thoughts and deeds of the delegates. Charles Cotesworth Pinckney added that the men from South Carolina and Georgia would "never be such fools as to give up so important an interest." [47]

On August 22, 1787, George Mason, a Virginia slaveholder who had been denied permission to free his two hundred slaves by the Virginia legislature, delivered a fiery antislavery address. With indignation dripping from his lips, Mason spoke: "This infernal traffic originated in the avarice of British Merchants! The British government constantly checked the attempts of Virginia to put a stop to it." His words were reminiscent of Thomas Jefferson's antislavery clause that had been expunged from the Declaration of Independence. Mason argued that the federal government must be given the power to regulate the slave trade in order to prevent slavery from spreading throughout the union. The hot-tempered Virginian struck sensitive nerves when he lambasted slavery as "inconsistent with the principles of the revolution, and dishonorable to the American character." He stated: "The Western people are already calling out for slaves for their new lands, and will fill that Country with slaves if they can be got through South Carolina and Georgia." Finally, he warned the convention that God always punishes national sins with national calamities, and the crime of

American slavery would some day bring divine judgment down upon the nation.[48]

Unmoved by Mason's verbal assault, Charles Pinckney argued that slavery was justified by its usage in ancient Greece and Rome and, according to him, the institution was also the cornerstone of modern societies such as France, Holland, and England: "In all ages, one half of mankind have been slaves." Charles Cotesworth Pinckney reiterated that "South Carolina and Georgia cannot do without slaves" and "it would be unjust to require them to confederate on such unequal terms." Luther Martin of Maryland reminded the delegates that the Revolutionary War had dramatically exposed military weaknesses associated with the enslavement of Africans. This was especially true in Georgia, where large numbers of blacks aided and supported the British during their two-year occupation of Savannah. Martin also raised the specter of bloody slave insurrections. The South Carolinian Rutledge boldly asserted that he would readily agree to exempt the other states from the obligation of assisting the slaveholding states in the event of slave rebellions. But despite his prideful boast, the final draft of the Constitution contained a key provision that required the federal government to help suppress all internal insurrections and rebellions.[49]

Abraham Baldwin joined the verbal fray by insisting that the individual states, not the federal government, should have the power to regulate the slave trade. The scholarly Georgian used carefully chosen words as he cautioned the convention to restrict its deliberations to "national objects alone." He maintained that slavery was purely a "local" issue, while observing that one of the dangers of centralization was the apparent desire of the "central states" to be the "vortex of everything." Baldwin stated that the people of Georgia fully supported the institution of slavery and would not accept any limitation or prohibition of the slave trade. However, he predicted that, if left alone, the state would probably "put a stop to the evil." James Wilson of Pennsylvania was not convinced, and questioned the wisdom and sincerity of Baldwin's assertion. Wilson stated that if Georgia was truly committed to the abolition of the slave trade, then no reason existed for her delegates to withhold their support for the proposed constitution.[50]

Baldwin and his fellow Southerners were not without allies in the North. Judge Oliver Ellsworth of Connecticut dryly noted that prohibiting the slave trade would be especially harmful to South Carolina and Georgia because so many of their slaves died in "sickly rice swamps" that fresh ones were in constant demand. Ellsworth argued that the morality and wisdom of the slave trade were issues that should be addressed by the individual states, not the federal government. The principle of "states' rights" dictated that the individual states should have the right to import black slaves without interference from the federal government. Rufus King of Massachusetts offered a pragmatic assessment of the debate. A constitutional prohibition against the African slave trade all but guaranteed that the Southern states would not consent to joining the Union. King concluded that it would be better to allow South Carolina and Georgia to import slaves than to go forward without them—"if they make that a sine qua non." [51]

The defiance of the Southern delegates and the willingness of their Northern colleagues to seek compromise reaped significant political dividends for both groups. The economic interests of commercial shippers in New England joined with those of the proslavery, agrarian South to effect a "bargain" that assured the adoption of the Constitution and affirmed the legality of American slavery. The Northern delegates secured the coveted elimination of a clause that required a two-thirds majority vote in the House of Representatives to pass any trade legislation. This delivered to the North what amounted to complete control of the regulation of commercial shipping and international trade. The Southerners walked away with explicit protections for slavery that were skillfully incorporated into the Constitution in five articles and clauses:

(1) The three-fifths clause (Article 1, Section 2) provided that 60 percent of all slaves would be counted in apportioning seats in the House of Representatives and assessing each state's contribution if a "direct tax" was levied.

(2) The slave importation clause (Article 1, Section 9, Par. 1) prohibited Congress from banning the African slave trade prior to 1808.

(3) The capitation or "head tax" clause (Article I, Section 9, Par. 4) declared that any federal tax had to take into account the three-fifths clause.

(4) The fugitive slave clause (Article IV, See 2, Par. 3) provided that no state could emancipate fugitive slaves and that they must be returned to their owners "on demand."

(5) Article V prohibited any amendment of the slave importation or capitation clauses before 1808.

Although the "peculiar scruples" of the delegates had led them to avoid using the word "slave" while crafting the historic document, the institution of slavery was intricately woven into the constitutional fabric of the United States of America. Angry abolitionists in the North saw through this political sleight of hand. Wendell Phillips called the new constitution "a pro-slavery compact," while three opponents in Massachusetts wrote that "this lust for slavery, [was] portentous of much evil in America, for the cry of innocent blood . . . hath undoubtedly reached to the Heavens, to which that cry is always directed, and will draw upon them vengeance adequate to the enormity of the crime." A generation later, abolitionist

William Lloyd Garrison declared that the document was "a covenant with death, an agreement with Hell." [52]

Prior to the Constitutional Convention, James Madison had written to Thomas Jefferson and predicted that South Carolina would not accept any limitation on the right to import slaves. After the delegates departed Philadelphia, he informed his friend that South Carolina and Georgia had been "inflexible on the point of slaves." Despite deep-seated reservations, even the Northerners who had spoken against slavery, in the end, were unwilling to risk jeopardizing the formation of the union of states simply to protect the rights of Africans. Although the Founding Fathers succeeded in giving birth to what would become the world's preeminent democracy, they were unable or unwilling to address the festering evil of American slavery. Delegate Luther Martin took note of the irony that cast a shadow over the framing of the Constitution. He observed that American patriots had waged a bloody revolution "grounded upon the preservation of those rights to which God and nature had entitled us, not in particular, but in common with all the rest of mankind—had ended by making a Constitution that was an insult to that God—who views with equal eye the poor African slave and his American master." [53]

Shortly after the convention adjourned, Thomas Jefferson hailed the men who had gathered and deliberated in Philadelphia during the summer of 1787 as "demi-gods." The Founding Fathers were gifted men, blessed with an abundance of vision, courage, and genius. However, in the final analysis, they proved themselves to be men, not gods or even demi-gods. The delegates were not immune to the human frailties of prejudice, self-interest, and greed. During the bicentennial celebration of America's birth in 1987, Supreme Court Justice Thurgood Marshall, the first African American to sit on the nation's highest judicial tribunal, argued that the true greatness of the "Miracle at Philadelphia" was not the "birth" of the Constitution but its "life." Marshall stated that the original

Constitution was not "perfect." He noted that it took decades of black struggle, civil war, and the Thirteenth, Fourteenth and Fifteenth Amendments to remove the stain of slavery from America's most sacred political document. In the final analysis, history has demonstrated that the Founding Fathers wisely constructed a constitution that granted succeeding generations of Americans the right to amend and perfect it.[54]

CHAPTER III

THE WAR OF 1812 AND THE
EMANCIPATION OF GEORGIA SLAVES

Thirty years after the final shots were fired in the Revolutionary War, Americans found themselves embroiled in another bloody conflict with England. This second war between England and America was tragic in its loss of life, but in many ways it was little more than a comedy of errors and confusion. In fact, American public opinion regarding the war was deeply divided because of widespread uncertainty regarding its cause. However, no such confusion or ambivalence existed among black men and women enslaved on coastal Georgia plantations. The war provided them with yet another opportunity to earn their freedom and the freedom of loved ones by bearing arms in a struggle against their former masters.

During the War of 1812, Georgia slave owners were once again tormented by the British strategy of emancipating and arming black slaves. In January 1815, British naval forces attacked and occupied the Sea Islands off the Georgia coast, setting the stage for the liberation and evacuation of more than four thousand Georgia and Florida slaves. The man responsible for masterminding this mass emancipation was Admiral Sir George Cockburn. Born into the British aristocracy, Cockburn rose quickly through the ranks of the Royal Navy. Before his forty-second birthday, he was promoted to the position of admiral and inducted into knighthood. His major military exploits included attacking and burning Washington, D.C. in 1814, and escorting Napoleon Bonaparte into exile on St. Helena Island.[1]

Early in 1813, Cockburn had unveiled his plan for the recruitment of a multiracial force consisting of freed slaves, Red Stick Creek and Seminole Indians, and Spanish, French, and British soldiers. Envisioned as a key war strategy, this unusual coalition would be hurled against American troops defending the southeastern United States. However, the admiral's plan was met with skepticism and indifference among British military and political leaders. They were concerned that implementation of the strategy would ignite slave insurrections throughout Great Britain's far-flung empire, as blacks in the Caribbean and elsewhere would try to follow the example of American slaves and rise up against their masters.

In December 1814, Cockburn was assigned command of all royal forces operating in the Atlantic along the Georgia-Florida coast. He continued to argue the merits of his plan, assuring skeptics it could be executed without inciting massive and bloody slave revolts. Early in 1815, following two years of discussion, Cockburn received permission to organize his multiracial fighting force. Military objectives included the attack and occupation of the Sea Islands off the Georgia coast; the emancipation of coastal slaves; the enlistment of one thousand black and white volunteers into the Royal Marines; and the evacuation of all freed slaves from American soil.

Once these objectives were secured, Cockburn and his motley troops planned to rendezvous with Captain George Woodbine and a war party of Creek, Seminole, and black warriors at the seaside village of St. Marys, Georgia. From there the British would launch attacks against Savannah, Charleston, and other major cities along the Atlantic coast. Although the rendezvous never took place, Woodbine did establish a fort in western Florida along the upper Apalachicola River, just south of the Georgia border. The enclave became known as the Negro Fort, a legendary stronghold for fugitive American slaves. In June 1816, the fort would become the site of a tragic battle in which some three hundred blacks, mostly women and children, were killed by American soldiers.

Phase one of Cockburn's plan was successfully launched on January 10, 1815, when fifteen hundred black and white British marines landed without opposition on the northern end of Cumberland Island in Camden County, Georgia. The black marines were former American slaves who had joined the elite Third West Indian Regiment of the British Colonial Marines during the invasion of the Chesapeake Bay area the previous winter. The presence of these free black men on Georgia soil emboldened coastal slaves and sent a wave of hysteria through the white population. By the end of January, the British had gained control of Cumberland, Jekyll, and St. Simons Islands. Phase two called for Cockburn to enlist several hundred emancipated black men in the British military. An official proclamation of emancipation was issued, promising all persons desirous of emigrating from the United States sanctuary on His Majesty's ships or on military posts that would be established along the American coast. According to the document, black and white men who enlisted, along with their families, would be taken as "Free Settlers" to British colonies in North America or the West Indies.

ESCAPE TO CUMBERLAND

Details regarding the British offer of freedom spread quickly along the coastal slave grapevine. Hundreds of Georgia slaves escaped from mainland and island plantations, and all but a few arrived at the British encampment on Cumberland Island in small boats and dug-out canoes. The black fugitives were a diverse lot that included men, women, and children of all ages. Testimony subsequently presented at 1824 hearings concerning slave-owner compensation provides extraordinarily detailed descriptions of the blacks who leaped at the chance for freedom.

Among the first to reach Cumberland was a man named Ben, who arrived at the British camp with his wife and child. He was also among the first to join the West Indian Regiment of the Royal Marines. Ben and his family escaped from the Thomas Ellis plantation on the Little Satilla River in Camden County. Seventeen other Camden County slaves fled from their master, William McNish, and landed on Cumberland during the second week of February 1815. Three other slaves from the McNish plantation—Polydore, Alick, and Jerry—also came to the island and joined the British marines.

African-born Tarquin made it to Cumberland around March 4, 1815. The twenty-seven-year-old slave and his four companions, William, Caesar, Charlotte, and Pricilla, had fled from Charles Floyd's plantation and found their way to the British encampment. William was "a prime likely fellow," thirty to forty years old; Caesar was thin and slightly built with very dark skin; his thirty-year-old wife, Charlotte, was also very dark with bushy hair "longer than is common among negroes." The couple brought along their infant daughter, Pricilla, who, according to their former master, was "much petted and nursed" by her mother. The four adults were all African-born members of the Gullah Tribe who had been "selected from prime cargo" and enslaved in America for twelve years prior to their escape.[2]

Also among the throng clamoring for freedom were six domestic slaves formerly owned by Henry Sadler, a St. Mary's merchant who later claimed the slaves had been "enticed away by the British." Included in the group were Patsy, an eighteen-year-old mulatto considered an "excellent servant" and valued at six hundred dollars; Letty, aged seventeen, "stout and short" and valued at five hundred dollars; fourteen-year-old George, described as "uncommonly smart" and valued at five hundred dollars; and Geoffrey, a thirty-seven-year-old field hand. By the first week of February, more than 450 blacks had crowded onto the island, forcing Cockburn to request additional uniforms. The admiral explained that the number of coastal slaves volunteering to serve in the British military was much greater than the number who stepped forward in the Chesapeake Bay area. Cockburn concluded the letter by assuring his superiors that he would transport all freed slaves to Bermuda at every available opportunity.[3]

Although financial losses associated with this exodus were substantial, many owners were more disturbed by the enthusiasm their supposedly loyal slaves exhibited toward the British invaders. Disappointment quickly turned to anger as they realized that all but a few of their most trusted slaves had fled to Cumberland. On St. Simons, 183 slaves belonging to James Hamilton escaped under the protection of British soldiers; Samuel Parker, a Camden County resident, lost 30 slaves and Peter Dibignon, a Jekyll Island planter, reported that 22 of his slaves had absconded to the British.

Despite the powerful lure of freedom, a handful of Georgia slaves refused to be enticed away by the invaders. These so-called "loyal" slaves decided to remain behind for various reasons. Some were too old and frail to travel, while others preferred the familiarity of slavery to the unknown realities of freedom. It is not unreasonable to assume that a legitimate bond of affection for their masters prevented a small number of longtime servants from answering the British call. Among those who remained was an elderly Negro named Daddy Titus, the only slave who did not flee the Fairfield Plantation in Camden County. According to Mary Floyd Hampton, the daughter of Fairfield owner John Floyd, "Daddy Titus fell on his knees" and actually begged the British troops "not to burn 'massa's' house for he had a great many children." [4]

At least four faithful Negroes were eventually granted their freedom by their owner as a reward for their loyalty during the British occupation and evacuation. They were members of a slave family living on Raymond Demere's St. Simons plantation. The four—Joy, a male slave, Rose, a female slave, and her sons, Jim and John—were eventually manumitted by a provision of Demere's will and an official resolution of the Georgia legislature. The slaves were cited for "their meritorious behavior and faithful conduct . . . when nearly all of the Negroes on St. Simons deserted and joined the British . . . ." According to the bequest, Joy and Rose protected Demere's property from British soldiers and hid a large sum of money they could have used to aid in their escape. Demere did not die until 1829, however, and by 1820 Georgia had prohibited all private manumissions, except by special act of the General Assembly. One year after his death and fifteen years after the British occupation, the legislature passed a resolution officially emancipating the four slaves. [5]

The inability of the undermanned Georgia militia to defend the coast prompted Thomas Spalding, a Sapelo Island slave owner, to organize a company of slave soldiers to protect his plantation. Spalding's head driver, a Moslem slave named Bu Allah or Ben Ali, commanded the troops, who were armed with eighty muskets supplied by the governor of Georgia. Allah allegedly assured his master that, in the event of an attack, he would stand and fight. He is quoted as proclaiming "I will answer for every Negro of the true faith [Islam] but not for the Christian dogs you own." Allah was a devout Moslem who thrice daily turned to the East, kneeled on his sheepskin rug, and prayed to Allah. He authored a rare thirteen-page document known as Ben Ali's "Meditations" or "Diary." The manuscript, written in complex Arabic dialect, has baffled and intrigued historians and religious scholars for decades. Upon his death, the pious slave was buried with his beloved Koran and prayer rug. [6]

Although the British admiral's emancipation strategy was primarily directed toward American slaves, it also attracted a growing number of fugitives from Spanish Florida to Cumberland Island. Their arrival should not have surprised the British because a copy of the emancipation proclamation had been posted earlier in the year on Fernandina Island, off the Florida coast. However, Spanish slaves seeking protection under the proclamation sparked a diplomatic firestorm between Spain and Britain, who at that time were enjoying peaceful relations. Although fugitive British and American slaves had been welcomed as free men and women in Florida for decades, the right of Spaniards to own slaves within the colony was protected by law. The issue: Did the British have the legal authority to grant freedom and sanctuary to fugitive Spanish slaves?

Florida Governor Sebastian Kindelan filed a written protest with Admiral Cockburn early in 1815. Kindelan claimed that Spanish slaves had taken refuge on Cumberland Island and he accused the admiral of offering freedom to those who joined the British army. He decried the loss of Spanish chattel and demanded the return of all fugitives to their Florida masters. In a letter dated February 13, 1815, Cockburn assured Kindelan that not a single Spanish slave had been transported to Cumberland by British ships, adding that only a few Florida fugitives were still on the island. To the Spanish governor's dismay, Cockburn flatly refused to help prevent future escapes or forcibly return any of the fugitives to Florida.[7]

Cockburn invoked his policy of noninterference in a case involving William Younge, a Florida slave owner, who asked for assistance in the return of three male escapees from his Fernandina plantation. Cockburn denied the request, explaining to Younge that the slaves could voluntarily return to Florida, but he refused to encourage or require them to do so. In an attempt to shore up strained diplomatic relations, he did grant aggrieved Florida slave owners the opportunity to speak with their fugitive slaves. Antonio Súarez was the first to take advantage of the new policy in an effort to reclaim a fugitive named Tony. But he ultimately fared no better than Younge. After locating Tony on Cumberland, Suarez tried to persuade him to trade his new-found freedom for reenslavement in Florida. The Spaniard returned to Florida disappointed and empty-handed.

Tension between Spanish slave owners and Cockburn continued to escalate, and nervous British officials in Bermuda eventually ordered the admiral to provide a rationale for his policy. On February 28, 1816, he wrote a long letter to his superior officer, detailing the legal and ethical reasons behind his course of action. He argued that, under the principles of positive law, simple assertions of ownership by Spanish slave owners were insufficient to prove their right to custody of the escaped slaves. He was certain all claims of ownership should be accompanied by incontestable documents that, prior to his acceptance, must be presented for consideration to a duly authorized court that would determine the legality of the assertion.

Secondly, Cockburn relied on the precepts of natural law, as embodied in English law, which prohibited him from accepting the notion that one human being could actually possess an absolute property right in another person. He wrote: "The spirit of Liberty is so deeply implanted in our very soul that a slave or Negro the moment he lands in England, falls under the protection of the laws and so far becomes a freeman." Cockburn maintained that since Cumberland Island was presently occupied by British soldiers, the resolution of all legal disputes should be based on British law. He sarcastically reminded the Florida governor that Spain had maintained a long-standing practice of granting freedom and land to fugitive British and American slaves in Florida. Cockburn ended with the assertion that he was unaware of any authority or legal precedent that required him to forcibly compel the return of the black fugitives to Florida.[8]

THE TREATY OF GHENT

The War of 1812 came to an abrupt and inconclusive end before the diplomatic conflicts between Spain and England could be resolved. Hostilities officially ended when the Treaty of Ghent was ratified by Great Britain on December 31, 1814, and by the United States on February 18, 1815. Terms of the treaty substantially restored the nations to their prewar status and provided for various commissions to deal with unsettled questions. Article 1, which required the return of all slaves evacuated by the British, became the focus of a contentious and long-running dispute between England and the United States. Despite the treaty's ratification, Cockburn did not acknowledge receipt of orders requiring the cessation of hostilities until March 1. In the interim, he continued to provide sanctuary for American and Spanish slaves on Cumberland Island.

On March 15, 1816, Sapelo Island slave owners Thomas Spalding and Captain Thomas Newell departed from Darien, Georgia, with authority from the governor to meet with Cockburn and negotiate the return of Georgia slaves and other property. The two men arrived on Cumberland the following day and were soon engaged in a heated argument with the admiral. The disagreement began when Spalding presented Cockburn with a copy of the *National Intelligencer* newspaper containing details of the treaty and its ratification. Cockburn informed the Georgians that unless they provided him with an authentic certified copy of the treaty, he would not honor its conditions. Spalding angrily demanded the return of all fugitive slaves who were presently living on Cumberland or on board British ships near the island when the treaty was ratified. The admiral informed the Georgians that, based on his interpretation of the treaty, only the fugitive slaves and property originally captured on Cumberland and still on the island at 11 P.M. on February 17, 1815, had to be returned. Cockburn was well aware of the fact that all but a few of the blacks and most of the property had already left the island. Despite loud protests from the Americans, he doggedly defended his position, although the British eventually did return eighty-one slaves and a few bales of cotton to one Cumberland Island slave owner.

On March 13, 1816, Cockburn, who was constantly reviled in the Savannah press as "a finished buccaneer" and "an accomplished vandal," finally acknowledged the ratification of the treaty and struck the Union Jack on Cumberland Island. Spalding subsequently charged that frantic Negroes were allowed to board British ships as late as March 16. Spalding and Newell, with Cockburn's permission, boarded the frigate *Regulus* to address a large group of fugitive Georgia slaves. Despite assurances that there would be no retaliation, only thirteen of the hundreds on board volunteered to return to their American masters. Spalding contended hundreds more would have stepped forward if not for the presence of British officers who discouraged them from doing so.[9]

COASTAL SLAVE DIASPORA

The exact number of slaves who gained their freedom during the British evacuation of Georgia's Sea Islands is unknown. Historian Mary Bullard, in a detailed study based on the registers of British evacuation ships, puts the figure at 1,483 black "super-numeraries." Other estimates range from 2,000 to 3,000. However, those figures do not include fugitive Spanish slaves or former slaves who found refuge among the Seminole Indians. Also, there is evidence that British naval officers may have intentionally understated the number of black evacuees to reduce England's financial liability during subsequent proceedings of the international Mixed Claims Commission.[10]

What is certain, though, is that the emancipation and evacuation of fugitive Georgia slaves: (1) ignited a fierce debate over slave-owner restitution; (2) sparked the passage of sweeping state tax-relief measures for coastal slave owners; (3) ushered in an era of increased repression of free black Georgians; and (4) spawned an unprecedented global manhunt. What's more, the newly free black men and women constituted a diaspora that swept over such diverse nations and British colonies as Canada, Bermuda, Ireland, Jamaica, and Cuba.

Even before the last evacuation ship sailed from American waters, a political storm began to rage in the Georgia legislature. In November 1815, Camden County legislator John Atkinson moved for the appointment of a special committee in the House of Representatives to draft tax-relief legislation for Georgians who had lost slaves and other property to the British the previous January and February. On November 17, the seven-man committee intro-duced a bill entitled "An Act for relieving the citizens of this state from paying taxes for property plundered and taken away by the British since the first day of January last." [11]

Meanwhile, in the state senate, Samuel Piles of Glynn County introduced a resolution denouncing the British for plundering the property of Georgians during the War of 1812. Senator Piles charged the British with making false promises designed to entice away approximately 1,000 black men, women, and children. He also lambasted the British officials for refusing to help Americans apprehend and return the former slaves now living in the "barren and frozen wilds" of Nova Scotia, Canada. [12]

The tax-relief legislation sailed through the house and senate and Georgia Governor David B. Mitchell quickly signed the mea-sure into law. The legislators also amended the state penal code by adding three offenses relating to the theft of slaves. Persons con-victed under the statute would be liable to the owner for the full value of the slave and imprisoned at hard labor for three to seven years. Mindful of the powerful influence the free black marines had over coastal slaves, the legislators also passed several repressive measures targeting free blacks.

Chatham County representative Isaac Minis moved for the appointment of a committee to prepare legislation that would prohibit the importation of any free person of color into the state of Georgia. The passage of this act heralded the beginning of a legislative movement that culminated in the prohibition of all private manumissions in Georgia. During the next session of the General Assembly, lawmakers passed a law that increased the penalty for free blacks found guilty of "inveigling" or "enticing away" a slave from his or her master's service. According to the statute, convicted blacks would be imprisoned for one year, after which they would "be sold to the highest bidder as a slave, for . . . the term of their natural lives." [13]

Georgia legislators also passed a resolution, along with several other southeastern legislatures, requesting the federal government to seek indemnification in an international court of law for slaves and other property lost during the War of 1812. In response to these requests, U.S. Secretary of State James Monroe was assigned the responsibility of negotiating with England on behalf of aggrieved American slave owners. Despite federal intervention, England refused to return a single slave or agree to any amount of compensation.

Slave owner hopes were temporarily buoyed by reports that scores of their former slaves were living in Bermuda under British protection. This led John Forbes, a Florida slave owner, to hurriedly sail to Bermuda in May 1815. Shortly after his arrival, Forbes requested and received permission to address his former slaves. The blacks listened intently, but the entire group rejected his overtures. Thomas Spalding and several other Georgians also went to Bermuda with hopes of opening negotiations with Cockburn's superior officer, Admiral Alexander Cochrane. Although the delegation was pleased with Cochrane's "sincerity of character," they nonetheless returned home without any commitments from the British.[14]

In May 1815 Secretary of State Monroe went outside diplomatic channels and hired Eli Magrueder, an American mercenary, to conduct a covert operation to recapture the former slaves. Magrueder was to secretly gather information regarding their whereabouts and devise a scheme to kidnap the blacks and return them to their former masters. Magrueder informed Monroe in mid-May that approximately one hundred former slaves were still in Bermuda, serving in the British Corps of Engineers. However, before he could kidnap them, the blacks were transferred to Ireland. Undaunted, the mercenary pressed on, offering the captain of a schooner ten dollars a head for each black the man would transport from Ireland to America. This plan also failed to materialize. Magrueder then informed Monroe that he was sailing to Trinidad, the Leeward Islands, and Jamaica to track down a persistent, but unsubstantiated, rumor that some of the blacks had been re-enslaved on British plantations.

On June 12, Georgia slave owner Spalding told Monroe he was convinced the majority of the former slaves had been resettled in Canada. He conceded his only remaining hope was that the brutally cold Canadian winter would drive the blacks back to the more hospitable Southern climate. His speculation would prove correct in part. The former American slaves did indeed suffer considerable hardships during the especially harsh winter of 1815-1816. The majority of them lived in two black settlements at Loch Lomond, Nova Scotia, and Melville Island. The lack of adequate food, clothing, and shelter, a devastating smallpox epidemic, and the prejudices of local British citizens made life extremely difficult. But none of them opted to return to a life of slavery.

In 1818 the emperor of Russia was asked to arbitrate the long-running dispute and determine whether the United States was entitled to restitution under Title 1 of the Treaty of Ghent. In 1822 he ruled in America's favor, and a mixed commission was appointed to determine the average value of the property plundered during the War of 1812. Slaves evacuated from Louisiana were valued at $580; those from Georgia, South Carolina, and Alabama, at $390; and all others at $280.[15]

American representatives presented evidence documenting the removal of 3,601 slaves; however, they offered to settle the dispute for an amount equal to the value of 1,650 slaves. British officials initially rejected the compromise, but in 1827 they ended the twelve-year dispute by agreeing to pay £250,000, or U.S. $1.2 million, for the official emancipation of the former slaves. This served as a fitting prelude to the parliamentary act of 1833 that abolished slavery throughout the British Empire. That historic statute would subsequently free more than 800,000 black slaves at a cost of £20 million pounds to the Royal Treasury.

CHAPTER IV

RED AND BLACK: ALLIES ON THE GEORGIA FRONTIER

The sable slave, from Georgia's utmost bounds
Escapes for life into the great Wahoo.
Here he has left afar the savage hounds
And human hunters that did late pursue;
There in the hammock darkly hid from view,
His wretched limbs are stretched awhile to rest,
Till some kind Seminole shall guide him thro'
To where by hound nor hunter more distress,
He in a flow'ry home, shall be the red man's guest.

—Albery A. Whitman, "The Rape of Florida"

The haunting image of fugitive Southern slaves following the North Star to freedom is a cornerstone of African-American history. Throughout their enslavement, black men, women, and children traveled the legendary Underground Railroad during their desperate escapes from bondage. Yet despite the historical allure of these harrowing journeys, only a few fugitive Georgia slaves actually reached the "Promised Land" in the North. For them, there was a shorter, more convenient route to freedom, through the dense swamps of south Georgia and north Florida. Decades before and after the American Revolutionary War, several thousand self-emancipated black Georgians sought refuge and found sanctuary in the land where the Seminole held sway.

Perhaps the Seminoles sympathized with the plight of fugitive slaves because they themselves were, in a sense, fugitives. During the early 1750s, tribal feuding within the Lower Creek nation had led to the secession of dissident members, who migrated south into an area now centered by the Georgia-Florida border. These Native Americans were called Seminoles, a name that appears to have been derived from *Cimarrón*, a Spanish word for fugitive or wild. In some instances the migrants established villages and camps close to Maroon settlements of fugitive slaves from Georgia, Alabama, and other Southern states. Decades of association, assimilation, and intermarriage led to the development of a unique Negro-Seminole culture and the creation of a powerful military alliance that lasted for more than half a century.

Beginning with the establishment of the Carolina colony in 1670, England and Spain had engaged in a protracted series of covert and overt hostilities that continued until 1763, when Spain ceded Florida to England under the terms of the Treaty of Paris. Prior to their withdrawal, the Spaniards had tried to destabilize the British colonies to the north by rewarding fugitive slaves from Carolina, and later Georgia, with freedom and land in Florida. Unlike the British, who encouraged fear and distrust between Native Americans and Africans, the Spanish encouraged their cooperation and enlisted the support of red and black men in defense of their colony. In 1739, as mentioned earlier, General James Oglethorpe and his British invaders were defeated at the Battle of Bloody Mose by a multiracial contingent of Spanish soldiers, blacks, mulattos, and Indians.[1]

After England gained control of Florida, the swamps and woods along the Georgia-Florida border ceased, at least temporarily, to be a safe refuge for fugitive slaves. During the first two decades of British rule, some of the more prosperous Seminole chiefs, recognizing the prestige that whites associated with the ownership of slaves, began to purchase blacks from slave traders. British officials also established the practice of giving black slaves—"King's gifts"— to some Seminole leaders as reward for their loyalty and service. However, the coming of the American Revolution dramatically changed the British relationship with fugitive American slaves, as well as with the Seminoles in Florida. Manpower shortages during the war forced British military leaders, like the Spanish who preceded them, to ally themselves with black and red men in order to shore up their depleted ranks.

The British strategy resulted in increased numbers of fugitive slaves living along Georgia's southern frontier. In 1776 General Charles Lee, commander of the colony's militia, informed the Continental Congress that Georgia slaves were escaping in ever-increasing numbers and seeking freedom among "the Exiles of Florida." Although he pleaded for assistance, pressing military concerns in other colonies prevented national intervention and the self-emancipated blacks lived peacefully during the Revolutionary War. Following the American victory, British-controlled east Florida became a primary staging area for the evacuation of white loyalists and their slaves, as well as hundreds of former American slaves who had supported the British war effort. One of the key conditions of the 1782 treaty that officially ended hostilities between England and her former colonies was a provision requiring the British to restore possession of Florida to Spain. Scores of blacks who did not join the British evacuation remained in Florida, further increasing the number of blacks who were living among the Seminoles.[2]

During the years following the Revolutionary War, fugitive Georgia slaves continued to escape to Seminole territory. Irate slave owners repeatedly petitioned Congress and the executive branch for assistance. Hoping to placate the Georgians, the United States government signed the Treaties of New York (1790) and Colerain (1796) with the Creeks in an attempt to secure the return of the fugitives. The Americans considered the Seminoles to be a part of the Creek Confederation. However, much animosity existed between the two tribes, and the Seminoles rejected any authority by the Creeks to determine the fate of their black allies who lived among them.

Three distinct groups of blacks lived among the Seminole: fugitive American slaves and their descendants; Negro-Seminoles who were the offspring of interracial liaisons; and legal slaves who actually belonged to Seminole masters. The governors of Spanish Florida accorded fugitive British, and later American, slaves the same rights and protections granted to Spaniards and Native Americans. One unidentified observer noted: "The Negroes dwell in towns apart from the Indians and are the finest looking people I have ever seen. They dress and look pretty much like the Indians, each having a gun, and hunting a portion of the time." As the slave grapevine spread glowing accounts of life among the Seminoles, fugitives from Georgia and other Southern states continued to swell Florida's black population during the post-Revolutionary period.[3]

According to numerous contemporary accounts, the Seminoles practiced a unique form of slavery that provided black "slaves" with all but complete equality with their Native American "masters." Whether acquired by gift, purchase, capture, or voluntary acquiescence, fugitive slaves preferred Seminole bondage to American slavery, for Seminole masters rarely attempted to control the activities of their so-called "slaves." The blacks owned axes, hoes, and other tools needed to build houses and raise crops. In exchange for their patronage, the blacks provided the Seminoles with a reasonable portion of their corn and other crops, while the rest would be used for sustenance and trade. Major General George McCall provided the following description of the Negro-Seminole relationship: "They are chiefly runaway slaves from Georgia, who have put themselves under the protection of Micanopy, or some other chief, whom they call master; and to whom, for this consideration, they render tribute of one-third of the produce of the land, and one-third of the horses, cattle and fowls they may raise. Otherwise they are free to go and come at pleasure." [4]

Seminole slaves often became valued counselors and interpreters who could establish communication between their Indian masters and the white man. Noted Negro-Seminole historian Kenneth Porter concluded that the symbiotic relationship resembled the medieval feudal pact between lord and vassal more than master and slave. A white observer once suggested that the slaves were actually more intelligent than their nominal masters, primarily because many of them were fluent in Spanish, English, and the Seminole language. By 1810, several hundred fugitive American slaves and their descendants were living in Seminole territory in scattered Negro towns and camps.

GEORGIA INVADES FLORIDA

For decades Georgia slave owners watched helplessly as their black bondsmen fled to freedom in Florida. Once on Spanish soil, the fugitives became subjects of the Spanish Crown and were protected from recapture, much to the dismay of their former masters. Georgians eventually realized that the most effective way to eliminate the troublesome slave refuge to the south—short of full-scale war with Spain—would be to annex the territory to the United States. They began to lobby the federal government to take jurisdiction over the poorly defended Spanish colony. According to Joshua Giddings, an abolitionist congressman, "An excitement . . . was raised in favor of annexation; and this anxiety to secure the slave interests of the South, soon extended to Congress, and infused itself into the Executive policy of the nation." The call for annexation was bolstered by American military leaders, who believed that the British were planning to retake the province from Spain. On January 15, 1811, the U.S. Congress met in secret session and authorized President James Madison to effect a covert takeover of Florida.[5]

President Madison commissioned George Mathews, a former governor of Georgia, to negotiate Florida's annexation into the United States. After Spanish authorities rejected his overtures, Mathews decided to take the colony by force. He organized a small army comprised mostly of Georgia residents and secretly crossed the St. Mary's River into northeast Florida. They planned to sow the seeds of rebellion in the colony, form an opposition government, and transfer jurisdiction over the colony to the United States government. With the support of American troops and gunboats, the so-called Patriot Army easily captured Fernandina Island off the Florida coast, and prepared to attack St. Augustine.[6]

Defeat of the Spaniards appeared certain, but intervention by Negro-Seminoles, Seminole warriors, and fugitive slaves quickly turned the tide of battle. The former slaves realized that an American victory would almost guarantee a return to slavery, and the Seminole slaves, too, dreaded the harsher, more restrictive slave codes of the Southern states. The Florida fugitives had long regarded the Spanish as bulwarks against reenslavement; consequently, black men armed themselves and rushed to aid in the colony's defense.

Tony Proctor, a black emissary from St. Augustine, convinced the Seminole chiefs that the Georgians planned to defeat the Spanish and take possession of Seminole land. Threatened by what they now recognized as a common enemy, allied bands of Negroes and Seminoles went on the warpath, plundering and burning plantations and farms along Georgia's southern frontier. As word of the Patriot invasion spread, scores of slaves escaped from plantations in Georgia and Alabama and joined the Florida resistance. The blood-curdling yells of black and red warriors were heard on both sides of the St. John's River.

On July 30, 1812, Lieutenant Colonel Thomas Smith informed his superiors of several Seminole depredations along the frontier and the escape of about eighty slaves. Smith also explained why he planned to send an expedition into Seminole territory: "They have . . . several hundred fugitive slaves from the Carolinas and Georgia at present in their Town & unless they are checked soon they will be so strengthened by desertions from Georgia & Florida that it will be found troublesome to reduce them." Two months later, Georgia Governor David Mitchell, who replaced Mathews as commander of the American troops in east Florida, claimed the governor of Florida had offered "freedom to every negro who will join his standard, and has sent a party of them to unite . . . with the Indians in their murderous excursions." According to Mitchell, the principal strength of the St. Augustine garrison consisted of black men. He noted: "most of our male negroes on the seaboard are restless and make many attempts to get off to Augustine, and many have succeeded." [7]

The St. Augustine garrison was comprised of four hundred Spanish and five hundred Negro soldiers. According to Mitchell, the Spanish were arming every able-bodied black man they could, and had reinforced the St. Augustine garrison with two companies of black troops from Havana, Cuba. The governor warned that, unless immediate steps were taken, the entire "southern country" would soon be engulfed in a bloody slave insurrection. Lieutenant Colonel Smith wrote a letter dated August 21, 1812, to Governor Mitchell informing him that "the blacks assisted by the Indians have become very daring." The American siege of St. Augustine was finally broken on September 12 when a band of about fifty red and black warriors, led by a black man named Prince, destroyed a wagon train escorted by U.S. Marines and Georgia volunteers. Although most of the soldiers escaped with their lives, the loss of supplies and ammunition eventually led to the complete withdrawal of Patriot troops from St. Augustine.[8]

Shocking details of the conflict soon began to emerge from the Florida thickets. There were numerous reports of armed, bloodthirsty "Negro Indians" who lurked seemingly behind every bush. Newspaper editors in Savannah and Charleston carefully inserted asterisks in their accounts of the battle, informing their readers that the deletions were necessary in order to maintain local security. Presumably, they feared widespread dissemination of information regarding the battle would encourage local slaves to rebel or escape to Florida.

Despite their failure to take St. Augustine, the Americans pressed their offensive in other parts of the colony. A second army of 250 Georgia militiamen from Milledgeville and Dublin was also mobilized and ordered to march south. The rapidly escalating conflict provided the Georgians with a pretext to expand the scope of the fighting. According to Governor Mitchell, they were hoping to incite the Seminoles to "take up the cudgels" in support of the Spaniards and their black allies. This provocation would allow the militia to march into Seminole territory and destroy a black town that had been growing under the patronage of the Indians.[9]

Major Daniel Newnan, commander of the Georgia militia, received orders in August 1812 to cross the border and attack the Seminoles. However, difficulty in obtaining horses, supplies, and ammunition delayed their departure, and more than half of the militiamen, many of whom had nearly completed their tours of duty, refused to go on the mission. On September 24, Newnan led a force of 116 men across the border deep into Seminole territory. After a four-day march, the Georgians encountered nearly 100 warriors, led by the aged chief King Payne and his brother

Billy Bowlegs. Payne was one of the first to fall as volleys from the frontier rifles of the militiamen ripped through the war party. The warriors quickly fell back and disappeared into the shadows of a nearby cypress swamp. Newnan's men took full advantage of the lull in the fighting by scalping the dead Seminoles, digging trenches, and erecting log barricades.

News of the battle reached several nearby Negro villages and approximately 100 black warriors joined the fight against the Georgia invaders. The fighting intensified, with the blacks displaying "conspicuous bravery" in the deadly struggle. Newnan later described them as having been the "best soldiers" on the field of battle. Casualties on both sides mounted as the bloody stalemate lingered for seven desperate days, until the American major ordered a daring nighttime withdrawal. Carrying the sick, wounded, and dying on stretchers, the militiamen set out for the Georgia border. According to historian Julius Pratt, what began as a "punitive expedition" had unceremoniously degenerated into an all-out retreat. Living for several days on gophers, alligators, and palmetto stalks, the Georgians barely avoided complete annihilation. Once again black and red guerrilla warriors had turned back an attempt by Georgia soldiers to conquer Florida.[10]

An enraged Governor Mitchell wrote a letter to Florida Governor Bernigno Garcia, chastising him for having the audacity to arm black men in defense of the Spanish colony. He argued that "common decency" should have compelled Garcia not to place weapons in the hands of fugitive slaves because of the "peculiar situation" existing within the Southern states. The Florida governor replied to Mitchell and explained that Spain allowed black men to serve in their militias, with status equal to that of other soldiers, throughout the Spanish empire. He sarcastically compared the Georgia governor's protest to that of a burglar requesting a homeowner to put down his "blunderbuss" and engage him "on equal footing with pistols."[11]

The failure of Newnan's expedition sent shock waves throughout the slave states. On January 24, 1813, Patriot leader John McIntosh complained in a letter to James Monroe, the U.S. Secretary of State, "Our slaves are excited to rebel and we have an army of negroes raked up in this country." McIntosh warned that Florida was on the verge of becoming a permanent refuge for fugitive slaves. Desperately in need of additional military support, he resorted to hyperbole by claiming that blacks soon would be dispatched across the border to incite slave insurrections throughout the United States. [12]

McIntosh's pleas did not go unanswered. The Georgia militia was quickly reinforced with two hundred mounted volunteers from western Tennessee. The Americans then marched back into Seminole territory, determined to eliminate further Negro and Seminole resistance. The militiamen were especially intent on extracting a measure of revenge on the black warriors. Brigadier General Thomas Flounoy issued general orders directing that every black man taken in arms should be executed without any consideration of mercy. This time the Americans completely overwhelmed their adversaries. The soldiers plundered and destroyed two principal Seminole towns, a Negro town, and several smaller villages; they also confiscated three hundred horses, four hundred cattle, and a large number of deer skins. No match for the larger American force, the blacks and Seminoles retreated westward toward the Suwanee River.

However, the American offensive came too late to salvage the ill-conceived plot to annex Florida into the United States. On April 18, 1814, President James Madison, under intense political pressure from congressional abolitionists, disavowed the actions of the Patriots and officially rejected annexation. The final nail was driven into the coffin on May 5, 1815, when General Buckner Harris, a brigadier general in the Georgia militia and key Patriot leader, was killed by a black war party.

DESTRUCTION OF THE NEGRO FORT

During the War of 1812, British Major Edward Nicholls rebuilt an old fort at Prospect Bluff on the Apalachicola River about sixty miles south of the Georgia border and supplemented the British garrison with fugitive slaves and Seminole and Red Stick Creek Indians. Following the ratification of the Treaty of Ghent in February 1815, the British and a small group of Creek chiefs abandoned the fort and sailed for London, leaving behind all the blacks, twenty Choctaws, eleven Seminoles, and a large arsenal of arms and ammunition, including ten pieces of heavy artillery.

Known as the "Negro Fort," the stronghold quickly became a beacon of freedom for slaves in Georgia, Alabama and the Carolinas. By 1816 approximately one thousand black fugitives had established residence at the fort and in the surrounding countryside. The lush fields and grazing grounds of the self-emancipated slaves extended fifty miles up and down the Apalachicola River. The fort, now under the command of a black chief named Garcon, was a thorn in the side of Southern slave owners. They successfully lobbied Georgia military and political leaders to ask the federal government for assistance in eliminating the worrisome slave refuge.

General Edmund P. Gaines, commander at Fort Scott in Decatur County, Georgia, informed the secretary of war on May 14, 1816, that scores of fugitive slaves had taken possession of an abandoned British fort on the upper Apalachicola River. This information was shared with General Andrew Jackson, the commander of the Southwestern Military District, who quickly concluded that the Negro Fort posed a serious threat to the institution of American slavery. Jackson directed a formal protest to the Spanish governor, demanding that immediate action be taken to destroy this black enclave. The governor replied that he wanted to suppress the "lawless banditti" manning the fort, but lacked the military resources needed to overcome the fugitives. At this point Jackson decided to take matters into his own hands. He ordered Gaines to destroy the fort, even though it was located on Spanish soil, and return all fugitive slaves taken alive to their former masters.[13]

In July 1816 the Negro Fort was besieged from the Apalachicola River by a small American fleet consisting of two gunboats and two troop transports. The force was led by Colonel Duncan L. Clinch and a young captain named Zachary Taylor, the future president. On July 17, a small crew from one of the gunboats was attacked by a band of black warriors. Three sailors and an officer were killed, although a lone survivor managed to escape by swimming to the opposite riverbank. The four dead Americans were stripped of all of their belongings and scalped.

Following an exchange of cannon fire on July 26, 1816, Clinch dispatched a delegation to the fort to demand an immediate and unconditional surrender. Garcon refused to surrender and boldly declared that no American vessel would be allowed to pass. The black chief swore he would blow up the fort rather than surrender his people to reenslavement. Ironically, Garcon's boast would soon be transformed into a tragic reality for the men, women, and children who inhabited it. To further demonstrate his utter contempt for the Americans, the black chief raised the British Union Jack and the red flag of defiance.

The fruitless demands for surrender were followed by another exchange of cannon fire, and according to Marcus C. Burk, a surgeon assigned to the Fourth Infantry, the Americans "were pleased with the spirited opposition, though they were Indians, Negroes and our enemies. Many circumstances convinced us that most of them [were] determined never to be taken alive." According to military records, the fight came to an immediate end after one of the gunboats managed to land a red-hot cannon ball in the fort's ammunition storeroom, causing a tremendous explosion. The Negro Fort was totally destroyed and 270 people, including many women and children, were killed. Buck later wrote: "The scene in the fort was horrible beyond description; The cries of the wounded and dying, mingled with the shouts and yells of the Indians rendered the confusion horrible in the extreme." Garcon and 40 others miraculously survived the explosion, but the black leader was captured and summarily executed. Survivors who did not escape were returned to lives of slavery in the Southern states. The destruction of the Negro Fort remained a closely guarded secret for more than twenty years, until the *National Intelligencer* obtained a copy of Colonel Clinch's official report and placed it in the hands of William Jay, an abolitionist congressman, who published the gruesome details surrounding the incident.[14]

The American victory effectively eliminated blacks as a military force along the upper Apalachicola River. The destruction of the fort also had a major impact on the development of future Negro-Seminole war strategy. Never again would they engage the better-armed Americans from a fixed, fortified position. Henceforth they would wage guerrilla warfare, fighting from the swamps and dense underbrush. The warriors would maintain well-concealed hideouts and secret caches of weapons, train their women and children to quickly move entire villages when threatened by enemy soldiers, and develop an uncanny ability to lure the Americans into deadly ambush.

Blacks not killed or captured at the Negro Fort joined other fugitives who had been living in the countryside and fled deeper into Florida. They took refuge with blacks and Seminoles living on the Suwanee River or reestablished themselves in a series of villages that extended along the seacoast to Tampa Bay. One of the few survivors of the blast who managed to escape was a black man named Abraham. He would become the trusted counselor to a powerful Seminole chief and one of the principal architects of the treaty that finally brought peace to Florida.

Several weeks after the destruction of the Negro Fort, the surgeon Buck, now stationed at Fort Crawford, Georgia, wrote a remorseful letter to his father regarding the grisly incident. "I [cannot] describe the horrors of the scene. In an instant hundreds of lifeless bodies were stretched upon the plain, buried in sand and rubbish, or suspended from the tops of surrounding pines. The brave soldier was disarmed of his resentment, and checked his victorious career, to drop a tear on one distressing scene." [15]

A SAVAGE AND NEGRO WAR

Although they suffered a demoralizing defeat at the Negro Fort, black and red men throughout Florida vowed to avenge the deaths of their brethren and allies. Unconfirmed reports told of a black chief named Nero, who led an army of six hundred men in daily military drills on the banks of the Suwanee River. Throughout the summer of 1817, a steady stream of fugitive slaves from Georgia and Alabama joined the Florida resistance, while black and Seminole raiding parties increased their attacks against white settlements.

By mid-1817 tensions along the Georgia-Florida border had reached a boiling point and renewed warfare appeared inevitable. In August, General Gaines of Georgia sent a message to Kenhagee, chief of the Mikasuki Seminole, demanding permission to conduct a slave-hunting expedition in his territory. "You harbor a great many of my black people among you at Sahwahnee," charged Gaines. He followed with a not-so-subtle threat: "If you give me leave to go by you against them, I shall not hurt anything belonging to you." Chief Kenhagee was not intimidated. He denied any knowledge of Negroes living within his territory and warned Gaines that no armed Americans would be

110

allowed to pass through his towns or over his land.[16]

On November 21, 1817, warfare broke out at Fowls Town, a Seminole and Negro settlement located about ten miles southwest of modern Bainbridge, Georgia. Major David E. Twiggs and 250 American troops killed four of the forty-five warriors living in the village. They drove the other inhabitants into the swamps and proceeded to plunder and burn all the homes and structures. This attack marked the beginning of what became known as the First Seminole War. Black and red warriors put on war paint and struck back at the Americans, attacking and overwhelming a boat transporting forty American troops, seven women, and four children along the upper Apalachicola River. All the Americans were killed, except four soldiers who swam to safety and one woman who was taken captive. Allied bands of Seminoles and Negroes increased border raids on Georgia plantations, killing settlers, carrying off livestock, and stealing or liberating hundreds of black slaves. Brutal back country warfare quickly engulfed Georgia's southern frontier.

Finally General Andrew Jackson, the legendary Indian fighter, was summoned by Secretary of War John C. Calhoun to take command of the troops at Fort Scott and restore order along the Georgia border. A bold and daring military commander, Jackson arrived at the fort in March 1818. He quickly moved his troops down the Apalachicola River to the ruins of the Negro Fort, where he oversaw the construction of a new fort. The future president demonstrated little patience or mercy for the red and black freedom fighters in Florida. Later that month, he proceeded to blaze a bloody path of destruction across northwest Florida. The American force of 3,300 men included 900 Georgia and Tennessee militia, 800 regulars, and a large contingent of friendly Creek warriors. According to historian Kenneth Porter, the principal objective of what Jackson described as a "savage and negro war," was the destruction of several frontier settlements that had provided refuge for fugitive slaves from Georgia and other Southern states for decades.[17]

Jackson's primary target was the black chief Nero's town and several smaller settlements located on the west bank of the Suwanee, about thirty-five miles from the mouth of the river. Hundreds of self-emancipated blacks lived there in cabins that were larger and better constructed than those of the Seminoles. They also cultivated large gardens that produced fruit, corn, potatoes, peas, beans, and rice, and maintained scores of cattle and hogs in fenced pastures.

In mid-April 1818 the advancing Americans were spotted by Seminole scouts who rushed to warn their black allies. Nero ordered the women and children to take refuge on the opposite river bank, while more than three hundred black men and an undetermined number of Seminoles frantically prepared to engage the Americans. Jackson divided his soldiers into three columns and unleashed a withering barrage. Although the Seminoles were quickly overrun, the black defenders held their ground in the face of the larger, better-armed American force. Jackson's right wing crumbled as the blacks poured gunfire into the American lines. A general charge was ordered, but the black men fell back, swam across the river, and disappeared into the swamps. According to Negro-Seminole accounts of the battle, after the fighting ceased Jackson ordered his men to search the surrounding forests for women and children who appeared to possess Negro blood. Those that were captured were placed in chains, marched back to Georgia, and sold to the highest bidders.

Although Jackson's official report contained not a single reference to the black men who fought and died on the banks of the Suwanee, numerous letters written by American soldiers described in detail the desperation of the warriors. According to Joshua Giddings, the Negro-Seminoles "preferred death upon the battle field, [sic] to chains and the scourge." The *Louisiana Gazette* reported that eighty blacks died in the battle, with an undetermined number captured and reenslaved. Although the *New Orleans Gazette* carried a similar account, the paper's editors also ridiculed the Seminoles for deserting the battlefield. The *New Orleans Gazette* even took the unusual posture of complimenting the blacks for "defending themselves with great courage" and displaying "greater resolution" in the heat of battle.[18]

The Americans relentlessly—abolitionist critics would later describe it as ruthlessly—marched on, destroying several Negro and Seminole towns in the process. They burned over three hundred well-built houses, confiscated crops and horses, and generally laid waste to the countryside between the Withlacoochee and Suwanee Rivers. Jackson's campaign was hailed by Southern slave owners who wanted to eliminate the slave refuge in Florida, but he was harshly criticized by antislavery advocates in the North. The "massacre" of blacks and Seminoles stirred the wrath of abolitionist congressmen who opposed using U.S. troops in what they derisively described as a slave-hunting expedition. The congressional outcry forced President James Monroe, who originally authorized the campaign, to issue a strict reprimand upbraiding Jackson for his unnecessarily brutal tactics. Georgia officials wanted the war fought to a definite conclusion, but Jackson knew that without the support of the Monroe Administration, hostilities could not continue. In May 1818, he received official orders from President Monroe directing him to end the conflict and dismiss his troops. Despite the inconclusiveness of Jackson's military campaign, the invasion effectively ended Spanish rule in Florida. Unable to defend its northernmost outposts, Spain signed a treaty of cession in 1819 that ultimately transferred possession of the Florida colony to the United States.

A NEGRO, NOT AN INDIAN WAR

The Second Seminole War began in December 1835 and lasted for seven bloody years. The conflict, conducted primarily as a slave-hunting expedition for the benefit of Georgia and Florida slave owners, was one of the costliest and most protracted so-called Indian wars in American history. Approximately fifteen hundred U.S. soldiers and an undetermined number of blacks, Seminoles, militiamen, and white settlers were killed during the fighting. The war reportedly cost the U.S. government more than $20 million. The federal government originally attempted to resolve the "Indian problem" in the Florida territory by restricting the Seminoles to reservations. A treaty council held at Moultrie Creek in 1823 had produced an agreement requiring the Indians to relocate to lands on the Apalachicola and Charlotte Rivers. Seminole leaders also agreed to return all fugitive slaves living in their territory to their American owners. But the chiefs, possibly as a result of Negro influence, returned few fugitives and refused to move to the designated reservations. The stalemate in Florida continued for several years.[19]

Finally in 1830, under the administration of now-President Andrew Jackson, the Indian Removal Act was enacted by Congress, requiring the removal of all Indian tribes in the southeast to western reservations. A commission was appointed to negotiate relocation with the Seminoles, and on May 9, 1832, a treaty was signed providing for the inspection of proposed reservation lands in the Oklahoma territory by a delegation of Seminole chiefs. During their inspection visit on March 28, 1833, the chiefs were allegedly coerced or bribed into signing the Treaty of Fort Gibson, which mandated the removal of all Florida Indians to Oklahoma by 1836. Seminoles throughout Florida were enraged by the treaty; they argued that the representatives at

Fort Gibson lacked the power to legally bind the entire Seminole nation. Among their many objections was the fear that their black allies, as well as their legal slaves, would be returned to American slave owners or claimed as the legal property of the Creeks, who were already living in Oklahoma. The red and black war chiefs vowed to fight to the death rather than voluntarily abandon their native and adopted land.

In December 1835 warfare erupted when Seminole warriors and bands of Negro-Seminoles and fugitive slaves, led by black subchief John Horse, fell on the sugar plantations of the St. John's River valley. Later that month, one hundred American soldiers and their commander, Major Francis L. Dade, were killed by red and black warriors near the Wahoo Swamp. According to Ransome Clark, the only white survivor of the battle, the Seminoles gave the black warriors the gruesome honor of scalping and looting the bodies of the dead Americans. The circumstances surrounding the death of a Lieutenant William Bassinger would be used to incite white Georgians. Bassinger, who had been critically wounded, rose from the ground and offered his sword in surrender, but according to Clark, the blacks mercilessly shot him down. Army officer John Casey wrote an emotional letter to Bassinger's brother: "We expect your Georgia volunteers . . . and let them know that your brother and my best friend after fighting til the last . . . was butchered by the Indian Negroes." [20]

During the first months of the war, approximately four hundred slaves escaped and joined the Negro-Seminole resistance. Described as being "more desperate than the Indians," the former slaves-turned-warriors spread panic and hysteria among whites in Florida and neighboring states. Fearing for their lives, white settlers abandoned their farms and plantations and sought protection from the United States military. During its most crucial phase, Major General Thomas Sidney Jesup proclaimed, "This . . . is a Negro, not an Indian war." [21]

Jesup assumed command of United States troops in Florida in December 1836. He was the first American commander in Florida to recognize that key black leaders more or less controlled their Seminole allies. He wrote: "Throughout my operations I have found the negroes the most active and determined warriors; and during the conference with Indian chiefs I ascertained that they exercised an almost controlling influence over them." Jesup was certain bloodshed would continue unless the black leaders received assurances that removal to Oklahoma would not result in their reenslavement. "The warriors" he observed, "have fought as long as they had life, and such seems to me to be the determination of those who influence their councils—I mean the leading Negroes." Jesup arranged, through a black emissary, a meeting with Abraham, the most influential of the black Floridians and the trusted counselor to Chief Micanopy.[22]

Abraham was a cunning and widely traveled man who had helped inspect the proposed western reservation in 1832 and later served as a negotiator and interpreter for the Seminole delegation that traveled to Washington, D.C. He became convinced that removal to the West with the guarantee of Negro freedom was a better option than continued warfare against superior American forces. Following a month of negotiations, Jesup and representatives of the major chiefs signed a peace treaty on March 6, 1837. The treaty provided that all "the Seminoles and their allies" who voluntarily surrendered and emigrated to the western reservation would be allowed to maintain their property and to live peacefully. Another key provision granted Seminole masters the right to transport any black slaves they may own, "their bona fide property," to Oklahoma. This language ignited heated protest from Georgia and Florida slave owners and would eventually lead to additional fighting and bloodshed.[23]

The allies stipulated in the treaty were the Negro-Seminoles and fugitive American slaves. Abraham had shrewdly made his

people's freedom a key condition of the treaty. However, the provision regarding Seminole masters and their so-called slaves
threatened to circumvent the entire peace process. The Seminole
chiefs and their black allies interpreted the provision to mean
that all fugitive slaves, including those who escaped during the
most recent fighting, would be protected from reenslavement.
This interpretation was originally shared by General Jesup. More
than any other American official, he believed the success of the
treaty was dependent on the support of the black leaders. "The
Negroes rule the Indians," he wrote. Unless the blacks remained
confident that their hard-won freedom would be preserved,
renewed warfare was inevitable.[24]

The war probably would have ended in the spring of 1837, but
angry protests by white slave owners, who had lost hundreds of
slaves during the war, forced Jesup to break his original promise. As
large numbers of Negroes and Seminoles gathered at the Tampa
Bay emigration camp, the general entered into a secret agreement
with some of the Seminole chiefs to return the more recent fugitives to their former masters. The arrival of slave owners from
Georgia and other Southern states alarmed the blacks who were
waiting to be transported to Oklahoma. On the night of June 2,
1837, Chiefs Osceola and Wild Cat, along with the young black
subchief John Horse, led a daring breakout from the camp. "All is
lost," despaired Jesup "and principally . . . by the influence of the
Negroes." Following his escape, the legendary Osceola developed
even closer ties with the Negro-Seminoles and the fugitive slaves in
Florida. His favorite wife, Morning Dew, was a descendant of fugitive Georgia slaves and fifty-two of the fifty-five warriors under his
command when he was finally recaptured were black. However,
Jesup realized that he would have to rely on a different strategy to
finally end the fighting in Florida. Having failed to end hostilities
by military force or diplomacy, he resorted to strategies based primarily on deceit. On three separate occasions the general would

capture hundreds of Seminoles and blacks while they were gathered under flags of truce during peace conferences.[25]

Hoping to avoid earlier mistakes, Jesup ignored the protests of slave owners and abandoned the idea of returning black fugitives to Southern plantations. He warned his superiors that the Florida blacks, many of whom had been born free, would instigate bloody insurrection if they were returned to slavery. Jesup recommended instead that they be transported out of the United States to an American colony on the African continent. An unidentified American soldier agreed with this assessment: "The negroes, from the commencement of the Florida war, have, for their numbers, been the most formidable foe, more bloodthirsty, active, and revengeful, than the Indians. . . . The negro returned to his original owner, might have remained a few days, when he again would have fled to the swamps, more vindictive than ever. . . . Ten resolute negroes, with a knowledge of the country, are sufficient to desolate the frontier, from one extent to the other." [26]

Jesup's insistence on transporting the blacks to Oklahoma led to his dismissal as commander of American troops in Florida. He was succeeded by now-Brigadier General Zachary Taylor, a slave owner and veteran of the Florida wars. Taylor surprised many Southerners when he also decided to honor the provisions of the treaty and preserve the freedom of his former adversaries. Instead of turning the blacks over to white slave owners, he placed them in the protective custody of the U.S. Marine Corps officer in charge of Indian emigration. Although Georgia slave owners made several attempts to gain legal possession of the former slaves and their descendants as they made their way westward, American military leaders, including Taylor, General Gaines, and General Jesup, successfully intervened on the blacks' behalf.

Between 1838 and 1843, approximately five hundred Negro-Seminoles and an undetermined number of fugitive slaves and their descendants boarded ships at Tampa Bay and eventually relocated to the western reservation. The emigration of these former slaves brought to a close their heroic and sometimes tragic struggle to live free in Georgia and Florida.

CHAPTER V

———

FREE BLACK GEORGIANS: BETWEEN SLAVERY AND CITIZENSHIP

Throughout the slavery era, black men, women, and children engaged in various forms of struggle to escape the chains of bondage. As previous chapters have shown, armed assault against former masters, military service in exchange for freedom, flight, and rebellion were some of the strategies Georgia's slaves employed. Yet from the earliest days of slavery in the state, there was a small but influential population of blacks who gained their freedom through peaceful means: manumission, industry, and thrift. Although they were more feared and despised than slaves, these free black Georgians managed to carve out a life for themselves against all odds, and they provided support and inspiration to the state's enslaved population.

Free blacks lived in a precarious world that hovered between bondage and citizenship. They were not slaves, but they were also not entitled to most of the rights and privileges enjoyed by whites. The prevailing opinion among the South's ruling white majority was that slavery was the absolute and irrevocable condition of the Negro. Thus, a "free" black person was an anomaly that engendered suspicion and hatred. In 1829 Congressman

Henry Clay of Kentucky offered a blunt assessment of what he considered to be the insidious threat posed by free Negroes:

> Of all the descriptions of our population, and of either portion of the African race, the free people of color are, by far, as a class, the most corrupt, depraved and abandoned.... They are not slaves, and yet they are not free. The laws, it is true, proclaim them free; but prejudices, more powerful than any law, deny them the privileges of freemen. They occupy a middle station between the free white population and the slaves of the United States and the tendency of their habits is to corrupt both. [1]

Free blacks were victimized by harsh legislative proscriptions that denied them citizenship rights, including the right to vote, to hold public office, to serve on a jury, or to testify against whites in court proceedings. A series of registration statutes limited their mobility, and they were required to carry on their person, at all times, a certificate documenting their free status. Free blacks lived under the constant fear of being kidnapped and sold into bondage by slave hunters and unscrupulous whites. They were also hampered by restrictive state and local economic sanctions that severely limited their ability to engage in certain occupations, earn a living, and accumulate wealth. Yet, despite these obstacles, free black Georgians established semi-independent churches, schools, and businesses that served the state's antebellum and postbellum black communities.

In Savannah, Augusta, and Milledgeville, free persons of color helped to establish several churches during the antebellum period where free and slave worshipers were exposed to Christian teachings. The First African Baptist Church of Savannah was officially constituted in 1788, just one year after the United States Constitution was drafted in Philadelphia. Free blacks owned and operated small businesses that produced income used to purchase the freedom of other family members, loved ones, and friends. Decades before the first shots were fired in the Civil War, free blacks in Savannah founded at least five "schools" that gave free and slave children access to a basic education. More importantly, by their mere existence, free persons of color offered Georgia slaves a striking contrast to the degradation of perpetual bondage. To the chagrin of many whites, free blacks were living proof that people of color could rise above the condition of slavery.[2]

Prior to the American Revolution, there were only a few free persons of color living in Georgia, and they were primarily light-skinned mulattoes born out of interracial liaisons between white men and female slaves. White fathers, stricken by conscience or moved by affection, sometimes manumitted these children by deed after a period of servitude or by will upon their death. On other occasions slave owners also manumitted the enslaved mother of their child or children. The growing number of mixed-race children in the state created some vexing legal problems: Were the mulatto offspring of white fathers free persons or slaves? Could these children inherit from the estates of their fathers?

In 1770 the Georgia legislature addressed this troubling issue by enacting a statute that clarified the legal status of mulatto children. According to the legislation, all Negroes, Indians, mulattoes, and mustizoes residing in Georgia, except those who had been legally freed, were declared to be slaves. Their children were also declared to be slaves and, more significantly, the legal status of the children was based on the condition of their mothers. In other words, the children of white men and enslaved women of color inherited the legal status of their mothers and nothing else. Although this legislation closed the door to freedom for some blacks, it inadvertently pried it open for others, as the children of free black women were now born free, even if their father was a slave. The law also benefited the small percentage of children who were born out of relationships between black male slaves and white women.[3]

While white lawmakers in the pre-Revolutionary War era focused on passing more restrictive laws intended to affect the status of free blacks, Georgia slave owners continued to manumit slaves in ever-increasing numbers. In November 1757, Issac Barksdale, an Augusta Indian trader, dictated through his will that his Negro "wench" Nancy and her two mulatto children be freed. Barksdale also provided for the freedom of another black woman, Nanney, whom he had "partly" freed prior to his death. The next year, the will of Margaret Pages of Savannah included a provision instructing her executor to free and educate a young mulatto slave named Peter. In 1762 John Heran, a Greater Ogeechee River planter, partially freed two mulatto children. The boy and girl, named Addin and Rachel, were the children of Diana, his female slave, and an unnamed white father. Both children were hired out to different individuals who were directed to free them after a specified period of service. Prominent Savannah merchant and landowner James Habersham freed a woman named Susannah in his will in 1767. In that same year, J. Prunieres of Savannah, "for divers good Causes and consideration," freed Tommy, the mulatto son of his female slave named Mary.[4]

Three years later, Daniel Ross's will directed his heirs to free Sally, a mulatto girl who was the daughter of his female slave named Phillis. Sally was required to live with a white guardian until she reached the age of fifteen. Ross also provided that the young girl be taught to read and be brought up in a decent and industrious manner. In a will dated February 4, 1771, Josiah Tattnall bequeathed freedom to two black women, Maria and Hagar. In that same year, Samuel Savery of Savannah freed a young mulatto slave named George Reaves Savery. In 1775 John Forbes's will directed that a mulatto girl named Dina, the daughter of his female slave named Babet, be freed and given 160 pounds sterling to be held in trust by her guardian. Forbes's will also bequeathed 200 pounds sterling to Janet, a free black girl who was residing at his house. In 1774 William Wylly of Savannah directed the executor of his will to manumit a mulatto boy named Ben. In 1796 the will of Absolom Davis of Elbert County granted freedom to Solvanah Randall, "a yellow woman" who was the daughter of one of his female slaves named Nancy.[5]

The second most common method of manumission in colonial Georgia was the "purchase of self," or buying one's own freedom from a slave owner. The legal right of a slave to purchase his freedom was recognized and protected by the Georgia courts. The availability of this process slowly changed the complexion of Georgia's free population because it opened the door to freedom for enterprising darker-skinned Negroes. The first recorded instance of a Georgia slave purchasing his own freedom occurred in 1772 when Peter Fleming paid his master the relatively small sum of five shillings. In 1782 a black woman paid David Brydie ten pounds sterling for her freedom. In that same year, John Galphin's will freed his Negro "wench" and her five children in exchange for her faithful service to him and a small amount of money. Two well-known black ministers, George Liele and Andrew Bryan, also purchased their freedom.

According to historian Herbert Aptheker, the purchase of one's own freedom, although "usually unobtrusive and rarely spectacular, nevertheless required great perserverance and a deliberate, cool courage." In many ways the process of self-purchase required more determination and fortitude than armed struggle or escape, for how could a slave, who by law possessed no rights and was property himself, accumulate the financial resources needed to purchase his own freedom?[6]

Several conditions had to exist before a slave could initiate this process: (1) the slave owner had to possess a desire to allow the slave to purchase his freedom; (2) the slave had to possess a skill or talent through which money could be earned; (3) the slave had to have the right or be given the opportunity to retain the money that was earned; (4) once the money was earned, it had to be saved or invested; (5) the owner would have to provide legal papers of man-umission in exchange for the money received; and (6) the legal right recognizing self-purchase or manumission had to exist in that state. In light of these many conditions, it is no wonder that the process often took years or even decades to complete. Enslaved blacks would sometimes go to great lengths to arrange a self-pur-chase opportunity with a willing slave owner. An extraordinary let-ter written in 1854 by Billy Proctor, an Americus, Georgia slave, to Colonel John B. Lamar is illustrative of this point:

> As my owner Mr. Chapman has determined to dispose of all his Painters, I would prefer to have you buy me to any other man. And I am anxious to get you to do so if you will. You know me very well yourself, but as I wish you to be fully satisfied I beg to refer you to Mr. Nathan C. Monroe, Dr. Strohecker and Mr. Bogg. I am in distress at this time, and will be until I hear from you what you will do. I can be bought for $1,000—and I think that you might get me for 50 Dolls less if you try, though that is Mr. Chapman's price. Now Mas John, I want to be plain and honest with you. If you will buy me I will pay you $600 per year until this money is paid, or at any rate will pay for myself in two years. . . . I am fearful that if you do not buy me, there is no telling where I may go, and Mr. C. wants me to go where I would be satisfied,—I promise to serve you faithfully, and I know that I am as sound and healthy as any one you could find. You will confer a great favour, sir, by Granting my request, and I would be very glad to hear from you in regard to the matter at your earliest convenience.[7]

Following the Revolutionary War, the number of free blacks increased dramatically in the Northern states. Desperate patriot leaders had been forced to recruit black men in order to shore up their depleted military ranks and as a result, hundreds of black slaves who served in the Continental Army or worked as military laborers were manumitted in exchange for their loyal service. By 1805 every Northern state had either abolished slavery or enacted a provision for gradual emancipation. The situation, however, was very different in the South. During the war, Georgia and South Carolina had refused to allow black men—slave or free—to join their militias. Thus, only a few black Southern patriots, such as Georgia's Austin Dabney and Monday Floyd, were able to earn the boon of freedom.

Although the struggle for American independence had little impact on the status of Georgia slaves, the spread of revolutionary ideas based on the "rights of men" led to a significant increase in the number of free blacks living in the state. The first federal census of 1790 revealed that 82,548 people lived in Georgia's eleven counties; of that number, 52,886 were white, 29,264 were black slaves, and 398 were free blacks. In 1792, Toussaint Louverture, a former slave who fought with the Franco-American force during the Battle of Savannah in 1779, returned to his native land of Haiti and led a successful revolt of black slaves (Haiti was called Santo Domingo prior to the revolution). The violent overthrow of French colonial rule forced thousands of frightened war refugees to flee to the United States in the ensuing years. Most of the migrants were white, although thousands of light-skinned free-black supporters of the French also arrived on American shores. The Americans welcomed the white refugees, but the mulatto immigrants were met with suspicion and contempt. Georgia and South Carolina quickly passed statutes barring West Indian free persons of color from entering their borders. Fearing that the fever of rebellion might be contagious, Savannah officials prohibited any ship from docking that had weighed anchor in Haiti. Later the federal government also banned free Haitians from entering the country, but these legislative efforts failed to stem the tide of immigrants who disembarked at Savannah,

Charleston, and other Southern ports.

By 1810 due primarily to the arrival of these light-skinned Haitians, the number of free blacks in Georgia had grown to 1,800—an increase of nearly 300 percent in twenty years. Savannah and the surrounding Chatham County had become the home of the largest and most affluent population of free blacks in the state. According to the 1810 federal census, 329 free persons of color lived in the city of Savannah alone, which nearly equaled the total number living in the state at the turn of the century. South Carolina witnessed a similar increase during the same twenty-year period; the number of free blacks living in that state more than doubled, to over 4,500.[8]

Concerned by this growing influx, the Georgia legislature passed the first law designed to regulate the entrance of free Negroes into the state in 1793. The statute required all free persons of color to register with local officials within thirty days of their arrival in Georgia and it gave them six months to secure a certificate from two or more magistrates demonstrating that they were honest and industrious persons. Anyone convicted of failing to abide by this law was subject to three months' confinement in jail. Yet this initial effort to regulate the movement of free blacks was relatively mild compared to the more stringent laws that would soon follow.

Local ordinances and statutes were also enacted to restrict and regulate the activities of free blacks. Those who migrated to Augusta had to pay one hundred dollars within thirty days of their arrival in the city or face incarceration. Free black Augustans were required to live in houses owned by their employers or secure a one-hundred-dollar bond to live in other parts of the city. Failure to abide by this ordinance could result in a fifty-dollar fine. Other municipal statutes restricted free blacks from selling beer, cake, or other small items on the street, except on parade days or during race week. The city prohibited free blacks from gambling or betting, and persons convicted of the offense were fined one hundred dollars. One of the most unusual ordinances prohibited free blacks from using candlelight in the kitchen or other area of their homes in the evening unless absolutely necessary. They could not venture out into the streets after nine o'clock without a pass; violators would be whipped. Free blacks were also required to secure written permission from the mayor or other local official to play a musical instrument within the city limits after dark. Another Augusta ordinance prohibited a white person from teaching a free black how to read or write; persons convicted of the crime would be fined. A free black convicted of trying to learn how to read or write was subject to whipping.

Despite aggressive efforts by state and local politicians to control Georgia's free black population, white slave owners continued to increase its numbers by private manumission and emancipation. In February 1795, Wilkes County planter Daniel Grant bequeathed freedom to all of his slaves, and granted the emancipated adults individual parcels of land. Grant was "fully convinced that perpetual slavery is most unjust and contrary to the spirit of the Gospel, and the Natural Rights of Mankind." In addition, Grant's will stated that all the freed blacks were to be granted the rights of Georgia citizenship. Surprisingly, the deceased slave master's unusual bequest was confirmed by the General Assembly in 1796. During that same year, the will of Anthony Haynes of Columbus freed ten of his slaves. In 1799 Joseph Posner of Louisville bequeathed freedom to a woman and her mulatto son. In a subsequent paragraph of his will, he refers to this woman as his wife and leaves her his entire estate.[9]

The proliferation of private manumissions alarmed Georgia lawmakers, who feared that the growing free-black population was a threat to the institution of slavery. At the beginning of the nineteenth century, Georgia lawmakers began to promulgate a series of laws that severely restricted the right of slave owners to free their slaves. They also passed increasingly repressive statutes that curtailed, and in some instances eliminated, the rights of free persons of color in Georgia. On the national front, white leaders were concerned that free blacks posed a serious threat to America's internal security. By 1810, the free black population in America had grown from a few thousand back in 1760 to more than 250,000.

AN ERA OF SUPPRESSION

In 1801 the Georgia legislature passed a statute that prohibited slave owners from freeing slaves except by an act of the General Assembly. According to the legislation, a fine of two hundred dollars would be imposed on anyone convicted of violating this law, and the slave or slaves in question would remain in bondage. Section three of the act prohibited court officials from recording any deed or document purporting to manumit a slave in the state. Failure to abide by this proscription rendered the entire document null and void. In 1808, a subsequent statute gave local justices of the peace and any three white landowners the power to rent out to farmers or artisans unemployed free blacks between the ages of eight and twenty-one. This semistate of slavery afforded aggrieved blacks the "right" to petition for a new guardian if they could prove that physical abuse had occurred.

Two years later, in 1810, the 1793 statute requiring the registration of free blacks was strengthened so that registration had to occur within ten days of their arrival in the state. The law also required that registration certificates include the free Negro's name, occupation, place of birth, place of origin, and reason for coming. Another provision required all free blacks to have a white guardian who assumed the authority to manage their legal affairs. Failure to comply with this mandate could result in a fine of thirty dollars and confinement in jail.

During the War of 1812, as discussed earlier, fifteen hundred black and white British Colonial Marines, commanded by Admiral George Cockburn, attacked and occupied Cumberland, Jekyll, and St. Simons Islands, off the Georgia coast. During the winter and spring of 1815, approximately four thousand fugitive slaves from Georgia and Florida answered a British proclamation of emancipation and eventually sailed away with these liberators. The significant role that free black soldiers played in this latest British invasion and the powerful influence they exerted over Georgia's slave population led to a legislative crackdown against free blacks in the state. The Georgia General Assembly promulgated a statute that covered almost every phase of the life of free persons of color.

In 1817 a law was passed that placed all unregistered free blacks under the control of the governor of Georgia. The governor was granted the authority to sell these blacks into slavery within sixty days or turn them over to the American Colonization Society, if that organization would agree to remove them from the state and pay all related expenses. While other Southern states, such as Virginia, Mississippi, and Tennessee, also required free black registration, no other state would enact a law as proscriptive as the one the Georgia legislature then passed in 1818.

According to the preamble of the 1818 legislation, "the principle of sound policy" considered in reference to white Georgians and "the exercise of humanity towards the slave population" dictated that the number of free persons of color in the state should not be increased by additional manumissions, or by admission of free blacks from other states or foreign countries. The lawmakers were concerned that scores of fugitive slaves were presently residing in Georgia, claiming to be free, although they had never been legally manumitted. These alleged fugitives were in the "full exercise and enjoyment of all the rights and privileges of free persons of color" and constituted "a class of people equally dangerous to the safety of the free citizens of this state, and destructive to the comfort and happiness of the slave population." According to the authors of the statute, the legislature was compelled to exhaust "all just and lawful means" available to suppress the individuals involved in these unlawful acts.[10]

This latest law mandated that the 1801 act be strictly enforced and the penalties be greatly increased for persons convicted of violating the statute. Legislators required all free persons of color in Georgia to register by the first Monday in March 1819. Instead of a three-month prison term and a fine, the penalty for failure to comply under the amended statute was enslavement. The clerk of the inferior court of the county in which free persons of color resided was required to make a registry of free persons that would contain the names, ages, places of birth, residence, date of arrival in the state, and occupation. After collecting a fee of fifty cents from each person registered, the clerk was then required to publish the list in one or more local newspapers. Any white citizen was granted the right to object to any black person on the list whom they believed was not legally free. A free black who failed to register and was found to be "enjoying the profits" of his labor would be immediately taken as a slave and sold at public auction to the highest bidder. In 1824 legislators repealed the provision authorizing the selling of free persons of color into slavery, although it was reinstated in 1859, on the eve of the Civil War.[11]

In addition, under the 1818 statute, every free person of color was required to keep in his or her possession a certificate of freedom. The act also required free black Georgians between the ages of fifteen and sixty to engage in public work at least twenty days a year. Section four prohibited the manumission of slaves by will and it also outlawed the practice of allowing slaves to purchase their own freedom. The legislators prohibited any slave from earning money in exchange for their labor, which made it even more difficult, if not impossible, for blacks to purchase their freedom.[12]

The final section of the draconian 1818 statute made it illegal for any free black or slave to purchase property by either direct or indirect conveyance from any white person who might reserve the title for that person of color. The law also stated that any property or interest in property conveyed to a free person of color by trust, will, testament, deed, or contract would be deemed to be wholly forfeited and void. The property in question would be sold to the highest bidder and the profits from the sale appropriated by the local government. According to the legislation, a small portion of the proceeds would be given to the white person who reported the transaction. Following its unanimous approval in the Georgia house and senate, Governor William Rabun signed the legislation into law on December 19, 1818.[13]

Although Georgia lawmakers had thus clearly expressed their intent to prohibit all manumissions, the process of private emancipation continued unabated. In fact, almost every session of the legislature witnessed the passage of special resolutions authorizing the manumission of Georgia slaves. Among the many examples were Sophia, the slave of Eli Fenn, who was freed by a legislative act in 1831 and was officially given the surname of Fenn; in 1834 Fanny Hickman, the wife of Paschal Hickman, a free black resident of Burke County, was freed along with their seven children. The legislature's most noteworthy manumission occurred in 1834 when a slave named Sam single-handedly saved the state capitol from destruction by fire. Grateful Georgia lawmakers appropriated eighteen hundred dollars to purchase the man's freedom from his owner.[14]

The promulgation of numerous laws designed to curtail private manumissions inevitably led to contentious legal battles between executors of the estates of deceased slave owners and angry heirs seeking title to human property. Scores of these cases were eventually appealed to the Georgia Supreme Court. Prior to the creation of the state supreme court in 1845, two superior court cases from different jurisdictions illustrated the inherent difficulties associated with interpreting the state laws that pertained to the institution of slavery. In 1822 one superior court held that a testate grant of freedom "subsequent to the Act of 1801, not sanctioned by the legislative authority is absolutely void, and produced no change in the condition of the slaves." In 1830, in the case of *Jordan v. Heirs of Bradley*, the superior court of Oglethorpe County ruled that a deceased slave owner could legally free his slaves if provisions had been made to remove the Negroes from the state of Georgia prior to their manumission. The judge concluded that the 1818 statute prohibited manumissions *only* if the freed blacks intended to remain in the state. Members of the Georgia Colonization Society used this ruling to encourage other slave owners to free their slaves after first relocating them to a state in the North or to the west coast of Africa.[15]

In 1853, in the case of *Bryan v. Walton*, Joseph Henry Lumpkin, the chief justice of the Georgia Supreme Court and a cofounder, along with Thomas R. R. Cobb, of the law school at the University of Georgia, rendered a lengthy opinion on the paradoxical legal status of free black Georgians:

> He may go and come without a domestic master to control his movements, but to be civilly and politically free, to be the peer and equal of the white man—to enjoy the offices, trusts, and privileges our institutions confer on the white man, is not now, never has been, and never will be, the condition of this degraded race.
>
> Our ancestors settled this State when a mere province, as a community of white men, professing the Christian religion, and possessing an equality of rights and privileges. The blacks were introduced into it, as a race of Pagan Slaves. The prejudice, if it can be called such, of caste, is unconquerable. It was so at the beginning. It has come down to our day. The suspicion of taint, even, sinks the subject of it below the common level. Is it to be credited, that parity of rank would be allowed to such a race?

He resides among us, yet is a stranger. A native even, and yet not a citizen. Though not a slave, yet he is not free. Protected by law, yet enjoying none of the immunities of freedom. Though not in a condition of chattlehood, yet constantly to it. The great principle of self-preservation demands, on the part of the white population, unceasing vigilance and firmness, as well as uniform kindness, justice, and humanity. He lives among us without motive and without hope. . . . His fancied freedom is all a delusion.[16]

Cleland v. Waters was probably the most sensational legal case involving post-mortem manumission to be argued before Georgia's highest court. George M. Waters, a deceased Gwinnett County slave owner, directed his executor to manumit thirty-two of his slaves, including William, his body servant, and the "future increase" of the female slaves named in the document. Prior to their emancipation, they were to be taken outside of the state to a place of their choice and set free. Waters acknowledged in the will that many of the slaves he desired to manumit were his lineal descendants, "bone of his bone and the flesh of his flesh." The will also contained an unusual clause that mandated the forfeiture of the interest of any named white heir who might resist his attempt to free the slaves. Despite this clause, a contentious legal battle ensued between Waters's children and the executor of Waters's estate concerning the legality and specific intent of the will.[17]

Williamina C. Cleland, the deceased slave owner's daughter, filed suit in the superior court of Gwinnett County in order to have the bequeath of freedom limited to William and the children of the female slaves. The judge ruled that all the slaves listed in the will and the future increase of the named females should be manumitted. Cleland's lawyers appealed the ruling to the Georgia Supreme Court, where it was argued during its October term in 1854. The justices ultimately upheld the lower court ruling, noting that the plaintiff's objection to the clause directing Waters's executor to remove the slaves to a place of their choice outside the state and then providing for their emancipation was unfounded. Surprisingly, they also determined that Waters intended to emancipate all the slaves listed in the will, including the future increase of the females.[18]

In a subsequent ruling involving the same litigants, however, Chief Justice Lumpkin went to great lengths to dispel any doubts regarding the state supreme court's unwavering support of the institution of slavery. He wrote:

> Slavery is a cherished institution in Georgia, founded in the Constitution and laws, and guarded, protected, defended by the whole spirit of her legislations; approved by her people; intimately interwoven with her present and permanent prosperity. Her interests, her feelings, her judgement and her conscience—not to say her very existence, alike conspire to sustain and perpetuate.[19]

All subsequent cases argued before the Georgia Supreme Court involving in-state post-mortem manumissions resulted in the invalidation of those wills. In 1859 the justices voided the will of Nathan Myrick of Monroe County because it directed that several of his slaves be freed and then removed from the state. Judge Linton Stephens, the stepbrother of Alexander Stephens, the future vice president of the Confederacy, wrote the opinion of the court. Stephens ruled that Georgia law prohibited in-state manumission and he added that manumission for even one hour within the state was illegal.[20]

Despite restrictive laws and a judiciary that was generally unsympathetic to their aspirations, free black Georgians managed to survive, and a few even prospered, in this slavery-dominated society. Using ingenuity, hard work, perseverance, and a willingness to accommodate the white majority, they built the foundation for a

POPULATION OF THE STATE OF GEORGIA BY RACE, 1790-1860

YEAR	FREE PERSONS OF COLOR	SLAVES	WHITES
1790	398	29,264	52,866
1800	1,019	59,404*	101,678
1810	1,801	105,218	145,414
1820	1,763	149,654	189,566
1830	2,486	217,531	296,866
1840	2,753	280,944	407,695
1850	2,931	381,682	521,572
1860**	3,500 (1,496 black 2,004 mulatto)	462,198 (425,208 black 36,900 mulatto)	591,588

Department of Commerce. Bureau of the Census. *Negro Population: 1790-1915*. Washington: Government Printing Office, 1915.

United States. Census Office. 7th Census, 1850. *The Seventh Census of the United States: 1850*. Washington: Robert Armstrong, Public Printer, 1853.

United States. Census Office. 8th Census, 1860. *Population of the United States in 1860*. Washington: Government Printing Office, 1864.

* *The Seventh Census of the United States: 1850* lists the figure as 59,404 while *Negro Population: 1790-1915* places the number of slaves in Georgia in 1800 at 59,406.

** The 1860 census further broke down the categories of free colored and slaves into black and mulatto.

post-slavery black community. Although their social status was far below that of whites, free blacks took advantage of biracial family ties, business relationships, and the support of some influential whites to amass a modest amount of influence and wealth. They were also aided by state and local officials who often failed to enforce many of the most restrictive laws. Especially in urban areas such as Savannah and Augusta, white officials discreetly looked the other way while free blacks ignored legal sanctions, earned money, purchased property, established semi-independent churches, and even operated schools for free and slave children.

FREE BLACK SAVANNAH

Savannah was the home of the largest and most affluent group of free black Georgians. By the beginning of the Civil War, the total number had reached 705, or 20 percent of the state's entire free black population of 3,500. And the wealthiest and most influential free black Georgians of that period were preachers Andrew Bryan and his nephew Andrew Marshall.

Andrew Bryan succeeded the legendary George Liele as the spiritual leader of Savannah's slave and free black population after the colonies won their independence from England. Liele had purchased his freedom shortly before the beginning of the Revolutionary War and had fled to British-occupied Savannah, where he ministered to black worshipers who found sanctuary in the war-torn city. After the war, as discussed earlier, he joined the British evacuation of Savannah in July 1782. But shortly before his departure for Jamaica, Liele preached a final sermon in the Yamacraw section of the city and baptized four black worshipers, Andrew Bryan and his wife Hannah, Kate Hogg, and Hagar Simpson.

According to one contemporary, Liele's successor Andrew

Bryan was a man of "good sense, great zeal, and some elocution." Although Bryan's owner supported his ministry, many local whites vehemently opposed the black preacher's proselytizing, charging that his primary goal was to stir up unrest among Savannah's slave population. His religious meetings were regularly broken up, and he and his brother were severely beaten, thrown in jail, and charged with sedition. Despite his incarceration, Bryan remained resolute, proclaiming that he "rejoiced not only to be whipped, but would freely suffer death for the cause of Jesus Christ." The two brothers were eventually exonerated of any wrongdoing and Bryan's master granted them permission to resume their meeting in a barn about three miles outside of Savannah.[21]

During the late 1780s, two white ministers, Thomas Burton and Abraham Marshall, aided the pioneer black minister. On January 19, 1788, Marshall officially constituted Bryan's church, the Ethiopian Church of Jesus Christ (later renamed First African Baptist), and also administered the full rites of ordination to the slave preacher. The certificate of ordination stated that the "beloved Andrew" had been called to the ministry and, after careful examination of his qualifications, he was appointed "to preach the gospel, and to administer the ordinances, as God in his providence may call." [22]

Following his ordination and the official recognition of the church he helped to found, Bryan's ministry and business prospered. By the end of the eighteenth century, he had become a successful drayman and managed to purchase his freedom and the freedom of his wife. His church became the center of Negro life in Chatham County and a place where free blacks could exercise their status and influence. They served as deacons and church mothers, formed their own temperance and benevolent societies, taught Sunday school, and sang in the church choir. According to Chatham County records and census data, the influential minister also owned eight "slaves."

It is important to note that so-called "slave" ownership among free black Georgians was not widespread. In 1830 census records show that 62 free black slaveholders in Georgia owned a total of 463 slaves, which represented only a fraction of the 217,531 slaves in the state. The largest number of black slave owners, 29, lived in Chatham County, followed by Richmond County with 13, and 3 each in the counties of Burke, Carroll, Fayette, and Randolph. Although some of the slaves were used as laborers, all but a few were "slaves" only in a technical sense. According to Carter G. Woodson, "the majority of the Negro slave owners were such from the point of view of Philanthropy." [23]

Herbert Aptheker provides additional insight:

> Many Negroes bought loved ones and were compelled to hold them in a nominal type of slavery. This occurred because in certain states at particular times laws were passed making emancipation or manumission extremely difficult. One way to evade these laws was by free Negroes purchasing slaves and, while exercising none of the prerogatives of a master, still maintaining the legal fact of enslavement. Thus may one account for the vast majority of cases of Negro slaveholders listed in census reports. [24]

In many instances a husband, wife, or lover would purchase the freedom of a spouse or mate. On other occasions a parent acquired the resources to purchase the freedom of their enslaved children or relatives. If the free black "slave owner" failed to have, or was prohibited from having, emancipation documents drawn and filed at the local courthouse, government officials and census takers would categorize these purchased individuals as slaves. Some free blacks also served as "middle-men," purchasing slaves from white owners and allowing the freed blacks to repay the debt with interest or by working for a period of time. Apparently at least one free black husband who purchased the freedom of his slave wife decided not to immediately emancipate her, preferring instead to place the woman on probation for a period of time to ensure obedience and loyalty. Woodson notes that this Charleston, South Carolina, shoemaker purchased his wife for $700; after discovering that she was hard to please and impossible to live with, he sold her for $750.

The slave and free membership at Andrew Bryan's church soon outgrew the building where meetings were held and he decided to organize a second black Baptist church. The Second African Baptist Church was established in 1802 under the leadership of Reverend Henry Cunningham, a former McIntosh County slave who had moved to Savannah and joined the First African congregation. Nine other free blacks assisted Cunningham in organizing the church, including five women: Elizabeth Cunningham, the pastor's wife, Susan Jackson, Silva Monnox, Leah Simpson, and Charlotte Walls.

In a letter written in 1800 to a Dr. Rippon, a white clergyman, Andrew Bryan offered the following assessment of his life and work:

> I enjoy good health, and am strong in body, tho' sixty-three years old, and am blessed with a pious wife, whose freedom I have obtained, and an only daughter and child who is married to a free man, tho' she, and consequently, under our laws, her seven children, five sons and two daughters, are slaves. By Providence I am well provided for, as to worldly comforts, (tho' I have had very little given to me as a minister) having a house and a lot in the city, besides the land on several buildings stand, for which I receive a small rent, and a fifty-six acre tract of land, with all necessary buildings, four miles in the country, and eight slaves; for whose education and happiness, I am enabled thro' mercy to provide.[25]

At the time of his death in 1812, Bryan was one of the wealthiest men in Georgia, black or white. The Savannah Association, an organization of white churches, passed the following resolution in his memory:

> The death of the Rev. Andrew Bryan, a man of color, and pastor of the first Colored church in Savannah sensibly affects the Association. This son of Africa, after suffering inexpressible persecutions in the cause of his divine Master, was at length permitted to discharge the duties of the ministry among his colored friends in peace and quiet, hundreds of whom through his instrumentality, were brought to the knowledge of the truth as "it is in Jesus." He closed his extensively useful and luminous course in the joyful hope of a happy immortality.[26]

Andrew Cox Marshall succeeded his uncle as the pastor of the First African Baptist Church in Savannah and ministered there for forty-one years, from 1815 to 1856. During his tenure, Marshall became embroiled in a bitter doctrinal dispute that eventually led him and a majority of his members to leave the original church and establish a rival congregation that became the First Bryan Baptist Church. The genesis of the conflict involved Dr. Alexander Campbell, the founder of the Disciples of Christ, who visited Savannah in 1832 and was invited by Marshall to preach at his church. Campbell espoused the controversial doctrine of Arminianism. He opposed the absolute predestination teachings of strict Calvinism and maintained the possibility of salvation for all Christians—white and black. Beyond his religious philosophy, Campbell had angered Southern whites when he formally proposed to the state of Virginia in 1829 his plans for the gradual government-financed emancipation of slaves.

Marshall's decision to invite Campbell into his pulpit infuriated the city's white Baptists, who helped stir discontent among the church's black members. The membership at First African Baptist became hopelessly split, worship services were disrupted by name-calling and fist fights, and city police were called in to quell a series of disturbances. After one particularly rancorous church service, several members were verbally abused and whipped by the city marshal. In 1832 Marshall and about sixteen hundred members officially withdrew from the original church located in Oglethorpe Ward and established the First Bryan Baptist Church in a structure purchased from local white Baptists.

In addition to being the preeminent black religious leader in the state, Andrew Marshall was also a successful businessman whose personal wealth exceeded that of a majority of Georgia's white residents. He was born around 1755, the child of a slave mother and a white father. His master manumitted Marshall in his will, but the executors of the estate refused to grant the bequest of freedom. Following a failed escape attempt, he was sold to a judge who brought the young slave to Savannah. As a young man, Marshall was assigned the responsibility of serving as his master's coachman. This enabled him to travel throughout the colonies and he found himself on several occasions in the company of General George Washington. After the Revolutionary War, when Washington became president and visited Savannah, Marshall was directed to serve as the revered general's body servant.

Marshall not only served his master, but he was also granted permission to operate what eventually developed into a successful dray business. Following in the footsteps of his uncle Bryan, he used the proceeds from this enterprise to purchase his freedom around 1808. Shortly thereafter, he purchased the freedom of his wife, their four children, his father-in-law, and stepfather. In 1824, Marshall owned real estate valued at $8,400 and profits from his business, which employed several free blacks, were invested primarily in real estate and stock in a local bank. He also owned one slave, possibly a relative, for a short period of time during the early 1830s. Marshall lived to be one hundred years old and, at the time of his death, owned a lot in Yamacraw that contained a single-family dwelling, a two-story stone building, and a wooden building; a lot in the village of Saint Gall; a four-wheeled carriage and horses; four shares of stock in the Marine and Fire Insurance Bank; and numerous other personal items.

Also listed among the wealthiest free blacks in antebellum Savannah was Anthony Odingsells. While still a minor, he inherited nine slaves and land on Wassaw Island from Charles Odingsells, a white slave owner who was probably his father. Proceeds from the land were used to maintain the young mulatto and provide for his education. Title to the land was transferred to him when he reached adulthood; he had already been freed earlier. In 1855 Anthony Odingsells owned eight slaves, assessed at $2,400, and two hundred acres of pineland in Chatham County. By 1860 he had increased his holding to two thousand acres, thirteen slaves, thirty-five milch cows, fifty sheep, and seventy-five pigs. Odingsells died on January 15, 1878, at the age of ninety-four. Despite the emancipation of his slaves at the end of the Civil War, Odingsells managed to retain his real estate, which was assessed at $2,000 at the time of his death.[27]

Although Bryan, Marshall, and Odingsells were the most high-profile members of Savannah's free black community, they were not representative of its entire membership. In fact, the majority of the city's free blacks were women and, on average, they were also its most prosperous; they constituted the majority of free black real estate owners in the area. In 1820 thirty-six free blacks owned property in the city assessed at $200 per parcel, totaling $31,250. Twenty-one, or 56 percent, of the homeowners were female. That same year, Chatham County tax records also showed that black women owned the majority of the free black homes assessed at $1000 or more.[28]

The ownership of real estate was extremely important to free blacks, male and female, because it was a clear indication of their status, wealth, and prestige in the community. Buying real estate became more difficult for free black Georgians, however, after 1830.

This was due primarily to growing hostility toward the free population and more stringent enforcement of the 1818 prohibition against black land ownership in Georgia. The increased hostility was probably caused by the widespread distribution in Savannah of David Walker's 1829 book *Appeal to the Colored Citizens of the World*, which advocated the violent overthrow of slavery. White fears were also heightened by the hysteria that swept through the Southern states following the Nat Turner rebellion in Virginia in 1831. Although the overall number of free black homeowners declined during the thirty years leading up to the Civil War, women managed to increase their percentage of ownership of the more expensive real estate. In 1858, seventeen of the nineteen free black homeowners whose property was valued in the $1000 or higher category were female.

According to local records, black women were the largest free black landowners in Savannah and they also owned the largest number of slaves. The most prosperous one was Ann H. Gibbons, who in 1850 owned two lots containing dwellings and four slaves. Two years later, her slaves were assessed at $2,200, which placed her net worth second only to that of Anthony Odingsells. As previously mentioned, black slave ownership was not very widespread and the majority of black-owned "slaves" during this period were actually relatives, loved ones, and friends. Still, the number of black slave owners in Georgia steadily declined after 1830. On the eve of the Civil War in 1860, there were only nine free black slaveholders in Chatham County, who owned a total of 19 slaves—only a small percentage of the county's total slave population of 15,417. [29]

Free black female Savannahians accumulated their wealth by inheritance from deceased husbands and relatives and by being a major part of the nonslave workforce. In the 1823 census, the 108 women appearing in Savannah's Register of Free Persons of Color listed the following occupations: washerwoman (30), seamstress (26), cook (17), vendor of small wares (11), housekeeper (5), and nurse (4). Other less-popular occupations included hairdresser, shopkeeper, and a keeper of the Oyster House. By 1860 significant changes had occurred in the occupational preferences of local free black women. Seamstress/dressmaker had become the occupation of choice for 121 women, far outpacing the 44 washerwomen listed in the federal census. Other popular categories included domestic servants (32), pastry cooks (20), and nurses (10). These hardworking women did not labor alone, for many free black men also loaned their skills and muscles in support of free black enterprise.[30]

Among the various occupations pursued by free black males, tailoring was a particularly successful one, especially for the Haitians who migrated to the city after 1792. Andrew Mirault owned a thriving tailoring business that was patronized by blacks and Savannah's leading white citizens. At the time of his death in 1828, he owned several pieces of real estate, six slaves, and his books contained accounts payable in the amount of $233.80. Andrew Morel, another Haitian tailor, owned two slaves who worked in his shop and in 1850 he owned property assessed at $1,600. Joseph Dubergier was yet another Haitian tailor who was also a slave owner but owned no real estate. Other business owners included Prince Gandy, a cooper, and John Gibbon, a carpenter, who owned seven and five slaves, respectively. The leading free black barbers in antebellum Savannah were Emanuel Waud and Jackson Regis; both were residential property owners.[31]

Although Savannah was the home of many of Georgia's more successful free blacks, there were others around the state who managed to accumulate sizable amounts of wealth. Wilkes Flagg of Milledgeville was born in Virginia in 1802 and eventually transported to Georgia and sold to the Fort family. He was taught to read and write by family members and also became a skilled blacksmith. His owners allowed Flagg to hire himself out to other whites and free blacks, by which he earned and saved enough money to purchase his freedom and the freedom of his wife and child. At the beginning of the Civil War, he owned his home and a blacksmith shop and had accumulated over $25,000. Flagg's Chapel Baptist Church stands today as a monument to the entrepreneurial talents of this self-emancipated black man.

Solomon Humphries of Macon gained permission from his owner to hire himself out, whereby he earned enough money to start his own business. Profits from the enterprise were used to buy his freedom and the freedom of his family. G. H. Dwelle was born into slavery in Columbia County in January 1833. After nearly thirty years of bondage, he purchased his freedom and that of his mother with money he earned as a cabinetmaker in Augusta. In 1866 he became an ordained minister and served as pastor of the Springfield Baptist Church for seven years. He later became a missionary in southwest Georgia, where he established several churches and worked for the Ebenezer Baptist Association.

A free black doctor named Gower developed a successful practice in Oglethorpe County. He received his medical education at a Northern college and by 1805 had earned a sparkling reputation as a skilled surgeon. Gower's medical career in Georgia ended abruptly when he and the wife of a local white merchant became romantically linked. The black doctor barely escaped with his life, fleeing Oglethorpe County with an angry lynch mob in hot pursuit. The harassment of free black business owners and professionals in Georgia was not uncommon. A petition authored by a group of white citizens and presented to the Atlanta city council clearly demonstrates this point: "We feel aggrieved as Southern citizens, that your honorable body tolerates a Negro dentist, Roderick Badger, in our midst, and in justice to ourselves and the community, it ought to be abated. . . . We the residents of Atlanta, appeal to you for justice." [32]

Despite the hardships and prejudice, free blacks benefited tremendously when they possessed a marketable skill and at least a rudimentary ability to read and write. As discussed earlier, the 1750 statute that legalized slavery in Georgia had also required slave owners to provide for the religious instruction of their slaves. Five years later, the legislature reversed itself and repealed this provision. According to the preamble of the new law, "the having of Slaves taught to write or suffering them to be employed in Writing may be attended with great Inconveniencys," so it was made unlawful to "teach or Cause any Slave or Slaves to be taught to write or . . . employ any Slave or Slaves as a Scribe in any manner or writing whatsoever." White persons convicted of violating this statute would be fined fifteen pounds sterling.[33]

Yet under this same statute, free persons of color were legally able to secure education and training for many decades. It wasn't until 1829 that the legislature passed another statute finally making it unlawful to educate Negroes—slave or free—in Georgia. A five-hundred-dollar fine and imprisonment could be imposed on any white convicted of teaching blacks to read or write. A free black convicted of the same crime would be fined or whipped. In addition, this law contained a provision prohibiting the circulation of pamphlets, papers, or any other material that might encourage slave insurrections. The penalty for violating this statute was death. In 1842, the Georgia legislature enacted another law that outlawed the sale or distribution of all printed books, pamphlets, writing paper, ink, and other writing materials to free blacks. In order to legally obtain these items, a free black had to receive permission from his white guardian. A white person convicted of violating this law could be fined not less ten dollars or more than fifty dollars. A second offense was punishable by automatic confinement.

Despite the legislation, free blacks continued to open and operate schools for free and enslaved black children in Savannah. Many of the statutes restricting access to education for free blacks were not enforced on the local level, and some whites made provisions for mulatto offspring to be educated. While scores of free black Savannahians earned a decent living through the ownership of small businesses, several blacks took an extra step, providing black children with reading, writing, and other skills. The most notable black teacher was Julien Fromontin, a native of Haiti who migrated to Savannah around 1818 and taught black children until 1844 in the school he established. Fromontin and local officials ignored the 1829 statute, for he continued to teach, more discreetly, for years after it was made law.

Mary Woodhouse also operated a school for about twenty-five to thirty slave and free black children in her home during the 1850s. Assisted by her daughter, Mary Jane, she provided her students with one to two years of basic reading, writing, and arithmetic before the children were transferred to another school, run by one Mary Beasley, where they received more advanced lessons. Although local white officials obviously were aware of these clandestine educational activities, they did not interfere. Susie King Taylor, who later became a teacher and laundress for the first all-black Union regiment and the author of a Civil War memoir, attended both of these schools. According to Taylor, the students carefully avoided detection going to and from school by wrapping their books in newspapers, carrying buckets as though on an errand, and taking circuitous and varying routes. The precocious young slave studied under Mary Beasley until May 1860, when the teacher informed Taylor's grandmother that she had taught the girl "all she knew" and that someone with greater knowledge had to be secured.[34]

Catherine Deveaux was another black educational pioneer who operated a school for black children prior to emancipation. Her husband, John, was a preacher in Savannah and she supported his ministry by teaching children how to read the Bible. Catherine eventually passed the responsibility of running the school to her daughter Jane, who expanded and improved the quality of the curriculum. Together they operated the school uninterrupted for almost thirty years. A surprised regiment of General William T. Sherman's soldiers found the school in session when they captured Savannah in December 1864. Jane Deveaux was subsequently hired by the Freedmen's Bureau, the federal agency charged with the

responsibility of assisting freed slaves, to teach at the school it established in the city the following year.

James Porter, a free black Charleston transplant and a future
member of the Georgia legislature, established a music school in
Savannah in 1854. He openly offered lessons in violin, piano, and
voice, as well as reading and writing classes, without harassment
from local authorities. The importance of these pioneer free black
educators cannot be overestimated. Whittington Johnson observes:

> Although their schools lacked up-to-date books, chalk-
> boards, and maps, teachers created a wholesome learning
> environment and provided their pupils with educational
> experiences that left a lasting impression. This training
> was especially important because many of the pupils, the
> first generation in their families to receive schooling, sub-
> sequently became community leaders. [35]

THE COLONIZATION MOVEMENT
IN GEORGIA

Increasing concern over the growing number of free blacks in
America led to the founding of the American Colonization Society
in Washington, D.C., in 1816. The society was the brainchild of
Reverend Robert Finley, a Presbyterian minister who served briefly
as president of the University of Georgia. Finley believed that
African colonization would provide America with the final solution
to its "Negro Problem." Hoping to prevent Southern secession
from the Union and a war over slavery, he tried to strike a delicate
balance between Northern abolitionists and proslavery
Southerners. During the early stages of the colonization movement, Finley's strategy appeared to be working. Several of the

groups that initially pledged their support to the American Colonization Society expressed varied and often opposing viewpoints regarding the source of the problems associated with slavery.

One group of supporters was comprised of white men such as Finley who opposed slavery but rejected the idea of immediate universal emancipation and the granting of citizenship rights to blacks. These Northern clergymen, philanthropists, and a few Southern slave owners argued instead for the gradual emancipation of slaves on the condition that they be transported from the United States and colonized in Africa. A second group of colonization advocates consisted primarily of Southern slave owners and political leaders who believed the growing number of free persons of color in America were a threat to the institution of slavery. These individuals generally opposed all private manumissions and argued that only blacks already freed should be allowed to emigrate from the United States. During the late 1820s, many of these men withdrew their support and became vocal critics of the Colonization Society because of its commitment to the removal and colonization of *all* blacks in America—slave and free.

A much smaller group of free and enslaved blacks supported the colonization movement because they were convinced that the Negro race would never receive full citizenship rights and equal justice in America. The earliest black proponent was Paul Cuffee, a Quaker ship captain who helped forty free blacks emigrate to Sierra Leone, Africa, in 1815. Other prominent black supporters of colonization during the antebellum period were James Forten, Absalom Jones, and Richard Allen, the founder of the African Methodist Episcopal Church. Scores of free black Georgians, in order to escape persecution and discrimination, eventually joined the movement.

Reverend Finley recruited some of the most influential white men in America to lead the African Colonization Society: Thomas Jefferson, James Madison, James Monroe, John Marshall, Francis Scott Key, congressmen Henry Clay of Kentucky and Daniel

Webster of Massachusetts. Bushrod Washington, an associate justice of the Supreme Court and the nephew of George Washington, was the society's first president. William H. Crawford of Oglethorpe County, an influential Georgia political leader and slave owner, served as one of the vice presidents.

According to the society's by-laws, the purpose of the organization was to "promote and execute a plan for colonizing (with their consent) the free people of color residing in our country in Africa, or such other place as Congress shall deem most expedient." In March 1819 Congress passed the Anti-Slave Trade Act that contained a one-hundred-thousand-dollar appropriation to be used by the American Colonization Society to return African slaves illegally imported into the United States. The following year, in January 1820, the first ship of eighty-eight black colonists set sail. In 1822 the society and the federal government established the free black colony of Liberia on the west coast of Africa. Its capital city was named Monrovia in honor of President James Monroe.[36]

In 1816 Robert Finley arrived in Athens, Georgia, as the newly appointed president of the state university, and eagerly set out to build Southern support for the colonization movement. He made several speeches in which he lauded the merits of colonization and he played a key role in establishing male and female auxiliary chapters in Augusta. Finley happily reported to a northeastern colleague: "With men of reflection the colonizing scheme is as popular here, as with you in [New] Jersey." His efforts to promote colonization ended prematurely when he contracted a fatal case of typhus in 1817. In a posthumously published article entitled "The History of the Rise, Progress, and Views of the American Colonization Society Extracted from the Memoirs of the Reverend Robert Finley, late President of Franklin College, Athens, Georgia," Finley wrote that the Colonization Society was founded to "repair the injuries inflicted by our fathers" on humanity. He argued that the benefit of black removal and colonization was threefold: white America would be "cleared" of blacks; the African continent would receive greater exposure to Christianity and civilization; and "our blacks themselves would be put in a better situation." Finley's untimely death slowed the growth of the society in the state, but the colonization movement continued to gain converts among white and black Georgians.[37]

Crawford informed the board of managers of the American Colonization Society in April 1819 that Georgia officials had seized thirty or forty Africans who were being illegally imported into the state by slave traders. An 1817 law provided that they be sold at public auction or turned over to the colonization society for transportation back to Africa. Reverend William Meade, the general agent for the society, was sent to Georgia to rescue the blacks from slavery. Georgia Governor William Rabun agreed to postpone the public sale while Meade solicited donations to pay the costs associated with their capture and return to Africa. According to Meade, "Some who had but little hope of our general enterprise declared their willingness to contribute for the ransom [sic] of these; and a few who intended to have become the purchasers at this sale, expressed a pleasure at the thought of their restoration to Africa, and proved their sincerity by uniting with the Society at Milledgeville." [38]

Although the state-supported manumission of the slaves demonstrated that support for colonization was present in Georgia, the majority of the white population became increasingly suspicious and critical of the organization. A resolution adopted by the Georgia General Assembly in 1827 is indicative of these changing sentiments:

At the first establishment of the Colonization Society, whatever may have been intended or avowed as its object . . . the general impression in the Southern States as to its object was, that it was limited to the removal, beyond the United States, of the then free people of color and their descendants, and none others. Under this impression, it once received the sanction and the countenance of many of the humane, the wise and patriotic among us.—It is now ascertained that this impression was false; and its officers ... now boldly and fearlessly avow that its object is and ever has been, to remove the whole colored population of the Union to another land; and to effect this object—so wild, fanatical and destructive in itself—they ask that the general fund, to which the slave-holding States have so largely contributed, should be appropriated for the purpose so especially ruinous to the prosperity, importance and political strength of the Southern States.[39]

The criticism emanating from the legislature was mild compared to the withering assault leveled against the American Colonization Society by fiery abolitionist William Lloyd Garrison. Garrison was an uncompromising advocate who fought for the immediate and unconditional emancipation of all American slaves. He was an early supporter of colonization, but he subsequently accused the society of being "the apologist and friend of American slaveholders." He charged that the organization "originated with those who held a large portion of their fellow-creatures in worse than Egyptian bondage" and that it was generally supported by them and under their complete control. Garrison pointed out that not one of the managers or officers of the society had emancipated his slaves and transported them to Liberia. Finally, he criticized the colonists for supporting the position that "no slave ought to receive his liberty, except on condition of instant banishment" from the United States of America. Although the movement came under attack from advocates on both sides of the slavery debate, historian Early Lee Fox observed that its fiercest enemies were the Garrisonian abolitionists and Southern slaveholders.[40]

Yet despite this vocal and sustained opposition, the fledgling Georgia colonization movement managed to recruit some enthusiastic supporters. The Jackson County American Colonization

Auxiliary Society held its inaugural meeting on April 2, 1825. Local supporters were keenly aware that the society's desire to remove and emancipate all American slaves was opposed by most white Southerners. This may explain the careful wording of a resolution that was unanimously adopted during the organization's annual meeting on September 1, 1827:

> Whereas this Society, notwithstanding the great discouragement arising out of the ill founded jealousies and fears of the South, relative to the ultimate designs of the North, and the Parent Society for Colonizing the free persons of colour, and such as may be by their respective owners from time to time emancipated; do, in the fullest confidence in the patriotism and philanthropy of the Parent Society, again renew to each other the solemn pledge of fidelity and perseverance. Believing (as we always have,) that it is one of the greatest National and Christian enterprises, and that the jealousies and fears of our fellow citizens do not arise from the want of equal patriotism, but from the want of correct information. [41]

By 1832 several auxiliary chapters of the American Colonization Society were functioning in counties around Georgia. Joining the Jackson County branch were Clarke, Burke, Putnam, and Baldwin Counties and Augusta, where male and female chapters raised money to support African colonization. Numerous white Georgians contributed to the fund, including Augustans George Hargraves and A. Campbell, who donated $1,350.00 and $1,000.00, respectively. During the ten-year period between 1846 and 1856, Georgia supporters contributed $12,669.90 to the American Colonization Society.

A few slave owners tried, with varying results, to will their entire estates to the society. In 1853 Francis Gideon of Fulton

County bequeathed all his slaves to the society with the expectation that they would be transported to Liberia. The administrator refused to carry out the testator's request and the American Colonization Society filed suit. The case was eventually argued before the Georgia Supreme Court during its August term in 1857. The court voided the will because the society's charter did not vest it with the specific authority to accept chattel property. In another case argued before Georgia's highest court in 1856, Francis J. Walker, a Burke County slave owner, directed his executors to liquidate his estate and transfer the proceeds from the sale to the society for the maintenance and transportation of eleven slaves to Liberia. The slaves to be freed were Louisa, a mulatto, and her three children, Green, William, and Elizabeth; another woman also named Louisa, a "light Negro," and her children, Catherine and Augustus; Sue and her son Harry; and Cecilia and her daughter Emily. Walker's executor, who was also his brother, filed suit and sought to have sections of the will pertaining to the manumission of the slaves declared null and void. The supreme court upheld the validity of the will because the manumissions were to occur outside of the state. The justices also directed the lower court to arrange for the transportation of the blacks to Liberia and make provisions for their continuing support.[42]

The estates of other deceased Georgia slave owners managed to avoid contentious legal battles and scores of slaves were manumitted on the condition that they first be transported to Liberia. The will of Zadock Simmons of Wilkinson County, probated in 1821, contained a provision freeing all of his slaves, provided that they be removed to the west coast of Africa and freed. Savannah attorney C. Bolton manumitted nine slaves to be sent to Liberia. The Negroes sailed for Africa on October 20, 1830, on board the *Carolinian*. In 1832 Georgia slave owner Dr. James Bradley transported 46 slaves to Liberia on board the *Jupiter*, where they were subsequently freed.

In 1830 Joel Early, a large Greene County slave owner and the brother of former Georgia Governor Peter Early, conditionally freed 30 slaves and arranged for their transport to Liberia. They sailed on board the *Brig Montgomery,* along with a large contingent of other black colonists. Some of the former Greene County slaves became dissatisfied with the harsh existence on the African continent and they asked for, and received, help from Early, who arranged for their return to Georgia.

In 1833, 180 black colonists departed Savannah on the ship *Hercules*; 150 were from South Carolina and the rest were from Georgia and Florida. This particular expedition generated a great deal of optimism throughout the American Colonization Society because many of the migrants were well-educated missionaries. It was hoped that they would spread the teachings of Christianity to the heathen African population. In November 1833, a ship set sail from Savannah with 83 black Savannahians and 14 other slaves who, upon direction from their owner, a Dr. Ripley, would be freed during the voyage. Cecilia D'Lyons, a free black thirty-five-year-old mother and her five children, ranging in age from seven to sixteen, joined a small group of Savannah emigres who sailed for Liberia in 1848. Prior to her departure, she persuaded several other free blacks to relocate to the West African coast.

In 1850 the will of Major Wood of Savannah provided for the emancipation of his 164 slaves on the condition that they be transported to Haiti, and he left a fund of $5,000 to cover their expenses. His executor decided that Haiti's proximity to the United States rendered his request unacceptable, so the blacks were taken instead to Africa. Two slaves, London Williams and Sally Tafts, sailed for Liberia on board the *Mary Caroline Stevens* in 1856, upon which vessel their owners, Savannahians M. A. Williams and J. B. Tafts, had instructed that they be manumitted. Also sailing on the *Mary Caroline Stevens* were 54 slaves who were to be emancipated by Elbert County slave owner Richard Hoff. He contributed $2000 to the American Colonization Society to defray the costs associated with their passage.

In 1836 the will of deceased slave owner Richard Tubman of Augusta directed his wife and executrix Emily Tubman to manumit all of his slaves. Tubman hoped to avoid the prohibition against intrastate manumission by establishing a fund in the amount of $10,000, half of which would be donated to the University of Georgia if the legislature allowed the freed blacks to remain in the state. He also stipulated that if the legislature rejected his offer, the money was to be used to relocate his former slaves to a section of "the United States best calculated to secure to them the rights and immunities of free persons of color." [43]

Emily Tubman decided that the most practical way to honor her late husband's request was to secure the assistance of the American Colonization Society. Early in 1837 she contacted the leaders of the national organization and its auxiliary in the state of Maryland. Representatives of the two organizations aggressively lobbied Tubman for her permission to colonize the soon-to-be emancipated slaves. Both groups faced growing budget deficits and were motivated by the availability of the $10,000 fund. John Latrobe, the corresponding secretary for the Maryland Colonization Society, eventually won Tubman's commitment and plans were developed to transport the blacks to Liberia. However, logistical problems complicated the expedition. Latrobe informed Tubman that the Maryland society could not send a ship to Georgia to receive the Augusta colonists. The Maryland blacks who were also scheduled to sail on the ship refused to dock in Georgia because they were afraid that they would be sold into slavery. Latrobe wrote to Tubman:

> We cannot call at Savannah for many reasons. As it is, the cry against us by the enemies of the colonization cause among the colored people is, that we send those who trust in us to Georgia. We could not make a shipment without

it being known of our intended calling at Georgia. . . . And that would make our emigrants desert. [44]

The Tubman slaves were forced to travel to Baltimore, where they boarded the brig *Baltimore* on May 17, 1837, and sailed for Liberia. The expedition consisted of 42 Tubman blacks and 4 other former Augusta slaves who were emancipated by "benevolent individuals." Following their arrival in Liberia, the former Augusta slaves developed a reputation for being industrious and hardworking. By 1839, they had established Mount Tubman as a thriving agricultural community. The settlement was surrounded by a sturdy eight-foot wall and a large cannon guarded the main gate. During the spring of that year, Tubman farms produced vegetables of the "highest quality" and they subsequently purchased a yoke of oxen to till the soil. By 1846, "Fort Tubman" had evolved into "a strong stockade capable of resisting any force that could be brought against it by the natives." [45]

Emily Tubman continued to correspond with and support her former slaves long after the initial fund had been depleted. The Liberian Tubmans accumulated wealth and influence throughout the nineteenth and twentieth centuries. Their adopted nation gained its independence from the American Colonization Society in 1847 and became a republic. In 1943 and again in 1951, William Vaccanarat Tubman, a descendant of the original Tubman settlers, was elected president of the Republic of Liberia.

The majority of the former Georgia slaves who returned to "Mother Africa," like the Tubmans, had little choice in the matter—except in rare instances, their former owners were the sole decision-makers. On the other hand, the free black Georgians who voluntarily joined the Liberian exodus did so because they believed that emigration was the only reasonable response to pervasive racial oppression. This belief became even more widespread following John Brown's bloody raid on Harper's Ferry in

1859. White Southerners blamed free persons of color for insti-
gating the incident and increased their efforts to expel free blacks
from the country and severely restrict the activities of the others.
State and local political leaders enacted harsh new measures
designed to crack down on free persons of color in Georgia. In
1859, the legislature eliminated the right of private manumission
when they prohibited *all* post-mortem emancipations within or
without the state. Faced with a new wave of hostility, hundreds of
free blacks chose to abandon life in America for the uncertainties
of the African continent.

Silas Pope, a free black Augustan, is one who heeded the call.
Pope purchased his freedom prior to 1860 for $1,072, and later pur-
chased the freedom of his forty-five-year-old wife, Louisa, and their
eight children. He informed the American Colonization Society that
his entire family was prepared to go to Liberia immediately. The
society granted the Popes free passage on a ship leaving in May 1860.
White colonization supporters reported that Pope was "delighted at
the prospect of being enabled to obtain a permanent home . . . which
he and his wife have been struggling [to secure] for many years."
Although about half of the black Georgians who migrated to Liberia
were already free, the majority of the state's free black population
opposed the idea of African colonization. They were influenced by
the advocacy of Northern abolitionists who castigated the American
Colonization Society as a tool of Southern slave owners. A heated
and prolonged debate over the wisdom of colonization reverberated
through Savannah's free black community.[46]

In a letter dated September 17, 1833, an unidentified free black
supporter of colonization in Savannah wrote a lengthy and revealing letter to the leaders of the American Colonization Society. The
writer acknowledged that several articles in newspapers and other
publications had provided him with insight into "the many difficulties and severe conflicts" that had slowed the progress of the
"holy and praiseworthy cause" of colonization. Responding to an

earlier inquiry regarding "the general sentiments of the free people of colour" in Savannah towards the American Colonization Society, he dolefully states, "I am ashamed to say." The Savannahian lashed out at the black opponents of emigration. "They seem," he wrote, "generally not be possess the feelings of men; for you can not by reasoning prevail upon them to leave this for Liberia." He was perplexed by their desire to stay in Georgia, "preferring the empty name of freedom to that genuine *liberty* which the coloured man can only enjoy no where but in Liberia." The free black writer concluded his letter by reaffirming his determination to sail for the African coast:

> I am determined to go, God being my helper; for my soul yearns after poor benighted Africa; and I pity the poor unfeeling, callous-hearted men of colour—particularly those who wear the holy appellation of Christian, and do not feel it to be their duty to go over and assist in this vast field of moral usefulness, and secure for themselves and those they ought to love as themselves, a country of liberty, together with its concomitant blessings.[47]

Whether the Savannah writer made good on his pledge to join the West African colonists is unknown. But several thousand other free black Americans did. By 1860 the American Colonization Society had assisted in the transportation of some 12,000 blacks to Liberia, including more than 1,200 from Georgia. Throughout its existence, the organization enjoyed the support of America's most influential white leaders, including President Abraham Lincoln, the eventual author of the Emancipation Proclamation. In the final analysis, however, the colonization movement never lived up to the lofty expectations of its founders. The American Colonization Society failed in large part because it could not maintain the support of two key groups, free blacks and Southern slaveholders.

The 12,000 colonists who were relocated to Liberia represented only a small portion of the 3.5 million slaves living in America by 1860. The belief that blacks were genetically inferior, and more specifically, that free blacks were a serious threat to the peace and prosperity of the nation, was a central tenet of the colonization movement. This philosophy chilled support among white abolitionists and free blacks. More importantly, colonization supporters naively ignored the fact that most free blacks simply did not want to go "home" to a continent from which they were generations removed. Finley, Crawford, and other colonization leaders failed to comprehend the important cultural and sociological transformations that had occurred within the free black community. Free blacks were not "Africans," they were "African Americans." For better or worse, America—not Liberia—was their home. It was a home that free African Americans were unwilling to exchange for a distant and forbidding land.

More importantly, Southern slaveholders realized that the gradual emancipation and removal of their slaves to Africa would result in enormous economic and political losses. Although a few conscience-stricken slave owners did provide for "deathbed manumissions" of their slaves, the majority of white Southerners opposed the colonization movement, except for the emigration of free blacks from America. Robert Finley's quixotic plan to save the Union by removing all blacks from American soil proved to be politically naive and practically impossible. Ironically, the vocal and sustained opposition of Southern slave owners and "radical" Northern abolitionists played a major role in undermining support for the movement. The failure of the African Colonization Society to garner long-term financial support from the federal government all but eliminated the opportunity for a peaceful resolution to the slavery controversy in America. After the colonization movement failed, the only remaining alternatives were Southern secession and civil war.

General James Oglethorpe, the founder of Georgia advocated against slavery.

The Savannah Settlement.

Job ben Jalla, the African prince who was rescued
from slavery by General James Oglethorpe.

Fort Mose, a fortress of freedom in the Florida Colony
for fugitive British slaves.

A Fort Mose militiaman.

Reverend George Liele, the first black man ordained
to preach in North America.

The signing of the United States Constitution.

Reverend Andrew Bryan, a free black Georgian and pastor of the
First African Baptist Church.

Savannah's first African Baptist Church (ca. 1790), one of the world's oldest black churches.

Admiral George Cockburn masterminded the emancipation
and evacuation of Georgia slaves during the War of 1812.

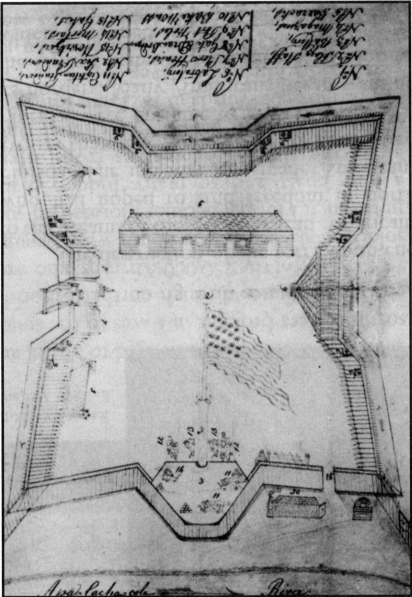

The Negro Fort, a fugitive slave stronghold on the
Appalachicola River in Spanish Florida that was
destroyed and rebuilt by American soldiers.

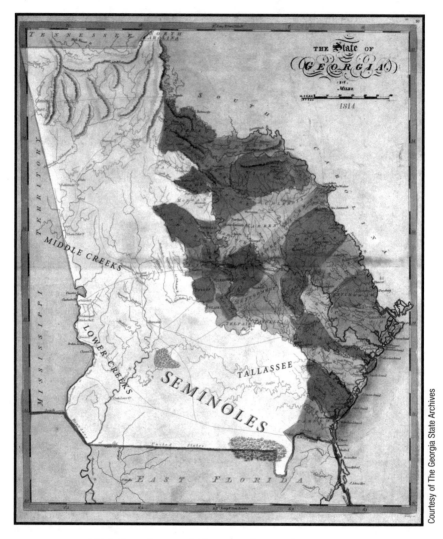

1816 Georgia map delineating Seminole territory.

John Horse, the Negro-Seminole subchief.

Abraham, the Negro-Seminole leader (center, top) and the Seminole
delegation that met with President James Monroe in Washington, D.C.

Reverend Andrew Marshall, a wealthy free black businessman
and pastor of the First African Baptist Church.

Before and after photographs of a fugitive Georgia slave
who joined the Union army.

Susie King Taylor, a nurse, teacher, laundress, and teamster
to the first black Union soldiers.

General Willliam T. Sherman meets with black ministers in Savannah.

CHAPTER VI

———

A WHITE MAN'S WAR

Shortly after the first shots were fired in the Civil War in April 1861, free black men in the North began to form militia units and volunteer for service in the Union army. Black volunteers realized that military service afforded them an unprecedented opportunity to prove their loyalty and manhood in the war against Southern slaveholders. More importantly, they were convinced that a Union victory would ultimately lead to the end of American slavery. Black and white abolitionists in the North heard in the roar of cannons at Fort Sumter the celestial trumpets that heralded the dawning of the Day of Jubilee. However, before black men could march off to fight for the liberation of their enslaved brethren, they first had to fight for the right to join the United States military.

A federal statute enacted back in 1792 prohibited black volunteers from serving in state militias or the U.S. Army and Navy. At the war's outset in 1861, President Abraham Lincoln adamantly opposed the enlistment of black men because he feared that their participation would change the meaning and purpose of the conflict. During the war's first eighteen months, the ever-cautious president reassured whites in the North and South that the conflict arose out of political differences concerning "states' rights," rather than a desire to abolish slavery. And in the early stages, the majority of white Northerners agreed with the idea that the Civil War was and should remain a "white man's war."

Lincoln rejected outright the persistent pleas of black and white abolitionists who wanted to transform the war into a crusade to destroy the institution of slavery. Despite a string of devastating military setbacks, an ever-dwindling pool of white recruits, and growing antiwar sentiment, as late as July 4, 1862, the president reassured Congress that he would not interfere with slavery where it existed. Several of his generals initially adopted the controversial policy of returning fugitive slaves who escaped to Union lines to their Southern masters. Their actions incensed abolitionists and severely diluted support for the Union war effort among some influential black leaders in the North. Elisha Weaver, editor of the *Christian Recorder*, the official newspaper of the African Methodist Episcopal Church in Philadelphia, publicly criticized the policy and counseled against black participation in the war. "To offer ourselves now is to abandon self-respect and invite insult," he wrote. Weaver argued that black men should not fight for a country that denied them the basic rights of citizenship and human dignity.[1]

Reverend J. Sella Martin, a prominent black minister and abolitionist, claimed that the Union army's refusal to grant sanctuary to fugitive slaves had convinced many Southern blacks to lend their support to the Confederate cause. At least some of them believed that by supporting the Confederacy, they might eventually secure increased citizenship rights for themselves and possibly elevate the status of their race. Although these sentiments may appear to have been unrealistic, General Robert E. Lee and other Southern officials would eventually seek to stave off defeat during the closing days of the war by advocating for the enlistment of slave soldiers. Several of the enlistment proposals would include provisions that required the emancipation of those slaves who served honorably in the Confederate army.[2]

One of the more eloquent and persuasive voices in favor of black enlistment in the North belonged to Frederick Douglass, the most influential black leader of the nineteenth century. Douglass was among the first to predict that the Civil War could not be won by the Union unless it was transformed into a struggle for the liberation of 3.5 million American slaves. He also believed that this transformation would not take place unless black men were allowed to fight and die on the fields of battle. Early in 1862, the fiery abolitionist wrote: "Once let the black man get upon his person the brass letters, US, let him get an eagle on his button, and a musket on his shoulder and bullets in his pockets, and there is no power on earth which can deny that he has earned the right to citizenship in the United States." He angrily denounced those who opposed the enlistment of black men in the Union army: "Let the slaves and free colored people be called into service and formed into a liberating army, to march into the South and raise the banner of emancipation." Douglass criticized the federal government's proscription against black soldiers as a "spectacle of blind, unreasoning prejudice" and he ridiculed President Lincoln and the Union for fighting with its "white hand" while allowing its "black hand" to remain tied.[3]

Whites in the North raised two primary objections to the enlistment of black troops. They believed first of all that white soldiers would be degraded and demoralized if they were forced to fight alongside black soldiers. More importantly, it was generally accepted that black men, especially former slaves, were unfit for service in the military because of their docile and cowardly nature. These same objections were raised by white Southerners during the subsequent debate regarding the enlistment of blacks in the Confederate army. All but forgotten by whites in the North was the fact that several thousand black men fought and died alongside American soldiers during the Revolutionary War and the War of 1812. In September 1862, Lincoln restated his opposition to Negro enlistment to a delegation of Indiana officials: "If we were to arm [Negroes] I fear that in a few weeks the arms would be in the hands of the rebels." The president predicted that black enlistment would turn fifty thousand bayonets from the loyal slaveholding border states of Kentucky, Maryland, Missouri, and Delaware against the Union.[4]

While the president was busy discounting the feasibility of allowing black men to fight in the Union army, coastal Georgia slaves were already engaged in a covert struggle for liberation. The occupation of the Sea Islands off the coasts of Georgia, South Carolina, and Florida by Union troops in December 1861 opened the floodgates for thousands of Georgia slaves, who followed in the footsteps of their forebears by fleeing to freedom behind enemy lines. After securing their freedom and that of relatives, some of the more courageous men and women sought to make more direct contributions to the Union war effort. These self-emancipated slaves participated in an underground guerrilla movement that harassed Confederate forces along the coast, aided in the escape of hundreds of mainland slaves, and spied on enemy fortifications and troop movements.

"MY GOD! ARE WE FREE?"

The Union assault on coastal Georgia actually began with the attack and capture of Port Royal, South Carolina, in November 1861. The reverberations of Yankee cannons booming just forty miles up the coast created near panic in Savannah. The city was quickly transformed into a ghost town, as the residents gathered as many of their possessions as possible (including slaves) and fled inland. Although two years passed before General William T. Sherman conducted his devastating March to the Sea, culminating with the capture of Savannah in December 1864, Union troops easily occupied Tybee, Wassau, and St. Simons Islands early in 1862. The rest of the Georgia coast, including Fort Pulaski in the Savannah Harbor, was brought under federal control by the end of March. The arrival of Yankee soldiers on Georgia soil signaled the arrival of the "Day o' Jubilo" for coastal slaves. Up and down the coast, black Georgians offered prayers of thanksgiving as they shed the chains of bondage.

During the first two and one-half years of the Civil War, Cumberland Island and the other Sea Islands once again served as hosts for black men, women, and children yearning to be free. Several "free island colonies" were established under the protection of the Union navy; the largest settlement was located on St. Simons Island at the mouth of the Altamaha River. By the end of 1862, more than six hundred fugitive slaves, mostly women and children, had crowded onto St. Simons, while hundreds more lived in smaller island settlements up and down the Georgia coast.

The exact number of slaves who escaped during this period is uncertain because navy officials failed to accurately record their arrival. According to historian Clarence Mohr, who conducted a detailed study of Georgia's slave exodus between December 1861 and October 1864, approximately twenty-five hundred fugitives succeeded in reaching Union lines. However, these figures do not include fugitive slaves who established themselves in maroon camps in the dense swamps along the coast or in isolated sections of the coastal islands. Some Georgia slave owners projected the number of fugitives to be much higher. A group of Liberty County citizens claimed in a petition dated August 1862 that twenty thousand was actually a low estimate of the number of slaves who had escaped from coastal plantations. Although historians debate the accuracy of that estimate, one fact cannot be contradicted: Georgia slaves demonstrated once again their willingness to risk life and limb in order to secure freedom for themselves and their loved ones. And once again, Georgia slave owners were surprised by the willingness of their supposedly loyal slaves to seek sanctuary and freedom among "foreign" enemies.

Early in 1862, Louis Manigault, a Savannah rice planter, observed: "This has taught us the perfect impossibility of placing the least confidence in any Negro. In too numerous instances those we esteemed the most have been the first to desert us. House Servants, from their constant contact with the family become more conversant with passing events and are often the first to have their minds polluted with evil thoughts." As soon as Georgia slave owners grasped the scope and impact of the slave exodus to the Union lines, they immediately began to remove their remaining bondsmen to more secure inland locations. This effort, called "refugeeing," resulted in the uprooting and removal of several thousand coastal slaves. Thousands of these slaves were reestablished on newly purchased plantations in southwest Georgia near the city of Albany in Dougherty County.[5]

Susie King Taylor, a young Savannah slave, wrote in her Civil War memoirs: "I wanted to see the wonderful 'Yankees' so much, as I heard my parents say the Yankee was going to set all the slaves free. Oh, how those people prayed for freedom!" A few weeks later she, along with her uncle and seven other family members, escaped to St. Catherine's Island. Following a two-week stay, Taylor and about thirty other fugitives were transported by federal gunboat to St. Simons Island. In scenes reminiscent of the British occupation of Cumberland some fifty years earlier, fugitive Georgia slaves arrived on St. Simons in small and large groups; individuals as well as entire families paddled their way to freedom in commandeered boats and dug-out canoes.[6]

These desperate escapes were often fraught with difficulty and danger, as evidenced by the trials of four brothers who planned and executed a daring escape from the Georgia interior. Leaving their youngest brother behind to care for their elderly mother, the

Wilson brothers, along with their sister and her children, fled down river in a dug-out canoe. The boat came under heavy fire from Confederate soldiers, who wounded every adult male on the boat. Despite their wounds, the fugitives eventually completed their desperate voyage to the coast, where they were taken aboard federal gunboats.[7]

Not all of the fugitive slaves succeeded in their attempts to secure sanctuary. In September 1862, twenty-three blacks joined in a mass escape from several Savannah River plantations. All but four managed to arrive at the prearranged rendezvous site on time. Two men and a woman with a child were left behind to face the wrath of pursuing slave-hunters, as the others got away in stolen canoes. The four unfortunate fugitives were quickly spotted as they tried to escape across a shallow creek. Bob, the leader of the group, was shot in the leg and immediately captured. The other black man was also wounded but continued to flee deeper into the Georgia swamps. After a harrowing pursuit of three or four miles, the mother and child literally collapsed from exhaustion and surrendered, but refused to disclose the whereabouts of their wounded companion. The three captured blacks were among the eighty-nine fugitive slaves who, according to Confederate records, failed to reach the Union lines.[8]

Although fugitive slaves faced the possibility of death or severe punishment if captured, many were determined to succeed. None was more so than the resolute grandmother who, on her second try, gathered twenty-two children and grandchildren on a stolen Confederate flatboat and floated forty miles down the Savannah River to freedom. When they were finally plucked from the murky waters by Union sailors, the elderly woman, clutching the youngest child to her breast, rose to her feet, raised her face toward the heavens, and exclaimed "My God! Are we free?" [9]

Late in December 1863, thirteen fugitive slaves from McIntosh County were taken aboard the U.S.S. *Fernandina* in St. Catherine's

Sound. The leader of the group was a twenty-seven-year-old black man named Cain who had been owned by William King, an infamous slave master who habitually brutalized and tortured his slaves. During the first week of January 1864, Cain risked his hard-won freedom, and possibly his life, in an effort to liberate several relatives who were enslaved near Sunbury, Georgia. He returned within a week with twelve relatives, including a forty-five-year-old woman named Grace, her five young children, her son-in-law Charlie, and her four grandchildren.[10]

Even though they were not allowed to enlist, a small band of blacks engaged in covert operations for the Union that helped undermine Confederate war operations and facilitated the escape of other Georgia slaves. One of the most daring black resistance fighters was Nat, who escaped from his Glynn County master shortly before the arrival of federal troops along the Georgia coast. By the summer of 1862, the resourceful fugitive had joined several hundred other former slaves who were living under Union protection on St. Simons Island. With the support and encouragement of Union commanders, Nat carried out numerous missions to rescue slaves and spy on Confederate fortifications. Described by white Savannahians as a "notorious runaway . . . and rascal," he was accused of killing two rebel soldiers and a white civilian. Local authorities also implicated Nat in the escape of more than one hundred Georgia slaves. On one particularly dangerous mission, he led six black men some thirty miles behind enemy lines to rescue their wives and children. During this expedition the men fought off two separate attacks on land and barely avoided capture by a Confederate river patrol.[11]

Nat eventually joined forces with another well-known resistance fighter named Harvey. The local paper chronicled their exploits and accused the two freedom fighters of being "spies, murderers, incendiaries and thieves." Nat and Harvey harassed enemy forces along the Georgia coast until they were shot to death by a

Confederate soldier in June 1864.[12]

Another member of coastal Georgia's black resistance was March Haynes, a literate fugitive who prior to the war had worked as a stevedore and river pilot at the port of Savannah. According to his Union allies, Haynes was a "pure, shrewd, brave, efficient man," who quickly grasped the historic implications of the Civil War. For several months following the Union invasion, he and his wife continued to live in Savannah, secretly gathering vital information for Union commanders, until growing suspicions among the white population forced them to seek refuge on the Sea Islands.[13]

General Quincy A. Gilmore of the Tenth Army Corps supplied Haynes with whatever resources he needed to carry out covert missions in and around Savannah. This included a sturdy, swift boat painted a drab color, similar to the hue of the Savannah River, in order to camouflage it from enemy river patrols. He was also granted the authority to recruit other black men to accompany him on his dangerous missions. Under the cover of darkness, the black commandos would land in the marshes below Savannah, enter the city, blend into the local slave population, and gather valuable information regarding Confederate troop movements and local fortifications. Other expeditions were conducted for the sole purpose of helping willing slaves to escape.

Because of his detailed knowledge of the river and its tributaries, Haynes easily slipped past rebel river patrols and literally delivered boatloads of Georgia slaves to freedom. He was shot in the leg during one mission, and on another occasion in April 1863 was arrested and jailed. On April 28 the *Savannah Daily Morning News* reported that a black man named March, the property of John C. Rowland, had been arrested and charged with the offense of harboring and "running off to the Yankees" several Savannah slaves. Haynes's ultimate fate is unknown.[14]

HUNTER'S REGIMENT

Despite the official ban on black enlistment, a handful of Union generals tried to organize Negro regiments in 1862. The first systematic attempt was conducted by General David Hunter, who assumed command of Union forces occupying key coastal towns and the sea islands of Georgia, South Carolina, and north Florida on March 31, 1862. Acting on vague orders from the War Department to arm fugitive slaves "if special circumstances seem to require it," Hunter set in motion a controversial plan to enlist black men in the Union army. From his headquarters at Beaufort, South Carolina, he sent a letter to the War Department in early April, requesting weapons, equipment, and fifty thousand pairs of scarlet pants for his proposed regiment of former slaves. Two weeks later the general issued a proclamation of emancipation that freed the slaves living on Cockspur Island, Georgia, near Fort Pulaski in the Savannah harbor.[15]

Hunter's early efforts were aided by Reverend Abraham Murchinson, a slave preacher from Savannah who had fled to the Union encampments shortly before Hunter's arrival. After a private meeting with the general, the elderly minister volunteered to serve as a Union recruiter among the fugitive slave population. On April 7, 1862, Murchinson called a meeting of all adult black males on the island and explained in stirring language the historic importance associated with the organization of America's first all-black regiment. According to a *New York Times* reporter, Murchinson's appeal "rose to eloquence" as he detailed the difficulties, hardships, and advantages of military life. Following his emotional speech, which was frequently interrupted by "amens" and applause, 105 black men—including scores of former Georgia slaves—volunteered for service and another 45 recruits stepped forward within seven days.[16]

Despite Murchinson's initial success, the recruitment process proceeded slowly, primarily because of determined efforts by Union soldiers and government officials to undermine the initiative. "We don't want to fight side and side with the nigger," wrote a corporal in the Seventy-fourth New York Regiment. "We think we are a too superior race for that." Union soldiers convinced many potential volunteers that the government planned to sell them back into slavery in Cuba, or that they would be forced to serve without pay. Many of the teachers and missionaries who had come to the Sea Islands to help the freedmen also opposed Hunter's enlistment plans. One of them wrote: "I don't believe you could make soldiers of these men at all,—they are afraid, and they know it." Another predicted that "Negroes—plantation negroes, at least—will never make soldiers in one generation. Five white men could put a regiment to flight." [17]

On May 8, 1862, acting without authority from the Lincoln administration, General Hunter boldly expanded his earlier proclamation of emancipation by freeing all the slaves in Georgia, South Carolina, and Florida. In fact, coastal slaves had been "free" since their masters fled in the face of invading Union soldiers that spring. But along with this decree, Hunter circumvented local opposition by ordering the mandatory conscription of all able-bodied black men between the ages of eighteen and forty-five. His proclamation and conscription order angered President Lincoln, as well as Treasury Department officials on the island, while raising suspicions among the newly freed slaves. Treasury officials wrote scathing letters to their superiors in Washington, complaining that forced conscription had disrupted their experiments with free black labor on abandoned rebel plantations. The federal officials also alleged that the former slaves reportedly equated the mandatory draft, with no guarantee of pay, with sale on the auction block.

Although early accounts that black men had been marched at gunpoint to the Union barracks were later proven false, Lincoln issued a harsh statement disclaiming any knowledge of Hunter's proclamation or conscription order. Men of less confidence would have been crushed by this presidential rebuke, but the general rationalized that Lincoln's public statements were little more than political posturing, designed to allay the fears of border state loyalists. (It was true that Lincoln had never missed an opportunity to reassure slaveholders in the loyal border states that he would not free or arm their slaves.) So Hunter based his optimistic conclusion on the fact that the president never expressed any *private* dissatisfaction with his emancipation decree.

The absence of official approval or support did not deter Hunter from stubbornly pressing forward with his controversial plan. Further recruiting took place during the summer of 1862 and the regiment eventually reached full strength with somewhere between 844 and 1035 soldiers commanded by white officers. Uniforms, equipment, and weapons were issued, and the men were exposed to a rigorous training regimen. The black soldiers quickly demonstrated a capacity for impressive drills and reviews, which delighted General Hunter and a constant stream of high-ranking army officers. On August 1, 1862, the enlisted men listened to a magnificent sermon delivered by a fellow soldier, which was followed by the presentation of "free papers," documents to verify their emancipation.

Hunter's efforts to raise a regiment of former slaves became the focus of a nineteenth-century media circus, as reporters and columnists from around the country filled newspaper columns with details and opinions regarding the historic experiment. Early assessments by the Northern press were harsh and unrelenting. A *New York Times* reporter warned that black enlistment signaled "nothing else than a determination to exterminate the white population" in the Southern states. Even worse, the writer predicted the inevitable development of a "disgusting" scenario: "The man that fights in the ranks and distinguishes himself is entitled to applause and promotion. A regiment of negroes will claim black officers, and will, if the qualities of command are found to exist, be entitled to them"—the problem being that white soldiers would eventually be forced to endure the indignity of serving under black officers.[18]

The editors of the *Boston Journal* joined the chorus of criticism surrounding Hunter's experiment. They were certain that the former slaves were incapable of exchanging "the cotton patch for the 'tented field'" or the "bucolic hoe for the death-dealing musket." From the midwest the *Chicago Tribune* weighed in: "He who imagines that these blacks are being organized *to be put in the forefront of battle*, or because of any inability to crush the rebellion without their assistance, *insults the loyal millions of the North, and the gallant army of the North; and none but a malignant traitor will entertain such a thought.*" The *National Intelligencer* added that the "rude negro of Southern plantations" was simply incapable of learning how to use a sophisticated military musket. A *New York Post* correspondent offered a more pragmatic evaluation. "Among military men," he wrote, "great differences of opinion prevail, but it is believed that, both with soldiers and officers, the movement will be popular when it is seen how completely it is in the interest of the white soldier as well as the black—by furnishing a force for those kinds of duty and those locations in which the black is safe, while the white soldier can only serve at a great hazard." [19]

Inevitably the United States Congress was dragged into the sizzling national debate. On June 9, 1862, Representative Charles Wickliffe of Kentucky, a Confederate sympathizer, passed a resolution directing the War Department to provide official details regarding Hunter's activities. Three questions were posed: Had Hunter organized a regiment of fugitive slaves? Had he been authorized to do so by the War Department? And had the War Department furnished him with weapons and uniforms? The request was forwarded to Hunter, who concluded that this was an excellent opportunity to place before Congress and the nation his enlistment plan and thereby force the Lincoln administration to grant him official sanction and the resources needed to build the regiment.

The general answered the first question by noting that no regiment of "fugitive slaves" had been or was being organized in the Department of the South. However, he sarcastically acknowledged the existence of a fine regiment of "men" whose former masters could best be described as "fugitive rebels." With tongue planted firmly in cheek, Hunter added that the "loyal persons" comprising the First South Carolina Volunteers were "working with remarkable industry to place themselves in a position to go in full and effective pursuit of their fugacious and traitorous proprietors." He answered the second question by referring to the authority that had been granted to his predecessor, instructing him to arm black fugitives if circumstances required it. He jestfully noted that the absence of a "fugitive masters law" made it necessary for the former slaves to organize themselves in order to pursue and capture their fugitive rebel masters, whose protection they were now without. Regarding uniforms, weapons, and equipment, Hunter admitted that he acted without specific authority, but he argued that the "liberty to employ men in any particular capacity implied with it liberty also to supply them with the necessary tools." Finally, the general proudly proclaimed that he had "clothed, equipped, and armed the only loyal regiment yet raised in South Carolina." [20]

The letter was delivered to the House of Representatives, and the Speaker ordered it be read to the entire body. The clerk could hardly maintain his composure as the congressional chamber reverberated with the uncontrolled laughter of the Republican majority. Of course, Wickliffe and his proslavery colleagues in the Democratic Party were not amused by Hunter's biting sarcasm. They promptly drafted a stinging resolution condemning the general for disrespecting the dignity of the House, but the proposal failed to win a majority vote. Although the letter generated a great deal of publicity throughout the North, it did nothing to change the federal government's official policy prohibiting the enlistment of black soldiers.

The following month Hunter sent yet another letter to the War Department, seeking official authorization to recruit fifty thousand black soldiers into the Union army. This request, like the others that preceded it, languished due to the equivocation and indecisiveness of the Lincoln administration. Having failed to gain official recognition from the War Department or pay for his sable soldiers, Hunter regretfully disbanded all but one thirty-eight-man company of the regiment in August 1862. The demoralized general was granted a sixty-day leave of absence and Company E, the only surviving unit, was sent to St. Simons to protect the more than six hundred fugitive slaves who were living on the island.

Lieutenant Charles Adams watched the breakup of the First South Carolina Volunteers with mixed emotions: "General Hunter's negro regiment was disbanded yesterday," he wrote in a letter to his father, "and now they have disbursed to their old homes. Its breaking up was hailed here with great joy, for our troops have become more anti-negro than I could have imagined." But Adams also expressed some reservations over the demise of the fledgling regiment: "I could not help feeling a strong regret at seeing the red-legged darkies march off. . . . Why could not fanatics be silent and let Providence work for a while. The slaves would have moved when the day came and could have been made useful in a thousand ways. As it is, we are Hamlet's ape, who broke his neck to try conclusions." [21]

"SAMBO'S RIGHT TO BE KILT"

Although Hunter's initial efforts failed to win the support of President Lincoln, he did succeed in forging a national debate over the enlistment of Negro soldiers. At the close of his first tour of duty at Beaufort on August 22, 1862, the impetuous general was convinced that he had set in motion a great train of events. By ordering general emancipation and organizing a regiment of former slaves, Hunter helped to make the status of the Negro a central issue of the war. According to a supportive Port Royal, South Carolina, newspaper editor, Hunter had done more "to set the mind of the country . . . considering the true issues of [the] war, than all the agencies of journalism, both Houses of Congress, and all the executive branches of the country combined." [22]

Although Lincoln had refused to embrace Hunter's initiatives, the president could not ignore the firestorm of indignation that arose throughout the Union after "Hunter's Regiment" was disbanded. Neither could he ignore the fact that the growing need for additional troops had led to a softening of opposition in the North to black enlistment. This shift in public opinion among white Northerners was sarcastically reflected in a popular song entitled "Sambo's Right to Be Kilt":

> Some say it is a burnin' shame
> To make the naygurs fight,
> An' that the thrade o' being kilt
> Belongs but to the white;
> But as for me, upon me sowl,
> So liberal are we here,
> I'll let Sambo be murthered in place o' meself
> On every day in the year.
> On every day in the year, boys,
> An' every hour in the day,
> The right to be kil't I'll devide wid him,
> An' divil a word I'll say.

The Republican-controlled Congress was quick to respond to the growing clamor for Negro troops. On July 17, 1862, two pieces of legislation were passed that pried opened the door for black men to enter the Union army. The Confiscation Act gave the president unlimited power to employ as many black men as necessary to help suppress the rebellion, while the second statute repealed the 1792 law that barred Negroes from serving in state militias. Four weeks later, on August 25, the War Department authorized General Rufus B. Saxon, Hunter's successor as provisional military governor of South Carolina, Georgia, and Florida, to recruit and organize fifty thousand black men for service as laborers in the quartermaster's department. He was also given the authority to arm, uniform, equip, and muster into the United States Army five thousand men of African descent for the express purpose of protecting the women and children of black laborers. White officers would be detailed to train the black recruits in military drill, discipline, and duty. Although it was not a full-scale endorsement of Hunter's original enlistment plan, these orders were the first to officially authorize the utilization of black troops in the Civil War. These were the orders that Hunter had literally begged for, but never received.

Meanwhile Company E, the surviving unit of Hunter's Regiment, had continued to drill daily on St. Simons Island, along with 150 other black fugitives, under the unofficial command of C. T. Trowbridge, a white sergeant. The soldiers had received no pay, and poor rations, and they were clothed in ragged uniforms. Despite these trying conditions, morale among the black men remained high. After their arrival on the island, Company E discovered that 25 black fugitives had formed a militia unit to defend themselves against Confederate attacks and mainland slave hunters. The soldiers were quickly recruited to assist in the pursuit of a Confederate landing party that had recently come ashore. The rebels were chased into a nearby swamp, where a heated gunbattle resulted in several black casualties, including the death of John Brown, the leader of the island militia who shared the same name as the famed abolitionist. The Negroes continued to search for the rebels, but the Confederates managed to avoid capture and eventually escaped on a stolen boat. Hungry, tired, and dirty, they reached the mainland and later recounted the details of their harrowing ordeal. "If you wish to know hell before your time," wrote one of the rebels, "go to St. Simons and be hunted ten days by niggers." [23]

In October 1862, Sergeant Trowbridge was informed that the United States War Department had officially sanctioned the enlistment of black soldiers. He was ordered to report, along with the remnants of Hunter's Regiment, to Camp Saxton at Beaufort, South Carolina, on November 15, 1862. The 38 men in Company E and approximately 50 other former Georgia slaves were mustered into the U.S. Army as Company A of the First South Carolina Volunteers. The regiment was placed under the command of Colonel Thomas Wentworth Higginson, a devout abolitionist who had been serving in the Massachusetts Fifty-Seventh Volunteers, doing picket duty near Beaufort. Although Higginson recognized the difficulty associated with transforming former slaves into soldiers, he gladly accepted the assignment. He wrote: "I had been an abolitionist too long and had known and loved John Brown too well, not to feel a thrill of joy at last on finding myself in the position where he only wished to be." Included among Higginson's new recruits were scores of former Georgia slaves who originally served in Hunter's disbanded ranks. These black Georgians became members of America's first Negro military regiment.[24]

THE EMANCIPATION PROCLAMATION

While much of the country's attention had been focused on the recruitment and training of black troops at Beaufort, several hundred miles to the north in Washington, D.C., President Abraham

Lincoln was on the verge of making a decision that would dramatically alter the complexion of the Union army and navy. During the summer of 1862, he informed two trusted advisors that he had decided to take full advantage of the slave element by issuing a proclamation of emancipation. Although Lincoln later declared that the Emancipation Proclamation was the moral and spiritual rebirth of American democracy, his original decision to issue the historic edict was based solely on military necessity. Following months of indecision, the president concluded that the war could not be won unless freed Southern slaves were allowed to bear arms in the conflict.

Lincoln also understood that the wholesale enlistment of black men in his army and navy would necessitate a radical transformation of Union war aims. Frederick Douglass had predicted that if former slaves were allowed to fight to preserve the Union, then the federal government could no longer deny them the right to manhood and citizenship. Lincoln finally realized that the South's slave population was one of the Confederacy's greatest military assets. Although only a few blacks actually fought for the rebels, a vast army of black slaves supported the Confederate war effort by serving as orderlies, teamsters, and military laborers. On the home front, slaves also supplied the labor for plantations, factories, arsenals, and mines. Military necessity required that this important element of the Southern war machine be removed from Confederate control.

During a July 21, 1862, cabinet meeting, Lincoln announced that he was drafting a proclamation that would free all slaves living in states still in rebellion as of January 1, 1863. Although the early drafts of the document contained no specific reference regarding the arming of blacks, Secretary of State W. H. Seward was concerned that the proclamation might ignite a political backlash among white Northerners. He bluntly observed that, because of recent military setbacks, the public might view the freeing of slaves as an act of desperation, "the last measure of an exhausted Government, a cry for help; the Government stretching forth its hand to Ethiopia, instead of Ethiopia stretching forth her hands to the Government." Lincoln accepted his secretary's advice and decided to withhold the proclamation until a Union victory could be claimed on the battlefield.[25]

On September 2, 1862, the president told Secretary of the Treasury Samuel Chase that his decision to emancipate Southern slaves was based solely on "military necessity and not because it was politically expedient or morally right." Following the limited Union victory at the Battle of Antietam, Lincoln decided to issue a preliminary Emancipation Proclamation on September 22, 1862. The document stated that, as of January 1, 1863, all persons being held as slaves in states still in rebellion against the Union "shall be then, thencefoward, and forever free." In other words, if the rebels would simply lay down their arms and rejoin the United States, they would be able to keep their slaves. It was no surprise that this final plea for compromise was rejected outright by Confederate leaders.[26]

During the first week of November, Senator Charles Sumner presented Lincoln with a copy of George Livermore's book entitled *An Historical Research: Opinions of the Founders of the Republic on Negroes as Slaves, as Citizens, and as Soldiers*. Livermore's book detailed the military contributions of black men, slave and free, on behalf of American patriots during the Revolutionary War. The president became very interested in the book and, according to Sumner, used it as a reference during his drafting of the final Emancipation Proclamation. One indication of the book's significance in shaping Lincoln's decision is the fact that the president presented the pen used to sign the document to Livermore.

On January 1, 1863, twenty months after the war began, Lincoln issued the Emancipation Proclamation. It contained a clause not included in the preliminary proclamation that authorized the enlistment of black men "into the armed services of the United States to garrison forts, positions, stations, and other places and to man vessels of all sorts in said service." In the concluding paragraph, Lincoln wrote that he "sincerely" believed that the proclamation was "an act of justice, warranted by the Constitution upon military necessity." Although few, if any, slaves were actually freed by the issuance of the document, it did remove all legal obstacles to the large-scale enlistment of black men in the United States Army and Navy.[27]

Lincoln's decision would have far-reaching consequences. Prior to the issuance of his proclamation, only a few independent efforts to organize black regiments had been initiated, in South Carolina, Kansas, and Louisiana; this would be the first national effort. The eventual enlistment of two hundred thousand black men in the Union military was the primary catalyst for the transformation of the war over "states' rights" into a crusade to abolish American slavery. In an unprecedented step, black men—the majority of them former slaves—would now officially be engaged in the war against their former masters.

CHAPTER VII

—

BLACK SOLDIERS AND THE
DAWNING OF THE JUBILEE

W hile momentous events were unfolding up north in Washington, D.C., General Rufus Saxon down in Beaufort, South Carolina, watched anxiously as the sixty-two men in Company A of the First South Carolina Volunteers drilled and prepared for battle. Early in November 1862, the "First South" had been ordered to conduct an expedition up the Sapelo and Altamaha Rivers into the Georgia interior. According to Saxon, the primary objectives of the expedition were "to bring away the people [Negroes] from the mainland, destroy all rebel salt-works, and to break up the rebel picket stations along the line of the coast." [1]

Between November 3 and 10, 1862, the First South Carolina Volunteers and a regiment of white soldiers conducted successful raids up and down the coast. They killed nine enemy soldiers, captured three prisoners at Darien, and spread havoc along the Georgia-Florida seacoast. Large quantities of rice, lumber, and other commodities were confiscated and approximately twenty thousand dollars' worth of horses, wagons, and other Confederate property was destroyed. According to one of the regiment's white officers, Colonel Oliver T. Beard, there was also an added bounty: "I started from St. Simon's with sixty-two colored fighting men and I returned to Beaufort with 156 fighting men (all colored)." The gleeful colonel explained his "recruitment process" as they proceeded across the Georgia countryside: "As soon as we took a slave from his claimant, we placed a musket in his hand and he began to fight for the freedom of the others." [2]

One of the primary targets of the black soldiers was the plantation of William Brailsford, a Georgia slave trader who also served as the captain of the Savannah Mounted Rifles. Brailsford was despised because of a slave-hunting raid he led on St. Catherine's Island the month before in which two black refugees were killed and four others captured. Clarence Mohr observes that Brailsford would probably have been a marked man even without the St. Catherine's raid, for several of the black soldiers had been enslaved on his plantation, including one Sam Miller, who was severely beaten by the planter when he refused to reveal the whereabouts of a fugitive slave. After "full consultation," the Union commanders agreed to extract an extra measure of revenge during their retreat back up the river. The regiment landed neared the plantation after sunset, routed a small Confederate garrison, and eventually burned numerous Brailsford structures, including the primary residence. Following the attack the black soldiers were ecstatic; some claimed to have "grown three inches," and Sam Miller proudly exclaimed: "I feel a heap more of a man." [3]

Colonel Beard wrote in his official report: "The colored men fought with astonishing coolness and bravery. For alacrity in effecting landings, for determination, and for bush fighting, I found them all I could desire—more than I had hoped. They behaved bravely, gloriously, and deserve all praise." A jubilant General Saxon later reported to the secretary of war that the expedition had been a complete success. He wrote: "It is admitted upon all hands that the negroes fought with a coolness and bravery that would have done credit to veteran soldiers. . . . There was no excitement, no flinching, no attempt at cruelty when successful. They seemed like men who were fighting to vindicate their manhood and they did it well. Rarely in the progress of this war has so much mischief been done by so small a force in so short a space of time." The exploits of the "First South" were also hailed by the thousands of black refugees living on the Sea Islands off the South Carolina-Georgia coast. On St. Helen, old Aunt Phyllis joyously repeated a slightly exaggerated account of the expedition: "Dey fought and fought and shot down de 'Secesh,' and ne'er a white man among 'em but two captains." [4]

Two months later a familiar and controversial figure, General David Hunter, rejoined the military operations in and around Beaufort. His dream of enlisting former slaves to fight for their own freedom was now a budding reality. Hunter quickly directed his officers to take a larger force of black troops on another expedition up the St. Mary's River between the Georgia and Florida line. Colonel Beard understood that the stakes were high: "Our success or failure may make or mar the prospects of colored troops." Two days later a force of 460 troops steamed up the St. Mary's aboard three ships, one of which, the *Planter*, had been "liberated" from the rebels by Robert Small, a legendary black river pilot. [5]

The St. Mary's expedition was designed to secure much-needed lumber supplies for Union encampments, even though white troops had failed in earlier attempts to find the materials in the same area. Corporal Robert Sutton, a former slave on the Alberti plantation near Woodstock on the Georgia side of the river, informed senior officers of the whereabouts of vast quantities of rebel lumber. Described by Higginson as "the real conductor of the whole expedition," Sutton performed his duties with courage and valor, while suffering three bullet wounds. During the expedition the black soldiers fought off a harrowing night attack and were constantly raked by Confederate sharpshooters from the banks of the river. [6]

The most poignant moment of the mission, however, occurred when Corporal Sutton returned to the Alberti plantation to confront his former mistress. After confiscating several torture devices found in the plantation slave jail, Higginson reintroduced "Corporal Robert Sutton" to his former owner. With indignation dripping from her lips, the woman exclaimed to Higginson: "Ah, *we* called him Bob!" *A New York Times* reporter subsequently filed an exuberant report: "Our colored troops are more than a match for any equal number of white rebels which can be brought against them. With a few horse carts to transport ammunition—these free men are all-sufficient to snuff out the rebellion." [7]

While the Northern press celebrated the early success of the "First South," white Georgians vented their anger over what they described as "cowardly" attacks against undefended civilian targets. As the second year of the war came to a close, the destruction of the South's slave-based economy became a major priority of the Union war command. Northern officers operating along the south Atlantic coast steadily increased the frequency of their strikes against plantations and industrial sites from Charleston, South Carolina, southward to Jacksonville, Florida. The gentlemen's war over states' rights had degenerated into a brutal winner-take-all war of attrition. While most white Georgians living along the coast had hurriedly "refugeed" to more secure inland locations, those who remained behind were victimized by military tactics designed to deprive them of their slaves and material possessions.

The Civil War general most often associated with the philosophy of "total warfare" was William Tecumseh Sherman. He believed that all Southerners bore "a collective responsibility" for the conflict and he resolved to "make war so terrible" that they would never again take up arms against the United States. The burning of Atlanta by Sherman's army in November 1864 and the devastating nine-hundred-mile march through Georgia and the Carolinas that followed represented the complete implementation of his policy. However, some eighteen months before Sherman boasted that he would "make Georgia howl," black soldiers introduced the concept of "total warfare" to the state by sacking and burning the town of Darien.[8]

THE DESTRUCTION OF DARIEN

Darien was established in 1734 by Scottish settlers who had been recruited to guard Georgia's southern frontier by General James Oglethorpe, the colony's founder. During Georgia's early years, Oglethorpe fought to prohibit slavery in the colony and his most loyal supporters had been these same Scots. As discussed earlier, in 1739 they even wrote and published a controversial antislavery petition that warned their fellow colonists that God would someday seek retribution from Georgia slave owners for their transgressions against humanity.

Over time, Darien's vocal antislavery minority was overwhelmed by the growing clamor for slave labor in the colony. By 1860 the town's population consisted of five hundred white residents and more than fifteen hundred black slaves. As was true throughout much of the South, relatively cheap slave labor had become the cornerstone of Darien's bustling economy. The focal point of the region's economic activity was the Darien seaport, where as many as thirty ships a day arrived and cleared cargoes of lumber, rice, and cotton. Negro slaves provided much of the heavy labor on the local docks, while thousands of their fellow bondsmen toiled on coastal rice and cotton plantations.

There were few, if any, Darienites, who cared to remember the antislavery legacy forged by the town's original settlers, or the prophecy, spoken 120 years earlier, that foretold the looming inevitability of slave retribution. But on a hot summer day—June

11, 1863—the people of Darien would watch that forgotten prophecy come true.

THE FIFTY-FOURTH MASSACHUSETTS

During the spring of 1863, twenty-five-year-old Colonel Robert Gould Shaw accepted an invitation by Governor John Andrews of Massachusetts to organize the first regiment of Negro soldiers in the North. The son of outspoken abolitionists, Shaw leapt at the opportunity to lead black men into battle against Southern slave owners. Although the regiment was credited to the state of Massachusetts, recruiting was actually conducted throughout the North. The ranks filled quickly and the young colonel was soon preparing the Fifty-fourth Massachusetts to fight for the liberation of their enslaved brethren. Two of the young men who volunteered for service in the regiment were Lewis and Charles Douglass, sons of the famed Frederick Douglass.

Down in Beaufort, South Carolina, General Hunter heard about the organization of the Fifty-fourth and petitioned the War Department to place the regiment under his command. The War Department responded favorably to his request and Governor Andrews began preparations to send his black regiment south. Prior to their departure, the Massachusetts governor decided to honor his sable soldiers with a military parade. On May 28, 1863, more than twenty thousand people gathered in Boston to cheer the nine hundred men as they marched through the streets of the city. An eyewitness noted that a military band played the John Brown song as the soldiers marched "over ground moistened by the blood of Crispus Attucks," the black patriot who had been among the first to die in the Revolutionary War. A *Boston Evening Journal* reporter wrote: "No regiment on its departure, has collected so many thousands as the Fifty-fourth. The early morning trains from all directions were filled to overflowing, extra cars were run, vast crowds lined the streets where the regiment was to pass, and the common was crowded with an immense number of people, such as only the 4th of July or some rare event causes to assemble." Shortly after one o'clock, the regiment marched to Battery Wharf, where they boarded a military transport and sailed for St. Simons Island, Georgia.[9]

The Fifty-fourth arrived on the island on June 9, 1863, and Shaw was officially introduced to Colonel James Montgomery, the commander of the Second South Carolina Volunteers. While Shaw had been busy organizing the Fifty-fourth in Massachusetts, Montgomery received instructions from General Hunter to begin organizing a second regiment of freed slaves along the Georgia-South Carolina coast. Unlike Shaw's experience, his initial recruitment efforts had been met with suspicion and evasiveness by the fugitive slave population. However, his persistence and determination eventually paid off, and within weeks the Second South Carolina Volunteers were ready for battle. Montgomery was a deeply religious man who possessed an even deeper hatred for slave owners. In a letter to his wife, Shaw described his military counterpart: "Montgomery is a strange compound; he allows no swearing or drinking in his regiment, and is anti-tobacco; but he burns and destroys wherever he goes with great gusto and looks as if he would have quite a taste for hanging people, whenever a suitable subject should offer." [10]

Although Hunter issued orders prohibiting unprovoked attacks against civilians, he also suggested that harsher measures might be justified under certain circumstances. The general informed his officers that "the wickedness and folly of the enemy" might sometimes require "the stern necessity of retaliation." These orders were originally issued early in June, after Hunter was angered by the passage of a statute by the Confederate Congress that required the execution of any white officer captured while commanding black troops. Hunter wrote a letter to Governor Andrews explaining his reasons and objectives for ordering the expeditions of attrition against Confederate civilian targets. He stated that the coastal raids were "the initial step of a system of operations which will rapidly compel the rebels either to lay down their arms and sue for restoration to the Union or to withdraw their slaves into the interior, thus leaving desolate the most fertile and productive of their counties along the Atlantic sea-board." Two days before the Darien raid, however, Hunter softened his original stance regarding the making of war against civilians by reminding Montgomery that "the right of war . . . is not to be lightly used, and if wantonly used might fall under that part of the instructions which prohibits devastation. All household furniture, libraries, churches, and hospitals you will of course spare." [11]

Shaw and the Fifty-fourth were still pitching their tents when Montgomery shouted out to the younger colonel, "How soon can you start on an expedition?" Shaw understood the challenge implied by the question, and without a moment's hesitation, he shouted back, "In half an hour." Montgomery planned to "present his compliments to the rebels of Georgia" by proceeding to the town of Darien. [12]

"I SHALL BURN THIS TOWN"

The expedition consisted of about four hundred black soldiers drawn from five companies of Montgomery's Second South Carolina, eight companies of Shaw's Fifty-fourth Massachusetts, and the all-white Third Rhode Island Battery. On June 10, 1863, the men boarded the *John Adams*. The next day, two more gunboats joined the expedition and sailed down the coast and up the Darien River. As soon as the gunboats came within sight of the town, the soldiers began to shell Confederate pickets and civilian residences along the banks of the river. The town of Darien consisted of about eighty homes, five churches, twelve stores, a few mills, and several storehouses containing rice, resin, and turpentine. The majority of Darien's white residents had already fled to such inland locations as Milledgeville and Albany, and those who remained behind were living about three miles north of the town in a settlement called the Ridge. A lookout alerted the Darienites that a Yankee landing party was approaching, but since only a small company of twenty rebel soldiers was available to guard the town, they decided to fall back and establish a line of pickets along the approach to the Ridge.

The mayor of Darien, who was also residing at the Ridge, was greatly disturbed by the fact that the Confederate soldiers were making no attempt to defend the town. He told them that if he were in command, some effort would be made to repulse the invaders. While the "few 'crackers' and paupers remaining in Darien ran frightened in every direction," the Union soldiers landed and marched into the town without "a single armed inhabitant to dispute" the attack. A Union officer described the scene: "The men began to come in by twos, threes, and dozens, loaded with every species and all sort and quantities of furniture, stores, trinkets, and such, until one would be tired of enumerating. We had sofas, tables, pianos, chairs, mirrors, carpets, beds, carpenters tools, books, china sets, tinware, Confederate shinplasters, old letters, papers." Large amounts of turpentine and resin were confiscated, as well as enough cows, chickens, rice, and corn to feed the soldiers for "at least a month." All livestock not taken were shot on the spot. Eyewitnesses later reported that the stench from the decaying carcasses could be smelled for miles in any direction.[13]

After the town "was pretty thoroughly disemboweled" and had been emptied of all its valuables, Montgomery turned to Shaw and announced, "I shall burn this town." Shaw replied that he did not want to participate in the burning of a defenseless town, to which

Montgomery stated that he would accept full responsibility for the act. "Why should I not burn it?" he asked, and added, "I could tell you stories about the misdeeds of slaves owners that would make your hair stand on end. Southerners must be made to feel that this is real war and that they [are] to be swept away by the hand of God like the Jews of old." He declared that the destruction of the town was justified because of the Confederate statute requiring the execution of any captured white Union officer who commanded black soldiers in battle: "We are outlawed, and therefore not bound by the rules of regular warfare." [14]

"The town of Darien is now no more," a Corporal Gooding told the *New Bedford Mercury*. Another Union soldier described, with some regret, the conflagration that consumed Darien: "It was a beautiful town, and never did it look so both grand and beautiful as in its destruction. As soon as a house was ransacked, the match was applied, and by six o'clock the whole town was in one sheet of flame. It was a magnificent spectacle, but still very few were found to gloat over it. Had we had a hard fight to gain the place, or had we taken a thousand slaves by its destruction, we would have had no complaints." However, any misgivings were quickly dismissed. "And I suppose we should have none anyway. The South must be conquered inch by inch, and what we can't put a force in to hold ought to be destroyed. If we must burn the South out, so be it." [15]

After the flames had died away, the Darienites came out of their hiding places on the Ridge and returned to survey the damage. They discovered that their town had been reduced to "one plain of ashes and of blackened chimneys." The only surviving structures were the white and Negro Methodist churches, a free black man's cabin, and two other white-owned houses. A despairing resident wrote, "It is a sad sight to see smoking ruins now. . . . The wretches shot the milch cows and calves down in the streets, took some of them on board their vessels and left the rest lying in the streets, where they still lie. They carried off every Negro that was in the place except one old African woman, named Nancy, who told them she was from Africa, and that she would not go again on the big water. . . . For myself I feel this calamity severely. You know I have lost heavily since the war commenced, but I still had a home left. This is now also gone." [16]

The fact that black soldiers played a major role in the raid only increased the anger of the Darien citizenry. "And to think it was burned by the cowardly Yankee Negro thieves," wrote an unidentified woman. According to a local planter the "destruction of Darien was a cowardly, wanton outrage, for which the Yankee vandals have not even the excuse of the love of plunder. [It merely] afforded a safe opportunity to inflict injury upon unarmed and defenseless private citizens, and it is in such enterprises that Yankee negro valor displays itself." The editor of the *Southern Watchman* lashed out at the Yankee invaders: "The Abolitionists and negroes have sacked and destroyed Darien in this state—one of our oldest towns. Destruction of property is to them a favorite pastime. They cannot whip our armies, and like Vandals, vent their spleen by destroying the labor of generations." This particular editor failed to acknowledge or consider that much of the "labor" mentioned in his column had been provided by generations of enslaved Negroes. [17]

Although the Northern press hailed the destruction of Darien as a great victory, Shaw was greatly disturbed by what he considered to be the needless destruction of civilian property. He wrote a letter of protest detailing his concerns to Governor Andrews and Hunter's adjutant, a Colonel Halpine. Several Southern historians have likewise harshly criticized Hunter's tactics, arguing that the general's decision to destroy the property of innocent civilians was improper and exceeded the bounds of civilized warfare. [18]

Shaw, who was later killed and buried in a mass grave with scores of his black troops, had no way of knowing that the burning of Darien was simply a prelude of what was to come. At the federal encampments around Chattanooga, Tennessee, General William Tecumseh Sherman was finalizing his plans for the invasion of Georgia. During the spring of 1864, Sherman's army swooped down into north Georgia and engaged Confederate forces in a series of bloody battles. Constantly flanking and outmaneuvering the entrenched rebels, he relentlessly pushed the desperate defenders back to the outskirts of Atlanta. Following a five-week federal siege, Confederate General John Hood reluctantly accepted the hopelessness of the situation and evacuated Atlanta. On September 2, 1864, Sherman occupied the city and dispatched a brief telegram to President Lincoln: "Atlanta is ours and fairly won." [19]

THE MARCH TO THE SEA

The capture of Atlanta, one of the South's most industrialized cities, was a major Union victory, but Sherman had no intention of permanently occupying or garrisoning the conquered city. He informed General Ulysses S. Grant of his plan to forcibly evacuate all civilians and burn the city to the ground. Following the destruction of Atlanta, he planned to lead his army on a daring three-hundred-mile march through the heart of Georgia to the Atlantic Ocean. After several weeks of intense lobbying, Sherman received permission from Grant to implement his controversial plan, which would soon transform him into one of the most revered and reviled figures in American history. His decision to evacuate and destroy the city infuriated Confederate leaders, who accused him of barbarity and inhumanity. Atlanta's mayor and aldermen protested that the looming evacuation would force thousands of innocent civilians into homelessness in the midst of winter. Sherman responded that his decision was not intended to "meet the humanities" but to end the war. He boldly declared:

> You cannot qualify war in harsher terms than I will. War
> is cruelty and you cannot refine it. . . . You might as well
> appeal against the thunder-storm as against these terrible
> hardships of war. . . . We don't want your Negroes, or
> your horses, or your land, or anything you have, but we
> do want and will have first obedience to the laws of the
> United States.[20]

General Hood denounced the "studied and ingenious cruelty" of the evacuation and informed Sherman that he would never surrender. "You came into our country with your army, avowedly for the purpose of subjugating free white men, women, and children, and not intend to rule over them, but you make negroes your allies, and desire to place over us an inferior race, which we have raised from barbarism to its present position. . . . Better die a thousand deaths than submit to live under you or your Government and your negro allies!" [21]

Before Sherman's sixty-two thousand-man army began their march on the morning of November 15, 1864, Union soldiers methodically set fires throughout the city. Historians still debate the extensiveness of the damage that was inflicted upon Atlanta; however, there is little debate that Sherman was determined to fulfill his promise to "make Georgia howl." As the fires blazed out of control, a dark cloud of smoke engulfed Georgia's second-largest city. Sherman observed the raging conflagration from a hill overlooking Atlanta but, as he wrote in his *Memoirs,* he quickly turned his attention to the task that lay ahead: "Then we turned our horses heads to the east; Atlanta was soon lost behind the screen of the trees, and became a thing of the past." [22]

In order to camouflage his true intentions, Sherman marched his army eastward over several parallel roads across a sixty-mile

front. There were two principal wings; the right—or Southern—
wing was commanded by General Oliver O. Howard, the future
head of the Freedman's Bureau. The left—or Northern—wing was
led by General Henry W. Slocum, who had seen extensive action at
the Battles of Bull Run and Gettysburg. The Union columns
moved slowly through Decatur, "a dilapidated village," and on to
Conyers, where Sherman spent his first night of the march. From
there he could see the granite face of Stone Mountain clearly out-
lined by the flickering lights of hundreds of campfires that
stretched for miles in the distance.[23]

The following day the soldiers marched through the village of
Covington, where hundreds of jubilant blacks crowded the road-
sides and cheered their blue-coated liberators. According to
Sherman, the former slaves were "simply frantic with joy." It was
here that Union soldiers first witnessed the religious fervor that
would accompany the liberation of Georgia slaves throughout their
three-hundred-mile march to Savannah. The majority of the newly
freed slaves failed to comprehend the military and political significance of the arrival of Sherman's army. To them it was a religious
event ordained by God—the Day of Jubilee.[24]

Born in secret slave-quarter worship services, the concept of the
Jubilee was the transmutation of Old Testament scripture that proclaimed a year of emancipation and restoration every fifty years.
The Year of Jubilee required the emancipation of all Hebrew slaves,
the restoration of alienated lands to their former owners, and the
omission of all land from cultivation. The devoutly religious and
mostly illiterate former slaves liberally interposed belief in the
Jubilee with other religious scriptures and parables. They professed
that Sherman's army was the personification of the Army of the
Lord, sent to rescue his chosen people. As Moses had been commanded to deliver the Hebrews from Egyptian enslavement, God
had now ordained Sherman to rescue American slaves from generations of bondage.

Freed Georgia slaves worshiped Sherman as their savior. "Whenever they heard my name," he wrote, "they clustered about my horse, shouted and prayed in their peculiar style, which had a natural eloquence that would have moved a stone." In a letter to his wife, Sherman later observed: "They [Negroes] flock to me, old and young, they pray and shout and mix my name with that of Moses, Simon and other scriptural ones as well as 'Abram Linkom,' the Great Messiah of 'Dis Jubilee.'" The general encountered a young black girl who was seemingly transfixed "in the very ecstasy of the Methodist 'shout'"; she hugged the regimental banners and jumped to touch his feet, believing that they were the "feet of Jesus." An elderly gray-haired black man gazed reverently at Sherman and exclaimed, "I have seen the great Messiah and the army of the Lord!" [25]

About four miles east of Covington, Sherman questioned another older black man lurking around the headquarters tents regarding the meaning and purpose of the war. "Do you understand about the war? Do you know it's almost over?" he asked. The old man said "that he had been looking for the angel of the Lord" since he was knee-high. His religious faith was buttressed by a healthy dose of political pragmatism: "I know you say you's fightin' for the Union, but I 'spect it's all about slavery—and you're gonna set us free." "Do all slaves understand that?" the general continued. The old man answered quickly, "Sholy does." "You must stay where you are," advised Sherman, "and not load us up with useless mouths. You'd eat up all the soldiers' food. If we win the war, you're free. We can take along a few of the young, strong men—but if you swarm after us, old and young, feeble and helpless, you'll just cripple us." [26]

Despite Sherman's oft-repeated warnings, the presence of Union troops on Confederate soil unleashed long-pent-up desires for freedom among the thousands of slaves who lived in the path of the conquering army. An exodus of unprecedented proportions unfolded across the heart of Georgia as more than nineteen thousand Negroes eventually followed in the wake of Sherman's army. Former slaves of all ages and conditions joined the march along the way to Savannah. According to General Slocum's official report, "Negro men, women, and children joined the column at every mile of our march; many of them bringing horses and mules, which they cheerfully turned over to the officers of the quartermaster's department." Hundreds of blacks came "on foot, on horseback, and in every description of vehicle . . . ox-carts, pack mules . . . [with] little nigs sprawling on top." They did not know where they were going or how long it would take them to get there, but the liberated slaves were willing to risk everything to find freedom. A Union officer asked one former slave who was struggling to keep up with the soldiers where he was going. The black man replied, "Don't know Massa; gwine along wid you all." [27]

According to reports, "vast numbers" of black women with small children also fell in behind the Union columns. This angered and distressed Sherman and his commanders. "Our wagons are too much over laden to allow for their being filled with Negro women and children or their baggage, and every additional mouth consumes food which required risk to obtain," one unidentified officer complained. Another officer discovered two four- or five-year-old boys hidden in a wagon, apparently abandoned by their mother. Scores of babies died from exposure and other diseases during the march and their bodies were simply left by the roadside. Others fell from perches on pack mules and drowned in swamps and streams. A mother of twelve ensured the safety of her children by tying their hands together so they would not become lost during the arduous march to Savannah. [28]

An Illinois soldier watched in amazement as the ever-growing throng of ragged and impoverished blacks swarmed in, around, and behind the Union columns. They appeared, he wrote, "like a sable cloud in the sky before a thunder storm. They thought it was freedom now or never, and would follow whether or no. . . . Some in buggies, costly and glittering; some on horseback, the horses old and blind, and others on foot; all following up in right jolly mood, bound for ease and freedom." [29]

Although some slave owners stubbornly continued to cling to the idealized notion of the loyal and devoted slave, they could not ignore the wholesale exodus of all but a few of their former bondsmen. Myrta Avary, wife of a Georgia slave owner, wrote: "We went to sleep one night with a plantation full of negroes, and woke to find not one on the place—every servant gone to Sherman in Atlanta. . . . We had thought there was a strong bond of affection on their side as well as ours!" A slave owner living near Macon complained, "They didn't even come to ask for advice. . . . When Sherman came along . . . every last skunk of 'em run away." [30]

Not only were former slaves anxious to join their liberators, they also provided them with important information regarding the local terrain, Confederate troop movements, and the locations of hidden food, jewelry, and other valuables. A Union soldier observed: "Let those who choose to curse the negro curse him; but one thing is true . . . they were the only friends on whom we could rely for the sacred truth in Dixie. What they said might be relied on, so far as they knew; and they knew more and could tell more than most of the poor white population." As foragers, no Union soldier could match their knowledge and skill in locating mules, horses, cattle, hams, bacon, silver, and the like. General Sherman took full advantage of this fact. One evening he sent several officers in search of a knowledgeable Negro. "I don't want a white man—I need some reliable information about roads and bridges." They returned with a black man who took pleasure in supplying information and poking fun at his former masters. "When the Yanks are far off, our people are very brave. They say the women and children could whip 'em—but when you come close, then how they git up and dust." [31]

However, not every Georgia slave welcomed the arrival of

Union soldiers. A minority chose to remain with their masters on the plantations. An Eatonton farmer proudly recalled, "Two of pa's Negroes went off.... Our other Negroes behaved splendidly. They were offered every inducement." Mary Ann Cobb wrote that the blacks on her Baldwin County plantation refused to follow the Yankees, except one twelve-year-old boy who she claimed was actually "stolen." Although feelings of loyalty to former white masters played an important role in their decisions, more pragmatic reasons also existed. Sherman openly discouraged all freed slaves, except the able-bodied, from joining his march to the sea. On several occasions he counseled black freedmen: "You're free . . . you can go when you like. We want men to come with the army if they choose to come, but we don't force any to be soldiers. We pay wages. But since you have family you should stay here and all go together later." Sometimes differences of opinion concerning whether to leave or stay strained the bond between husbands and wives. After a Union officer explained to an elderly couple that they were free, the woman pointed her finger and shouted at her husband, "How come you sittin' there? You s'pose I been waitin' sixty years for nothin'? Don't you see the door's open now? I'm goin', you hear? I'm gonna follow my child and go 'long with these people till I drop in my tracks." [32]

With little or no Confederate opposition to impede their progress, the black march to freedom was soon transformed into a traveling Negro religious revival. "To them," a Wisconsin soldier wrote, "it was like the bondsmen going out of Egypt." Major George Nichols, a Union staff officer, concluded that the majority of the freed slaves accepted "the advent of the Yankees as the fulfillment of the millennial prophecies." Although the great majority of the federal soldiers possessed a strong anti-Negro bias, some found it difficult not to be affected by the outpouring of religious fervor. "The whole land seemed to be inhabited by negroes," recalled an unidentified soldier, "and the appearance of the army inspired them with a profound religious sentiment and awakened in them the most extraordinary religious emotion." [33]

Another soldier at a campsite near Milledgeville observed: "The colored people hailed with demonstrative delight the advent of the union army. 'Bress de Lawd! Tanks to Almighty God, de Yanks is come,' they cried, and [they] wanted to hug the soldiers, often touching the dress of some of the officers, who marched nearest the sidewalks, as the afflicted of old touched the garments of the Great Master." Wherever "Massa Sherman" went, he became the singular object of praise, jubilation, and worship. As he rode through a crowd of cheering middle Georgia blacks, they pressed their heads against his horse and held onto his stirrups. Jubilant former slaves proclaimed that Sherman was "the Angel of the Lord!" [34]

Although he was revered by the freed blacks, Sherman was, at best, a reluctant liberator of Southern slaves. He disliked the institution of slavery, but the enigmatic general also stated that, if given a choice, he would not abolish or modify it. He opposed extending full citizenship rights to blacks or allowing them to join the Union army. Sherman argued that, congressional enactments notwithstanding, the Negro could not be raised to the intellectual level of the white man. Critics in the North complained that he often demonstrated a complete disregard for the well-being of black refugees during his march through Georgia. He answered his detractors by asserting that his decisions were based solely on military necessity and that his only objective was to defeat the rebels.

Sherman's reputation of being unsympathetic or even hostile to the Negro race was primarily shaped by three events: (1) His orders issued in Atlanta that allowed the prohibition of all blacks, except those who could be of service to the army, from joining the march. (although these orders were ignored by thousands of black followers, his critics argued that others were unnecessarily left behind); (2) The general's refusal to enlist black men in his army; and (3)

The deaths of black refugees at Ebenezer Creek following their abandonment by one of his generals. Controversy and criticism surrounding these issues dogged Sherman from Atlanta to Savannah and throughout the remainder of his life. Even though he constantly sought to define himself strictly as a military man, he was not totally oblivious to his political environment. Following his triumphant arrival in Savannah, he confided in a friend that mistakes or missteps on the "Negro Question" could "tumble my fame into infamy." [35]

Inevitably the presence of thousands of grateful black women in and around Union camps led to interracial sexual liaisons and all-night celebrations that reverberated with the sounds of laughter, songs, and fiddles. According to Private David Cunningham, who also served as a correspondent to the *New York Herald* newspaper, at night black and white couples made love all about the camps. The most favored women rode by day in Union supply wagons and lived "luxurious lives" dressed in fine clothing and jewelry confiscated from Confederate homes. Cunningham claimed that Sherman's orders directing his army to "forage liberally" on the countryside were soon converted into unlimited licenses to secure items that were used to entice black women. Boxes were ripped apart, closets ransacked, and "the finest silks, belonging to the planters' ladies, carried off to adorn negro wenches around camp." He added: "It would be vexatious to the Grand Turk or Brigham Young if they could only see how many of the dark houris were in the employment of officers as servants and teamsters. I have seen officers themselves very attentive to the wants of pretty octoroon girls, and provide them with horses to ride." [36]

Sherman and his commanders were almost certainly aware of these illicit activities, but they apparently did nothing to discourage the behavior. In fact, Sherman became the subject of a widespread Confederate rumor accusing him of also maintaining a black mistress. Gertrude Clanton Thomas of Burke County wrote an angry letter to his wife informing her of the alleged affair after the Thomas plantation was ransacked by Union troops:

Mrs. Gen. Sherman:

Last week your husband's army found me in possession of wealth, tonight our plantations are the scene of ruin and desolation. You bade him Godspeed on his fiendish errand, did you not?—Desolate homes, violate the sanctity of firesides and cause the "widow and orphan to curse the name of Sherman for the cause" and this you did for what? To elevate the Negro race. Be satisfied Madame your wish had been accomplished. Inquire of Gen. Sherman when next you see him Who had been elevated to fill your place? . . . Did he tell you of the mulatto girl for whose safety he was so much concerned that she was returned to Nashville when he commenced his vandal march? This girl was spoken of by the Negroes whom you are willing to trust so implicitly as "Sherman's wife." Rest satisfied Mrs. Sherman and the apprehension of your Northern sisters with regard to the elevation of the Negroes. Your husbands . . . are most of them provided with "a companion du voyage—" [37]

For many young black men, Sherman's army provided the opportunity to find employment and, for the first time, to earn compensation for their labor. Although Sherman prohibited black men from enlisting, he understood the importance of securing their muscle and brawn for the difficult march. The former slaves became servants, teamsters, scouts, foragers, cooks, and pioneers. Hundreds helped to build bridges, repair roads, gather food, wreck Confederate railroads, and destroy telegraph lines. From Atlanta to Savannah, they marched along with the soldiers, "earning their way as part of the army." A disgruntled white Georgian complained, "They [the army] offer $12 pr month. . . . Many are going off with them." Lucy McCullough, a former slave, recalled that the Yankees "pick[ed] out de stronges' er Marse Ned's slave mens en take 'em 'way wid 'em." Despite Sherman's prohibition, many of the young men still longed to join the Union army. "An immense number of 'contrabands' now follow us . . . who intend going into the Army," wrote one soldier.[38]

Although thousands of black men were already serving in the Union army by the fall of 1864, Sherman ignored General Ulysses S. Grant's advice to "clean the country of Negroes and arm them." His refusal ignited a firestorm of criticism among Northern abolitionists and state recruiting agents. Although he never changed his stance on the matter, he would eventually be forced to officially renounce his opposition to black enlistment. Following a meeting with Secretary of War William Stanton and twenty black Savannah ministers during the second week of January 1865, Sherman would issue Field Order Number 15, which stated in part that "young and able-bodied negroes must be encouraged to enlist as soldiers in the service of the United States, to contribute their share toward maintaining their own freedom, and securing their rights as citizens of the United States." Scores of young black men who had joined the march through Georgia subsequently enlisted in the Twenty-first United States Colored Troops. They were originally known as the Third, Fourth, and Fifth regiments of the famed South Carolina Volunteers.[39]

But before Sherman would offer this historic proclamation, he faced the daunting prospect of completing his daring march. On November 20, 1864, he stopped at the Henry Farrar farm located a few miles east of the city of Madison. Following his stern lecture to Farrar's wife regarding Southern war guilt, several of the Negroes living on the farm stepped forward to complain of cruel treatment by their former master. "He whups us with strops, hand saws and paddles with holes cut in 'em—and then rubs salt in the wounds."

They also informed the soldiers of the existence of a large red blood-hound on a neighboring farm that had been used on numerous occasions to track down fugitive slaves. A Union officer ordered his soldiers to kill the dog, and when the blacks heard the echo of a shot and the dying howl of the animal, they shouted with joy.[40]

Throughout the remainder of the march, Sherman's troops methodically killed nearly every dog in their path. Carrying out the order to the extreme, one soldier snatched a small poodle from the arms of his distraught slave mistress. The woman pleaded, "Leave my baby alone—she's all I've got! She's no bloodhound—she's a house pet." Well, Madam," the soldier replied, "we can't tell what it'll grow into if we leave it behind." The animal was taken away and presumably killed.[41]

One evening Sherman stopped to take supper at an abandoned plantation. After he finished his meal, he sat astride a chair, immersed in thought, with his back to a glowing fire. After a while an old black man emerged from the shadows, holding a flickering candle in his hand. He used the light to study the features of Sherman's face. Sherman asked, "What do you want, old man?" The man answered, "Dey say you is Massa Sherman." He acknowledged that he was General William Tecumseh Sherman and asked why the man wanted to know. Trembling uncontrollably, the old man stated, "Jest to know if it's so!" He then began to mutter, "Dis nigger can't sleep dis night." Sherman then inquired as to why he was so frightened. The old man explained that he wanted to make sure that the soldiers were really "Yankees." On a previous occasion Confederate soldiers had disguised themselves in blue coats and the unsuspecting blacks who welcomed them as liberators had been beaten unmercifully by the rebels. The officers reassured him that they were his friends and offered him a drink of liquor, which was readily accepted. Soon the old man was talking freely, comfortable in the knowledge that his life-long dream of emancipation had been realized.[42]

Sherman and his army were now only twenty-five miles from the city of Milledgeville, capital of the state of Georgia at the time. Panic gripped the city as most of the residents rushed to escape the approaching Yankees. According to Anna Marie Green, the daughter of the superintendent of the state insane asylum, the Georgia legislature conducted a chaotic, emergency session on November 19, 1864. "The scene at the State House was truly ridiculous, the members were badly scared, such a body of representatives made my cheeks glow with shame." The legislators passed a statute that immediately drafted all white men in Georgia—except legislators and judges—into the army. They also appropriated three thousand dollars to secure a train to transport the lawmakers out of Milledgeville and adjourned "to the front . . . to meet again if we should live at a place as the Governor may designate." As hundreds of white and black war refugees streamed from the city, Governor Joseph Brown went to the state prison and offered 126 convicts full pardons if they would agree to join the Confederate army. All but a few accepted his offer. But it was too little, too late. On November 22, 1864, federal troops, without opposition, occupied Georgia's capital.[43]

Sherman was still a few miles outside the city when the first advance regiments of cavalry rode into Milledgeville. In order to escape the late November chill, he stopped to warm himself in a Negro cabin. To his great surprise, the general discovered that he was on one of several plantations owned by General Howell Cobb, one of the "head devils" of the Confederacy. Observing that the blacks were ragged and near starvation, Sherman ordered that all the food on the plantation be distributed to them. "Come on!" he shouted. "We're your friends. You needn't be afraid of us. All this is for you—corn, wheat, molasses." Sherman then instructed his officers to "spare nothing" and burn all the plantation buildings.[44]

Some twenty miles ahead, the regimental bands played "Yankee Doodle," as the columns of Union soldiers marched triumphantly into Milledgeville. They sang the national anthem as the Stars and Stripes replaced the Confederate flag above the capitol dome. Throngs of jubilant Negroes rushed into the streets and gathered along the sidewalks to cheer their Northern liberators. The soldiers playfully called out to the joyful blacks, "Come on! Come on, Sambo! Come on, Dinah!" A young black woman rushed out and hugged two soldiers. "Yes, I'm gwine!" she exclaimed. "But some of you's gotta marry me." The white residents who chose to remain behind stayed in their homes, although Sherman sarcastically noted that Governor Brown, Georgia's constitutional officers, and members of the legislature had "ignominiously fled, in the utmost disorder and confusion . . . some by rail, some by carriages, and many on foot." [45]

The general established his headquarters in the governor's mansion, where scores of frightened residents sought an audience with him to request protection for their homes and businesses. Despair and desperation consumed Georgia's fallen capital: "We were despondent" wrote Anna Marie Green, "our heads bowed and our hearts crushed—the Yankees in possession of Milledgeville. The Yankee flag waved from the Capitol—Our degradation was bitter." [46]

With hundreds of drunk and rowdy soldiers cheering them on, some of the men conducted a mock session of the legislature in the statehouse. A Speaker and other officers were elected and the soldiers roared with laughter as the "legislators," many of whom were suffering from "bourbon fits," were laid out unconscious on the floor. "Mr. Speaker, a point of order!" shouted one of the representatives. "I believe it is the custom to treat the speaker." "Yes," the Speaker responded, "I believe it is the custom." To a deafening chorus of cheers, the Speaker pulled out a bottle of brandy and swallowed its contents. Then a special committee marched back into the chamber singing "We Won't Go Home Until Morning" and they began a spirited debate over the propriety of Georgia's decision to secede from the Union. Resolutions were quickly passed repealing the Ordinance of Secession, with admissions that the decision was "highly indiscreet" and "a damned farce." Another committee—Sherman's army—was appointed and directed to whip Georgia and the other Confederate states back into the Union. The session was finally adjourned when frantic soldiers rushed into the chambers and shouted, "The Yankees are coming! The Yankees are coming!" The drunken, boisterous soldiers— mocking the departed members of the Georgia legislature— cringed in terror and fled the building.[47]

The soldiers then proceeded to ransack and loot the statehouse. Books, legislative documents, and furniture were thrown out of windows and trampled under foot by men on horseback. Soldiers rummaged through the books and carried away those that interested them. A Union sergeant described the situation as "a very bad exhibition of a very lawless nature." Major James Connolly witnessed the confiscation of hundreds of books: "It is a downright shame. . . . I am sure General Sherman will, some day, regret that he permitted this." If Sherman opposed the actions of his men, he did nothing to stop them. Connolly refused to engage in the plunder: "I don't object to stealing horses, mules, niggers and all such *little things*, but I will not engage in plundering and destroying public libraries." [48]

Bedlam reigned as the soldiers looted the deserted government office buildings. Millions of dollars' worth of unsigned (and worthless) Confederate currency was burned by the bundle or used to light pipes and cigars. What was left of the state arsenal—muskets, spears, bowie knives, and swords—was distributed to the marauding soldiers. The state penitentiary was emptied of its remaining inmates and set afire. Private homes were looted and gardens stripped clean. But, to the surprise of the majority of Milledgeville's residents, only the penitentiary, arsenal, and magazine were burned.

On November 24, 1864, Sherman's army began to vacate Georgia's capital. By nine o'clock the next morning the last Union brigades crossed over to the east bank of the Oconee River, leaving in their wake a totally ransacked and dispirited city. The editor of the local paper wrote: "A full detail of all the enormities . . . would fill a volume, and some of them too bad to publish. In short, if an army of Devils just let loose from the bottomless pit were to invade the country, they could not be much worse than Sherman's army." [49]

DEATH AT EBENEZER CREEK

Brigadier General Jefferson Davis (no relation to the Confederate president) commanded the fourteen thousand men of the Fourteenth Corp who formed a part of the left wing of Sherman's army. They had cut a northerly path from Atlanta through the heart of Georgia, hoping to mislead rebel commanders into believing that their primary destination was Augusta, instead of Savannah. The freed slaves who fell in behind Davis's columns had no way of knowing that the general was a proslavery Unionist who possessed little sympathy for the plight of black refugees. Although his men had marched, almost unimpeded, across more than two hundred miles of enemy territory, they were finally halted by the rain-swollen waters of Ebenezer Creek on December 3, 1864. The creek rose near the village of Springfield in Effingham County, some thirty-five miles west of Savannah, and flowed north into the Savannah River. Following several days of heavy rain, Ebenezer Creek had been transformed into a one-hundred-foot-wide and eight-foot-deep river—virtually impassable without a bridge.

To make matters worse, Confederate cavalry commanded by Major General Joseph Wheeler were aware of the situation and had initiated sporadic attacks against Davis's rear pickets. Davis ordered his engineers to construct a pontoon bridge across the creek and, two days later, the entire Fourteenth Corps crossed safely over the hastily built structure. According to Colonel Charles Kerr of the Sixteenth Illinois Cavalry, an official messenger was told to mislead the black refugees into believing that fighting was occurring on the other side of the creek and that they should not cross the bridge until all the soldiers and wagons had done so. Immediately after the soldiers reached the opposite bank, the pontoon bridge was taken up, without a single black being allowed to cross. Kerr recalled the chaos that ensued: "I . . . witnessed a scene the like of which I pray my eyes may never see again." The Negroes rushed to the water's edge, raising their hands and begging the Union commanders for protection. Their prayers and pleas fell on deaf ears. Crying out in anguish, hundreds of black men, women, and children rushed into the stream, where many were swept away by the swift currents. Kerr wrote: "I speak of what I saw, and no writer who was not on the ground can gloss the matter over for me. It was claimed this was done because rations were becoming scarce; in short, that it was a military necessity. There was no necessity about it. It was unjustifiable and perfidious and my soul burns with indignation as I recall it." [50]

Another eyewitness, John Hight, a chaplain from Indiana, noted that as soon as the black refugees understood their dire predicament, "there went up from that multitude a cry of agony." Someone shouted "Rebels!" and the panic-stricken Negroes "made a wild rush. . . . Some of them at once plunged into the water and swam across. Others ran wildly up and down the bank, shaking with terror. . . . Some were drowned—how many is not known." A muscular black man was among the first to dive into the rushing waters; with "head high and eyes rolling in terror," he swam until he reached the far bank. Scores of the women carrying small children in their arms rushed in behind him and were quickly swept downstream and drowned. Union soldiers standing on the opposite bank tossed logs and pieces of wood in the stream in a desperate attempt to save those who were fighting against the deadly currents.[51]

Several black men fashioned a makeshift raft out of wood and blankets and, although it sank several times, managed to ferry a large number of women and children to safety. At one point a black woman riding on the raft lost her balance and tumbled into the water. Her husband managed to drag her back on board, and they reached the shore soaked but thankful. "I'd rather drown myself than lose her," the man exclaimed. An elderly couple made it across and the old man cried out: "Praise the Lord, we got away from the Rebels . . . . We got troubles on our road but bless the Lord, it will be all right in the end." Private Harrison Pendergast of the Second Minnesota stated that he saw at least one hundred blacks "huddled as close to the edge of the water as they could get, some crying, some praying, and all fearful that the rebels would come before they could get over." A lone black man continued to steer the makeshift raft back and forth across the creek until the last column of Union soldiers disappeared from sight.[52]

Shortly thereafter, a detachment of rebel cavalrymen rode up and recaptured scores of terrified Negroes who had been abandoned by their Yankee liberators. Although his statements were contradicted by Northern eyewitnesses, Confederate General Wheeler later claimed that the black refugees were unharmed and eventually returned to their former masters. A Northern journalist provided a different account: "The waters of the Ogechee and Ebenezer Creek can account for hundreds who were blocking up . . . [the Union] columns, and then abandoned. Wheeler's cavalry charged on them, driving them, pell-mell, into the waters, and mothers and children, old and young, perished alike!" [53]

Although most Union soldiers possessed little sympathy for the black refugees, the events at Ebenezer Creek infuriated many of the battle-hardened troops. Major James A. Connolly of the 123rd Illinois infantry found it difficult to contain his emotions: "The idea of five or six hundred black women, children and old men being returned to slavery by such an infernal Copperhead as Jeff C.

Davis was entirely too much." He did not mince words when he told fellow staff officers that he considered Davis's abandonment of the blacks to be "inhumane" and "barbarous." Although he was certain that his statements would be relayed to Davis, and that a reprimand from his "serene Highness" was forthcoming, Connolly declared, "I don't care a fig." Fully aware that his vocal criticism could also cost him a promotion, he added, "I am determined to expose this act of his publicly." Connolly made good on this threat by writing a letter of protest to the Military Committee of the United States Senate; he also showed the letter to General Absalom Baird, who promised to encourage newspaper editors in the North to print stories relating to the incident.[54]

Private Pendergast also lambasted Davis—whom he presumed to be a Christian—for the cruel treatment of the former slaves. "Where can you find in all the annals of plantation cruelty anything more completely inhuman and fiendish than this? Legree was an angel of mercy in comparison . . . this barbarous act has created a deep feeling against Davis in this Division." Pendergast hoped the matter would be reported to President Lincoln and that Davis would be court-martialed for his actions. A doctor in another unit declared that Davis was undeserving of a court martial and suggested instead that he should be hanged as "high as Haman." Chaplain Hight was livid: "Davis is a military tyrant, without one spark of humanity in his makeup. He was an ardent pro-slavery man before he entered the army, and has not changed his views since." [55]

General Sherman was not present at the crossing and apparently took no official action against Davis or his junior officers. He probably believed, or hoped, that any criticism concerning the incident at the creek would be lost in the celebration of his triumphant arrival in Savannah. He was wrong. The ghosts of the unnumbered dead who drowned at Ebenezer Creek would haunt the general as he basked in the glory of military conquest.

"GLORY BE TO GOD, WE ARE FREE!"

Savannah was taken without a major battle in December 1864. The city's nine thousand Confederate defenders escaped across the Savannah River to Hutchinson Island under the cover of night, over a pontoon bridge constructed with the assistance of slave laborers. Sherman's march to the sea was hailed around the world as one of the great military victories of the nineteenth century. Predictably, black Savannahians viewed the arrival of their liberators from a more religious perspective. As he rode through the streets of the city, Sherman observed, "the negroes are having their 'jubilee.'" Reverend James Simms, a minister who would become one of the first blacks to serve in the Georgia legislature, recalled, "When the morning light of the 22nd of December, 1864, broke in upon us, the streets of our city were thronged in every part with the victorious army of liberty; every tramp, look, command, and military movement told us that they had come for our deliverance . . . and the cry went around the city from house to house among our race of people, 'Glory be to God, we are free!'" [56]

General Oliver O. Howard, a Sherman commander, noted that December 21, 1864—the day federal soldiers first appeared in Savannah—was "a day of manifest joy" for local blacks. Howard posed a rhetorical question: "Wasn't it a visible answer to their long-continued and importunate prayers? Certainly so it all appeared to these simple souls who met our columns of troops at every point in crowds, and with arms akimbo danced and sang their noisy welcome." A black woman exclaimed to a Union soldier, "I'd always thought about this, and wanted this day to come, and prayed for it and knew God meant it should be here sometime, but I didn't believe I should ever see it. I bless the Lord for it." Another black woman joyously proclaimed, "It's a dream, sir—a dream!" [57]

The realization of black Savannah's dream of freedom also signaled the arrival of a terrible nightmare for the city's white residents. Although the surrender and occupation of Savannah was a devastating blow, local whites were especially disturbed by the hero's welcome extended to Yankee soldiers by freed slaves. Georgia slave owners were once again angered by the willingness of former slaves to desert. In March 1865, Savannahian Richard Arnold informed a friend in the North: "Almost every house servant in the city has left his or her place." Elizabeth Mackay Stiles wrote to her son: "Old Andrew stays with the Mackays & helps them nicely—so does Lizzy Rose & Peggy—all the rest took french leave." One female member of Savannah's aristocracy told a Union officer: "It is terrible, sir! All my slaves have left me." She was mortified by the possibility that she would have to try to earn a living by submitting "to the disgrace of giving lessons in music." Even Charles Hardee's faithful old cook and nursemaid, Mom Jinny, could not resist the intoxicating lure of freedom. As 1864 drew to a close, white Georgians began to fully accept the meaning of Sherman's successful campaign through their state: Southern defeat and humiliation were almost inevitable. Savannahian Fanny Cohen summed up the feelings of all but a few whites when she wrote in her diary that December 1864 was "the saddest Christmas that I have ever spent." [58]

"THE FRUIT OF OUR OWN LABOR"

Sherman's daring march through the South earned the general national and international acclaim. However, this admiration was not universal. Detractors in the North argued that the general's triumph was illusory because he had prolonged the war by allowing two rebel armies to escape prior to capturing Atlanta and Savannah. Angry abolitionists and radical Republicans in Congress charged that he had betrayed the true cause of the war by discouraging liberated slaves from following and joining his army. The stinging criticism was, in large part, due to the fact that several of his officers followed through on earlier threats to expose the tragic incident at Ebenezer Creek.

As the chorus of criticism grew louder in the North, a letter arrived from his friend Henry Halleck, who was President Lincoln's chief of staff. Halleck informed Sherman that almost everyone had praised his military triumph, but there were some who were raising serious questions regarding his character and reputation. "There is a certain class having now great influence with the President . . . who say that you have manifested an almost *criminal* dislike of the negro and that you . . . repulsed him with contempt! They say you might have brought with you to Savannah more than fifty-thousand, thus stripping Georgia of that number of laborers . . . but that, instead . . . you drove them from your ranks." [59]

Sherman sent a quick reply to Halleck categorically denying the "cock and bull story." He claimed that not a single Negro had been turned away from his ranks and the general offered a half-hearted explanation regarding the actions of his commanders at Ebenezer Creek: "Jeff Davis took up his pontoon bridge, not because he wanted to leave them [Negroes], but because he wanted his bridge. He and Slocum tell me they didn't believe Wheeler killed one of them." Years later Sherman was still chafed by the criticism: "Because I had not loaded down my army by the hundreds of thousands of poor Negroes, I was construed by others to be hostile to the black race." [60]

On January 11, 1865, Lincoln's Secretary of War Edward Stanton arrived unexpectedly in Savannah. The outcry in the North had prompted administration officials to dispatch Stanton to gather facts surrounding Sherman's treatment of black refugees and to once again urge the general to enlist black men in his army.

Sherman was dismayed that his military success could not shield him from criticism regarding his policies toward Southern blacks. Stanton questioned him about the conduct of his commanders during the crossing at Ebenezer Creek. The general defended Davis: "I assured him that General Davis was an excellent soldier, and I did not believe he had any hostility to the blacks." Stanton produced a newspaper clipping detailing the events of the crossing at Ebernezer Creek, prompting Sherman to summon Davis into the room. Davis proclaimed his innocence and explained that his men had acted solely out of military necessity. Although he admitted that some Negroes had drowned trying to cross the rain-swollen creek, he stated that Confederate soldiers did not kill any of those trapped on the opposite bank of the river.[61]

Davis was excused and Stanton then asked Sherman to assemble a group of local black leaders so that he could engage them in a face-to-face discussion regarding the future of their emancipated race. The general invited twenty ministers and lay leaders from Savannah's black community to meet with the secretary on Thursday, January 12, 1865, at 8:00 P.M. in Sherman's headquarters, located in the home of Charles Green, a wealthy Savannah cotton broker. The purpose of the meeting was to ascertain from black leaders what they wanted for their people. Stanton later intimated to a friend that the meeting marked the first time that a representative of the United States government had ever gone to the "poor debased people to ask them what they wanted for themselves." Exactly one month later, a verbatim report of the meeting was placed in the hands of abolitionist Reverend Henry Ward Beecher, who distributed copies to his congregation. On February 13, 1865, the *New York Daily Tribune* printed the text of the discussion in its entirety.[62]

The designated spokesman for the delegation was sixty-seven-year-old Garrison Frazier, who formerly served as pastor of the Third African Baptist Church. Frazier had been a slave until shortly before the Civil War, when he purchased freedom for himself and his wife for one thousand dollars in gold and silver. During the meeting he demonstrated astute political insight and diplomacy in his carefully spoken responses to Stanton's probing questions.

Other key members of the twenty-man delegation were William J. Campbell, age fifty-one, the pastor of the First African Baptist Church, who had been manumitted by his mistress's will in 1849; John Cox, age fifty-eight, the pastor of the Second African Baptist Church, who had purchased his freedom for eleven hundred dollars in 1849; and Ulysses L. Houston, age forty-one, the pastor of the Third African Baptist Church, who was freed by Union soldiers. Houston would be among the first of his race to serve as a state senator in the Georgia General Assembly. Also present were William Bentley, age seventy-two, the pastor of Andrews Chapel Methodist Church, who was emancipated by the will of his master at the age of twenty-five; William Gaines, age forty-one, who had served as a Methodist pastor for the last sixteen years and was owned by Confederate Senator Robert Toombs and his brother Gabriel until freed by Union soldiers; and James Porter, thirty-nine, who was born free in Charleston, South Carolina. Porter became a lay preacher and served as president of the board of wardens and vestry at St. Stephen's Protestant Episcopal Colored Church of Savannah. During the Reconstruction period he represented Chatham County in the Georgia House of Representatives. The youngest member was James Lynch, age 26, who was born free in Baltimore, Maryland, and served as the presiding elder of the Methodist Episcopal Church and a missionary to the Department of the South.

Stanton began what amounted to an interrogation by asking Frazier to elaborate on his understanding of the meaning of the Emancipation Proclamation. Frazier responded: "So far as I understand President Lincoln's proclamation to the Rebellious States, it is, that if they would lay down their arms and submit to the laws of the United States before the first of January, 1863, all would be well, but if they did not, then all the slaves of the Rebel States would be free henceforth and forever." Stanton followed with a question regarding the meaning of slavery and the freedom that had been granted by Lincoln's proclamation. "Slavery is receiving by *irresistible power* the work of another man, and not by his *consent*. The freedom promised by the proclamation, is taking us from under the yoke of bondage, and placing us where we could reap the fruit of our own labor, take care of our selves, and assist the Government in maintaining our freedom." [63]

The third question involved two of the most vexing issues facing the Lincoln administration: Could emancipated slaves be relied upon to care for themselves, and how might they assist the federal government in the war against the Confederate states? Frazier's answer eventually formed the philosophical basis of Sherman's revolutionary Field Order Number 15 that temporarily transferred "possessory title" of 600,000 acres of confiscated Confederate land to 40,000 freed slaves. The wise pastor must have known that he was speaking on behalf of 3.5 million slaves who were literally standing on the threshold of freedom. In simple terms, Frazier articulated the hopes, dreams and aspirations of his people. "The way we can best take care of ourselves, is to have land, and turn it and till it by our own labor—we can soon maintain ourselves and have something to spare." He added that freed slaves should be allowed to work the land until they were able to save some money and purchase it. Recognizing that the abolition of slavery was dependent on the defeat of the Confederacy, he stated that freed slaves could be of greatest assistance to the federal government by volunteering to fight in the Union army.[64]

Sherman and Stanton listened carefully to the thought-provoking answers provided by the venerable Savannah preacher. The secretary took notes and occasionally stared in amazement at Frazier, whose ideas impressed him as being "shrewd, wise and

comprehensive." He later observed that Frazier possessed the ability to discuss complex racial issues "as well as any member of the
Cabinet." Stanton was reportedly surprised by the intelligence of
the black preachers, and he went away from the meeting with
"new hopes for the future of the colored race." The next question
concerned an issue that would prove to be a continuing source of
racial conflict and tension throughout American history: "In what
manner would you rather live—scattered among the whites or in
colonies by yourselves?" [65]

"I would prefer to live by ourselves," stated Frazier. "There is a
prejudice against us in the South that will take years to get over; but
I do not know if I can answer for my brethren." Aware of some
internal disagreement over this point, he paused to allow the other
men to speak. Only James Lynch, the twenty-six-year-old free-
born minister from Baltimore, disagreed. Lynch, who could be
described as more radical than his black colleagues, insisted that
whites and blacks should be allowed to live together in integrated
communities.[66]

After more than an hour of questioning, Stanton politely asked
Sherman to leave the room. The secretary posed a final question to
the delegation regarding their opinion of the general. Frazier spoke
forthrightly: "We unanimously feel inexpressible gratitude to him,
some of us called upon him immediately upon his arrival, and . . .
he met us . . . as a friend and a gentlemen. We have confidence in
General Sherman, and think that what concerns us could not be
under better hands." Once again Lynch broke ranks with the other
men. He refused to offer an opinion of the general because of the
"brief nature" of their acquaintance. Although he did not openly
criticize Sherman, Lynch's refusal was obviously intended to con-
vey some reservations concerning the treatment of black refugees
during the march to the sea.[67]

To his credit, the general maintained his outward composure
after being asked to leave the room, but he was seething inside.

Insulted and embarrassed, Sherman later observed that the secretary had "catechized Negroes concerning the character of a general who had . . . conducted 65,000 men successfully across four hundred miles of hostile territory, and had just brought tens of thousands of freedman to a place of security." [68]

Following this meeting, Stanton instructed Sherman to devise a plan for the provision of food and shelter for the former slaves of Georgia, South Carolina, and Florida. By January 1865, Savannah was literally overflowing with black refugees, even though thousands had already been shipped to the Sea Islands off the coast of South Carolina. Each day hundreds of black refugees arrived on the coast "after long marches and severe privations, weary, famished, sick, and almost naked." [69]

The answers provided by Reverend Frazier and his delegation during the meeting with Sherman and Stanton formed the basis of a temporary solution to the problems associated with the emancipation of Southern slaves. On January 16, 1865, Sherman issued his Special Order Number 15, which stated in part that "The islands from Charleston south, the abandoned rice fields along the rivers for thirty miles back from the sea, and the country bordering the St. John's River, Fla., are reserved and set apart for the settlement of the negroes now made free by the acts of war and the proclamation of the President of the United States." Each Negro family would be given a "possessory license" to forty acres of tillable land and would maintain complete control over their affairs. All white men, with the exception of authorized military officials, were prohibited from residing on what became known as the Sherman Reservation.

On February 2, 1865, a mass meeting was held at the Second African Baptist Church in Savannah. More than one thousand blacks gathered inside, while hundreds more stood in the churchyard. Hosted by General Rufus Saxon, the provisional military governor of Georgia, South Carolina, and Florida, the purpose of the meeting was to explain the details of Sherman's order. According to

S. W. Magill, the highly emotional gathering was "one of the most remarkable meetings ever held in the city of Savannah." An expectant hush fell over the crowd as Saxon rose to speak. "I have come to tell you what the president of the United States has done for you," he began. In unison the audience shouted, "God Bless Massa Linkum." "You are all free!" proclaimed Saxon. The church erupted with words of praise and exhortation. Men and women shouted, holy danced, and sang hymns of thanksgiving. The spiritual outpouring spread to the growing mass assembled on the church grounds, and they too joined the celebration. "Glory be to God! Hallelujah!" and "Amen!" were repeated over and over again.[70]

Saxon was followed to the podium by Reverend Mansfield French, a member of his staff, who proceeded to explain the realities and implications of the order. He encouraged the former slaves to "be good citizens, truthful and honest" and to demonstrate to their former masters that they could take care of themselves. "If I were in your place," he concluded, "I would go, if I had to live on roots and water, and take possession of the islands." The freedmen shouted their unanimous approval of his suggestion. Their most earnest prayers had seemingly been answered.[71]

The Sherman Reservation contained more than 435,000 tillable acres and, by the spring of 1865, more than twenty thousand blacks had established themselves up and down the southeastern coast. With the assurance of Secretary Stanton that the federal government fully supported the policy, Saxon divided the reservation into 40-acre tracts. Sherman also provided the black settlers with hundreds of mules and horses confiscated during his march from Atlanta to Savannah. For the former slaves of Georgia, South Carolina, and Florida, the Jubilee prophecy had been fulfilled. In many ways, Sherman's order was more revolutionary than Lincoln's Emancipation Proclamation. The general had summarily authorized the confiscation of over half a million acres of Confederate land and its redistribution to former Southern slaves.

Thousands of freedman were granted "temporary" possession of a sizable portion of the land that they and their ancestors had tilled for generations.

In mid-January 1865, Sherman and his army left Savannah and continued their march of devastation into South Carolina and North Carolina. Although he urged General Grant not to garrison the city with black troops, that is exactly what occurred during the following spring. In March, the First South Carolina Volunteers— renamed the thirty-third United States Colored Troops—arrived in Savannah, along with the fifty-fourth Massachusetts regiment. By the beginning of April, more than twenty-three hundred black Union soldiers were stationed there.

The reaction from many white Savannahians was predictable. One resident wrote: "Some of the troops stationed here are negroes, which adds to my discomfort." The black soldiers were the target of ridicule and sneers from both white Southerners and white Union soldiers. The *Savannah Republican*, a pro-Union newspaper, acknowledged that much animosity existed between "our best soldiers and many citizens, against the colored soldiers." They encouraged all parties to "respect their uniform . . . no matter what their complexion may be." The *Republican* urged tolerance and understanding: "The colored troops, since their arrival in the city, have behaved in a soldierly manner, never seemingly forgetting that they are placed here to preserve, rather than disturb the order and quietude of our city." Although the presence of black soldiers angered white Savannahians, a growing number of Southerners believed that black soldiers—dressed in gray—might be the last, best hope for the crumbling Confederacy.[72]

CHAPTER VIII

———

BLACK MEN IN GRAY?

During the final months of the Civil War, the frenzy for Southern independence that marked the beginning of the conflict had dissolved into the sobering reality of impending defeat. Proud white Southerners watched in disbelief as hopelessness and despair spread across the face of the Confederacy. As casualties and desertions mounted, and the pool of potential recruits dwindled, some rebel leaders began to consider what had been unthinkable at the beginning of the war: the enlistment and emancipation of slave soldiers.

The winter of 1864 and the spring of 1865 witnessed a dramatic shift in opinion throughout the rebel states regarding the utilization of black soldiers. The issuance of the Emancipation Proclamation by President Lincoln on January 1, 1863, had provided the North with a fresh source of manpower and a decided strategic advantage. Lincoln's about-face dramatically exposed the inherent military weakness associated with the enslavement of Negroes. The severely undermanned Confederate military was now in the untenable position of having to engage an enemy without (advancing Union forces) and defend against a newly aroused enemy within (former slaves who could now fight for their freedom).

These dire military circumstances led an increasingly vocal group of Southerners to begin speaking openly about the military necessity of utilizing black soldiers. Like their Northern adversaries, they grudgingly concluded that blacks would fight only if their service was conditioned on emancipation from slavery. Although the failure to implement this controversial policy would all but guarantee defeat, opposition in the South to slave enlistment and emancipation remained fierce and determined. Entrenched beliefs in Negro inferiority and huge financial investments in the institution of slavery prevented the majority of whites from supporting such a radical restructuring of their society.

Yet despite this widespread opposition, white Southerners reluctantly began reexamining the purpose and meaning of the Civil War. Was the South fighting to preserve the institution of slavery or to win independence from the United States of America? Would white Southerners be willing to sacrifice slavery in order to secure new troops to help stave off defeat? If Southern slaves were willing to fight for the North in exchange for their freedom, why not offer them the same opportunity in the Confederate army? In the wake of Sherman's destruction of Atlanta and his devastating march to Savannah, this historic, and often bitter, debate consumed the Confederacy.

As early as January 1864, following a series of crushing defeats and the looming prospect of a major spring offensive by Sherman's army, a small group of Confederate leaders argued that desperate measures had to be considered. At a meeting near Dalton, Georgia, General Patrick R. Cleburne developed the first official Confederate proposal for the enlistment of black soldiers. He stated that the Confederacy had spilled much of its "best blood" in the war, but after three years of fighting, the "fruits" of the struggle "have slipped away from us and left us nothing but long lists of dead and mangled." As Cleburne and his senior officers struggled to devise a plan to defend Georgia against the impending Union invasion, he sent the proposal to Confederate President Jefferson Davis. He urged Davis to take immediate steps to train "a large reserve of the most courageous of our slaves" for battle and that a guarantee of freedom be offered within in a reasonable time "to every slave in the South who shall remain true to the Confederacy in this war." Cleburne had been moved to propose this controversial step after witnessing the valor of former slaves who were now fighting to preserve the Union: "If they [Negroes] can be made to face and fight bravely against former masters, how much more probable is it that with the allurement of a higher reward, and led by those masters, they would submit to discipline and face dangers?" [1]

Convinced that implementation of Cleburne's proposal would ignite a severe political backlash, Davis quickly decided to suppress the document. Over time, however, the declining fortunes of the Confederacy would ultimately force many white Southerners, including Davis, to rethink their stance on the issue. Georgian Sam Clayton was among those who lobbied the Confederate president: "The [new] recruits should come from our Negroes, nowhere else. We should do away with pride of opinion, away with false pride, and promptly take hold of all the means God has placed within our reach to help us through this struggle. . . . Some say that Negroes will not fight. I say they will fight." On September 29, 1864, an anonymous writer from Augusta urged Confederate Secretary of War James Seddon to implement slave enlistment: "Promise them [slave soldiers] freedom when the war is over. Compensate the owners, of course, with interest-bearing bonds. All the able-bodied men might be used certainly as effectively as the Yankees use them against us." [2]

On November 7, 1864, Davis opened the final session of the Confederate Congress by voicing his "official" disapproval of slave enlistment. "I must dissent," he stated, "from those who advise a general levy and arming of slaves for the duty of soldiers." However, he opened the door to the possibility by stating that should the alternative be presented between subjugation to the North or the utilization of black soldiers, there was "no reason to doubt what should be our decision." Although he refused to fully embrace slave enlistment, Davis initiated a new phase in the debate by calling for the impressment of an additional forty thousand slave laborers and their eventual emancipation.[3]

The promise of freedom was a radical departure from existing Confederate policy. It was clearly an attempt by Davis to lay the groundwork for the eventual enlistment of black Confederate soldiers. He argued that although slaves were property and possessed no rights as citizens, they still bore an obligation to protect and support the Confederate government. Davis maintained that once a slave contributed to the Confederate war effort, his status as a person would somehow take precedence over his enslaved condition. Thus, according to this line of reasoning, the government would be obligated to purchase slave laborers from their masters and grant them freedom in exchange for their service.

Reaction to Davis's statements was intense. Samuel Boykin, editor of the *Christian Index* in Macon, denounced even the discussion of the possibility of slave enlistment and emancipation: "Such a question ought never to have been agitated. Its discussion is fraught with infinite mischief." In a subsequent column he raised additional objections: "The army will be a propitious school wherein to teach the slaves many things inconsistent with . . . servitude . . . the use of firearms; a sense of self-reliance [and] a vague perception of equality with the white race." Even worse, the Baptist editor was repelled by the thought of having to live in a South populated by thousands of emancipated black war veterans. "They would remain in our midst as freedmen, entitled it is to be presumed with the rights of citizenship. . . . To deny these after the promise of freedom, would be . . . an outrage upon truth and justice." [4]

The *Macon Telegraph and Confederate* also carried letters of opposition and support. "Randolph" claimed that enlisting slave soldiers "would in the eyes of Christendom, heap deep and dire disgrace upon the South and put a final end to an institution, to which the South is indebted for all that makes her superior." Another writer named "Sydney" disagreed; he believed that it would be better to sacrifice slaves on the fields of battle rather than additional white men. "If the exigency demands [more] men . . . in God's name, do not sacrifice every white man in the Confederacy in preference to taking a few negroes from their fondling masters. There is [sic] in the Confederacy one or two hundred thousand able bodied negroes not engaged in agriculture. Many of them . . . can very well be spared." Nowhere in Georgia was opposition to slave enlistment and emancipation more determined than at the *Augusta Chronicle and Sentinel*. On December 21, 1864, even as Sherman's army was marching triumphantly through Georgia, editor Nathan Moore cautioned against "rash and dangerous experiments" that could jeopardize the Southern social order.[5]

But following the surrender of Savannah and the defeat of a large Confederate army at Nashville, a growing number of white Georgians began to rethink their opposition to black enlistment. By far the most significant change involved the transformation of war purposes—from preserving slavery to winning independence. As the authors of *Why the South Lost the Civil War* astutely observed, prior to 1864 Southerners could fight for both, but by the fall of that year it had become an either-or proposition. A Georgia preacher counseled his son: "We are fighting first for our liberty and independence, not for our interests." During the first months of 1865, Georgia newspapers were filled with letters and editorials that enthusiastically supported the arming and emancipation of slaves. On January 5 the *Macon Telegraph and Confederate* published a strongly worded editorial by John Forsyth of the *Mobile Register* who wrote that it was time for the South to abandon one of its most cherished institutions. "In the foreground of this picture of national military disaster, we shall not fail to discover, torn up root and branch, the institution of domestic slavery. . . . With such reverses and pressed as we are, is it folly to hesitate to avail of it and fill our depleted army?" Supporters of the various slave enlistment plans argued that their adoption would also serve to secure European recognition and "neutralize that large party in the North whose sympathy and interests were mainly employed with the Negro." [6]

In January 1865 General Robert E. Lee, commander of the Confederate military, joined the raging debate. In an extraordinary letter, he stated his unqualified support for the enlistment of black men in the Confederate army:

> We should not expect slaves to fight for prospective freedom when they can secure it at once by going to the enemy, in whose service they will incur no greater risk than ours. The reasons that induce me to recommend the employment of Negro troops at all render the effect of the measures I have suggested upon slavery immaterial, and in my opinion the best means of securing the efficiency and fidelity of this auxiliary force would be to accompany the measure with a well-digested plan of gradual and general emancipation. I think we must decide, whether slavery shall be extinguished by our enemies and the slaves be used against us, or use them ourselves at the risk of the effects which may be produced upon our social institutions. My own opinion is that we should employ them without delay. [7]

Lee's endorsement generated widespread support, but many Southern politicians and journalists were unmoved by his appeal. In a lengthy editorial, the editors of the *Charleston Mercury* lashed out at the Confederate commander: "General Lee, the advocate, if not the author of this scheme, of nigger soldiers and emancipation is said by those who are acquainted with the families . . . in Virginia to be a hereditary Federalist and a disbeliever in the institution of slavery." Despite the endorsement of the South's preeminent military leader and the looming prospect of unconditional surrender, the Confederate senate on February 8, 1865, rejected a resolution directing the committee on military affairs to pass a bill that would require the immediate enlistment of Negro soldiers. Stung by criticism of his earlier proposal, Jefferson Davis publicly maintained his opposition to slave enlistment and emancipation, but he confessed his true feelings in a letter to John Forsyth in February 1865: "All arguments as to the positive advantage or disadvantage of employing them [blacks] are beside the question, which is simply one of relative advantage between having their fighting element in our ranks or those of the enemy." On February 11, 1865, a second measure to enlist two hundred thousand black soldiers was introduced by Congressman Ethelbert Barksdale. On February 18 General Lee wrote to the congressman and declared that the measure was not only expedient but absolutely necessary, and that black men "will make good soldiers." On the question of emancipation, Lee did not mince words: "Those who are employed should be freed. It would be neither just nor wise . . . to require them to serve as slaves." [8]

Although Southern politicians were slow to endorse the plan, there was growing support for black enlistment among the men who were "doing the fighting and the dying" on the battlefields. In February 1865, near Petersburg, Virginia, four separate Georgia regiments declared that they were ready to "make soldiers" out of all willing black slaves. A week later, General John B. Gordon polled the Second Corps of the Army of Northern Virginia and discovered that the majority of eighty-six hundred officers and soldiers were "decidedly in favor of the voluntary enlistment of the negroes as soldiers." The men of the Forty-ninth Georgia Regiment responded to critics who believed that fighting alongside black soldiers would be a fate much worse than Northern defeat. "When in former years, for pecuniary purposes, we did not consider it disgraceful to labor with negroes in the field or at the same work bench," explained the Georgia soldiers, "we certainly will not look upon it in any other light at this time, when an end so glorious as our independence is to be achieved." An Augusta soldier serving in Virginia voiced his support: "If Congress agrees that the 200,000 negroes ought to be put in, I will fight by them. . . . Many of the men wish to see the negroes in the field." [9]

However, the majority of Southerners clung to the belief that the South was fighting to preserve and expand slavery, and they realized that arming and emancipating slaves would be the death knell for the institution. The fundamental theory undergirding American slavery was that the Negro was an inherently inferior being, incapable of the civilized or courageous behavior that soldiering required. Thus, if a slave was declared capable of fighting in the Confederate army, it had to be assumed that he possessed the characteristics of a man, and if he was a man, then his natural condition could not be that of a slave. In March 1865, a Mississippi newspaper editor argued that the enlistment and emancipation of blacks would represent "a total abandonment of the chief object of this war." He then posed a crucial question: "Why fight one moment longer, if the object and occasion of the fight is dying, dead or damned?" In Virginia another editor explained that "if our people are not capable of vindicating their title to property in negroes, then they ought to quietly surrender the question, stop the war, abolish slavery, and confess themselves eternally disgraced." Referring to the slave enlistment proposals, Confederate Senator William Graham of North Carolina wrote: "With such wild schemes and confessions of despair as this, it [is] high time to attempt peace." [10]

No one placed the Southern dilemma in better perspective than two well-known Georgians, General Howell Cobb and Governor Joseph Brown. In an address to Georgia legislators, Brown stated that God had created blacks to be slaves and not soldiers; if the South admits or establishes the fact that black men are capable of military service, "we destroy our whole theory that they are unfit to be free." The governor pointedly concluded that "when we arm the slaves we abandon slavery." Howell Cobb described slave enlistment as "the most pernicious idea" that had been suggested since the war began. Cobb bluntly asserted that "you cannot make soldiers of slaves or slaves of soldiers. The day you make soldiers of them is the beginning of the end of our revolution. If slaves make good soldiers, our whole theory of slavery is wrong." For men like Cobb and Brown, the prospect of arming black men and allowing them to fight for their freedom was far more troubling than defeat and subjugation by the North.[11]

Georgia congressman Warren Akin had also pondered the implications of black enlistment upon the Southern social order:

> I can only say it is a question of fearful magnitude. Can we prevent subjugation, confiscation, degradation and slavery [to the Union] without it. If not will our condition or that of the negro, be any worse by calling them into service. If I were convinced that we will be subjugated, with the long train of horrors that will follow it, unless the negroes be placed in the army, I would not hesitate to enrol [sic] our slaves and put them to fighting.

An anonymous writer concluded, "I see but one alternative left us, and that is to fill up our army with negroes. I have no doubt but they can be made good soldiers as the population our enemies are importing from Europe. . . . If you do not put them in the field they will very soon be taken from us and made to take up arms against us."[12]

On March 8, 1865, with the support of Lee and Jefferson Davis, the Confederate senate reversed itself and passed a resolution directing the Military Affairs Committee, which had held the measure for weeks, to send to the full senate a bill authorizing the enlistment of black soldiers. The act read in part:

> In order to provide additional forces to repel invasion, maintain the rightful possessions of the Confederate States, secure their independence and preserve the institution, the President . . . is hereby authorized to ask for and accept from owners of slaves, the services of such number of able bodied negro men as he may deem expedient, for and during the war, to perform military service in whatever capacity he may direct.[13]

The measure, which passed the senate by one vote on March 13, authorized Davis to organize the black soldiers into military units under rules and regulations established by the secretary of war. During their tour of duty, black Confederate soldiers were to receive the same pay, rations, and clothing as white troops in the same service. The Confederate president was authorized to enlist up to three hundred thousand blacks from the various states, provided that not more than 25 percent of the male slaves in any one state were called to service. However, the fifth and final section of the statute severely limited the effectiveness of the preceding sections by stating that "nothing in this act shall be construed to authorize a change in the relation which the said slaves shall bear toward their owners, except by consent of the owners and of the State in which they may reside." [14]

This language reflected a key element of radical Confederate political ideology and thought. Under the Confederate Constitution, "states' rights" were superior to the powers of the national government, Union or Confederate; sovereignty of the individual states could not be abridged—not even in the case of "military necessity" or national emergency. Thus, the inalienable right to traffic, buy, and own slaves was derived solely from the states and only consenting slave owners and the individual states could provide for the enlistment and/or emancipation of slave soldiers. In other words, Southern slaves who served in the Confederate military would not be guaranteed their freedom by the Confederate government. Davis tried to remedy this critical defect in the enlistment legislation by issuing an executive order that offered an indirect promise of emancipation to slave soldiers.

Ex-Confederate Colonel William Oates, a Civil War historian, observed: "A Negro who did not have sense enough, under that law, to have deserted to the enemy at the first opportunity would have been too much of an idiot to have made a soldier. No sensible Negro would have volunteered under that law—unless it was for the purpose of availing himself of the opportunity it would have given him to desert to the other side, where he [would] have obtained his freedom." Oates was convinced that if the measure had been passed one year earlier, when the subject was first broached by Cleburne, and in lieu of the fifth section a general decree of emancipation had been ordered, more than three hundred thousand black soldiers would have taken the field in support of the Confederacy. But the financial, cultural, and political investments in slavery were too great. Although defeat and unconditional surrender were the inevitable alternatives, Southern political leaders could not bring themselves to strike what would have been a decisive blow against the institution. Oates sadly concluded: "After slavery was practically dead the Confederacy clung to its putrid body and expired with it." [15]

Despite the absence of a general decree of emancipation, the Confederate war department proceeded to appoint recruiting officers in each of the Southern states. On March 17, 1865, Jefferson Davis stated: "We shall have a Negro army. Letters are pouring into the departments from men of military skill and character asking authority to raise companies, battalions, and regiments of Negro troops." The *Augusta Constitutionalist* confidently predicted that "quite a number of patriotic negroes" would step forward to join the Confederate army "upon the first call." The editor of the *Columbus Enquirer* urged local readers "to take the matter [of black enlistment] into their own hands, and, by inducements, urge the negroes to volunteer." In Macon two separate black recruitment efforts were initiated. Private James B. Nelson of the Sixteenth Georgia Battalion established a recruitment headquarters in a Bibb County store and Captain Thomas J. Key set out to organize a volunteer regiment of three or four hundred Negro soldiers. Key appealed to slave owners to "emancipate such negroes as will volunteer in the Confederate service, promising them after we shall gain our independence, and they should desire to return to their old homes, that proper provisions will be made for them and their families and fair wages given." He counseled Georgia slave masters who preferred defeat over black emancipation and enlistment: "Better to give up half your negroes to defend your homes, than let them fall into the clutches of the North, to be used as spies and guides, and to aid in your utter ruin." [16]

Before the slave enlistment plan could be fully implemented, however, the last two Confederate armies in the field hoisted the white flags of surrender. General Lee surrendered to General Ulysses S. Grant at Appomattox courthouse on April 9, 1865, and the final nail was driven in the Confederate coffin when General Johnson surrendered his army to General Sherman on April 14. With these acts of submission, the Confederate States of America ceased to exist. After the war Jefferson Davis recalled that he had once warned a member of the Confederate Congress who opposed slave enlistment and emancipation that if the South ultimately lost the war, "there should be written on its tombstone, 'Died of a theory.'" A key element of that theory was that black men were cowardly, subhuman beings, incapable of possessing the qualities that military service required. History has left unanswered an intriguing question: Could the defeat of the South be attributed to the fact that Confederate leaders waited too late to embrace the enlistment and emancipation of black soliders?

"SLAVERY IS ABOLISHED AND . . . THE NEGROES ARE FREE"

The Civil War officially ended in Georgia on April 30, 1865, when Governor Joseph Brown surrendered the last regiments of Confederate troops to Union commanders. Northern leaders moved quickly to supplant local and state civil authority with military rule. General Sherman had already placed Savannah and Macon under federal occupation, and this status was extended throughout the state during April, May, and June. Augusta and Athens were occupied during the first week of May, while Atlanta and Milledgeville were reoccupied by the end of the month. Brunswick, Darien, Thomasville, Columbus, Albany, and scores of smaller Georgia towns and villages were systematically placed under what Southerners derisively referred to as "bayonet despotism."

In areas not penetrated by Union forces during the war, the arrival of occupation troops signaled emancipation to jubilant Georgia slaves. Ella Gertrude Thomas, a white resident of Augusta, recorded in her diary the events surrounding the arrival of Union soldiers in that city: "Fri. morning a large force of Yankees came marching into Augusta, the drums beating & colors flying—surrounded by a large crowd of Negroes. . . . Tonight the impression is general that Slavery is abolished and that the Negroes are free." Tom Singleton, a former slave, recalled the day Union cavalrymen rode into Athens: "I was standing on the corner of Jackson Street when they said freedom had come. That sure was a rally day for the

Niggers, about a thousand in all were standing around here in Athens that day." [18]

To the dismay of many white Georgians, hundreds of black soldiers were used to help garrison Union military outposts throughout the state. According to historian C. Mildred Thompson, "Garrisons where colored troops were established were centers for disturbance. Hotheaded young Southern men would not brook the lording insolence of blacks in brass buttons. And Negro soldiers everywhere had a bad influence on the freedmen of the neighborhood, encouraging them to idleness and arousing in them a feeling of distrust or hostility to their white employers." Eliza Frances Andrews, a Wilkes County resident, expressed the deep-seated animosity many whites felt toward black men dressed in blue: "it did seem a pity to break up a great nation about a parcel of African savages. . . . Since the Yankees have treated us so abominably, burning and plundering our country and bringing a gang of Negro soldiers here to insult us, I don't see how anybody can tolerate the sight of their odious flag again." Similar complaints were raised in Augusta, Savannah, Darien, and other cities by whites who charged that the presence of black soldiers encouraged freedmen to commit an endless series of petty thefts, robberies, and nighttime raids on unguarded chicken houses and pig pens. [19]

Shortly after the shackles of slavery were broken, black Georgians began to test the boundaries of their newfound freedom. One former slave recalled: "Right off colored folks started on the move. They seemed to want to get closer to freedom, so they'd know what it was—like it was a place or a city." John Eaton, a Union officer, witnessed this mass movement on Southern roads: "Imagine if you will a slave population . . . rising up and leaving its ancient bondage, forsaking its local traditions and all the associations and attractions of the old plantation life, coming garbed in rags or in silks, with feet shod or bleeding, individually or in families and in larger groups." Although white Georgians were angered by what they perceived to be idle "Wanderlust," this movement by freed blacks was not without meaning or purpose. Historian Robert Gamble offers an interesting analysis: "A closer examination of this flux ... reveals a significant development in the Negro community ... which lies deeper than mere restlessness, [it was] an attempt to knit together the fabric of a true family life." When asked where he was going, a former slave replied, "I'se got a wife . . . in Virginia ... [and] I am going to look her up and fetch her home." John E. Bryant, a Freedmen's Bureau agent, wrote to his wife: "I wish you could see this people as they step from slavery into freedom ... families which had been for a long time broken up are united and oh! Such happiness." Dusty Southern roads were crowded with black men and women as they wandered from plantation to plantation, county to county, city to city, and across state boundaries in search of family members and loved ones who had been sold away. John Richard Dennett, a Northern correspondent, encountered a former slave from Georgia slowly making his way up the east coast toward Virginia, in search of a wife who had been placed on the auction block and purchased by the highest bidder.[20]

The majority of Georgia's postwar black migrants were freedmen who had been enslaved on rural plantations. They quickly realized that greater personal freedom and protection existed in and around the cities garrisoned by Union soldiers. By the spring of 1865, the state's urban areas were practically overflowing with unemployed and impoverished Negroes. The *Athens Southern Banner* lashed out at the growing number of black refugees who crowded into the college town: "Can anybody tell where so many idle Negroes come from? Like the frogs of Egypt, they seem to be everywhere and in everybody's way." The influx of freedmen and the refusal of white landlords to lease their dwellings to blacks (even if they could afford to pay) created a critical housing shortage. Blacks were forced to congregate in settlements of hastily built shanties on the outskirts of many Georgia cities. They were often joined by urban freedmen, who preferred life in the newly established ghettoes to the relative confinement of the servant's quarters located near the residences of their former masters. Living conditions were deplorable and basic sanitation all but nonexistent in these primitive shantytowns.[21]

A *New York World* correspondent writing from Washington, Georgia, observed: "I have passed places inhabited by crowds of freedmen where in hot summer weather the stench was so great that I had to stop up my nose and cross to the other side of the street." Francis Andrews graphically described the blacks crowded in a local slum as a "teeming . . . pile of maggots." In Macon, a Northern missionary working in another shantytown discovered eleven blacks, including six children, living in a rickety hut covered by a tin roof and a few bundles of rags. Listed as all of their worldly possessions were three crude stools, one chair, five pounds of bacon, a bag of meal, and a dozen cooking utensils.[22]

In Atlanta, John Trowbridge, a Northern reporter, described the makeshift housing of local freedmen as "wretched hovels, which made the suburbs look like a fantastic encampment of gypsies with ragged fragments of tin roofing from the burned government and railroad buildings, kept from blowing away by stones placed on the top." Some white Georgians took pleasure in sarcastically referring to these settlements as "Sherman towns." In Savannah, Columbus, Augusta, and Washington, Georgia local officials and Union officers soon decided to eradicate local slums by forcing their inhabitants to relocate to the countryside. Officials in Macon took a more direct approach: they emptied the shanties of their black occupants and burned them to the ground.[23]

During the first few months of freedom, the great majority of blacks were forced to scavenge for food, clothing, and shelter in order to avert starvation and death from exposure to the elements. Abolitionist Frederick Douglass observed that American slaves had been set free—"free to the wind, free to the rain, free to suffering and want, free to the wrath of their former masters. They had no land, they had no tools, and they had no capital." In January 1865 the citizens of New York City were among the first to respond to General Sherman's call for assistance to help feed the 19,000 destitute black war refugees who had followed his troops to Savannah. The American Missionary Association and other abolitionist and religious groups also contributed money, food, and clothing. Although much needed and well-intentioned, these private, independent relief efforts were inadequate to meet the growing needs of Georgia's impoverished black and white population.[24]

The mounting death toll from dysentery, smallpox, and other diseases led some white Georgians to conclude that the black race was literally on the verge of extinction. Judge C. H. Sutton of Clarkesville declared in July 1865 that the American Negro would simply die out within fifty years. Prior to the establishment of Freedmen's hospitals in Savannah, Atlanta, Augusta, Macon, and Columbus, black Augustans addressed the critical medical needs of local freedmen by forming a freedmen's "aid society." The society used the money generated through local subscriptions to establish a hospital, secure the services of a doctor, and hire a black midwife.

In March 1865 Congress moved to address the complex social and economic problems associated with the liberation of 3.5 million Southern slaves by creating the Bureau of Refugees, Freedmen, and Abandoned Lands. Generally known as the Freedmen's Bureau, the purposes of this federal welfare agency were to provide food, clothing, and medical care for poor white and black war refugees; to settle black freedmen on abandoned or confiscated lands; to help freedmen make the transition from slavery to freedom; to assist in negotiating work contracts with white employers; and to establish freedmen's schools for adults and children.[24A]

Before the measure could be fully implemented, however, President Abraham Lincoln was assassinated on April 14, 1865. His successor, Andrew Johnson of Tennessee, was sympathetic to

Southern interests and decided to moderate many of the Union policies designed to punish ex-Confederate officials and to assist the former slaves. Johnson's amnesty order of May 29, 1865, restored the lands confiscated by Sherman's Field Order Number 15 to their former owners. It gave black settlers until the end of the year to abandon their farms and directed Bureau agents and the army to forcibly evict all freedmen who refused to allow the return of white landowners. The majority of black settlers were allowed to remain on their plots until the crops they had planted were harvested, but thousands of freedmen simply abandoned their crops in the fields.

Although Georgia's coastal blacks were badly disillusioned by the loss of their farms, the situation would have been much worse except for the appointment of Major General Oliver O. Howard as commissioner of the Freedmen's Bureau. Howard was a thirty-five-year-old Maine native who served as one of Sherman's commanders during the march to the sea and later founded Howard University in Washington, D.C. His first task was to appoint individual commissioners to oversee the affairs of all the former Confederate states. State commissioners were directed to assist *all* refugees and to introduce a system of free and compensated labor for the freedmen; act as courts of law where no courts existed; serve as the freedmen's friend of the court where they were not recognized as citizens; and establish the institution of marriage among the freed slaves. In June 1865 Howard appointed General Rufus Saxon commissioner of the Freedmen's Bureau in Georgia; a few months later, Brigadier-General Davis Tillson would succeed Saxon in that position.[25]

The first challenge faced by Saxon and Freedmen's Bureau officials in Georgia was providing food, clothing, and shelter to thousands of destitute black and white war refugees. This task was made more difficult by the fact that the Bureau lacked an organizational structure and many of the agents hired in the South were unsympathetic to the plight of the freedmen. Bureau agents initially refused to assist Savannah blacks, but they did provide relief to the six thousand impoverished whites in the area. This policy was subsequently overruled, and by the fall of 1865, Saxon had appointed some two hundred Bureau agents, stationed around the state, who were actively engaged in the Reconstruction effort. Agents distributed three pounds of bacon, a peck of cornmeal, and a pint of molasses to each adult freedman on a weekly basis. Although historians have roundly criticized the Freedmen's Bureau as being corrupt and inefficient, it played a key role during those early months in relieving human suffering and easing the transition from slavery to freedom.

A PASSION FOR EDUCATION

Beyond the need for basic food, clothing, and shelter, Georgia freedmen also possessed a burning desire for education. "In the first days of freedom," writes historian Lerone Bennett, "the freedmen demonstrated a passion for education which has perhaps never been equaled in the history of the world." Just days after Sherman occupied Savannah, local black ministers formed the Colored Education Association. Its leader was Reverend James Lynch, a well-educated black minister of the African Methodist Episcopal Church, who later became secretary of state in Mississippi. The by-laws of the association provided for the establishment of several tuition-free elementary schools that would be supported by voluntary subscriptions. The executive board was comprised of nine black men who in turn interviewed and hired fifteen black teachers and acquired several buildings to be used as schools. In an ironic twist, they established the Bryan Free School in the building that was formerly a Savannah slave market. Holding pens once used to confine slaves awaiting sale on the auction block were dismantled to create more space for seating and tables. Louis Toomer, who operated one of Savannah's clandestine schools for free and slave children prior to emancipation, was hired to serve as the "principal teacher." By January 1, 1865, black Savannahians had raised eight hundred dollars and more than five hundred children were enrolled in classes.[26]

According to W. E. B. Du Bois, Savannah's fledgling education initiative attracted blacks of "every age and shade, eager for [the] book learning which seemed to them the key to their advance." Reverend J. W. Alvord, a white minister affiliated with the American Tract Society of Boston, Massachusetts, wrote: "The interesting fact in this whole organization is that it is wholly their own. The officers of the Assoc. are all colored men. The teachers are all colored." On the first day of school, the students met at a local church and then marched through the streets of Savannah to their assigned schools. Reverend William T. Richardson, a white minister affiliated with the American Missionary Association, later exclaimed: "This army of colored children moving through the streets seemed to excite feeling and interest second only to that of Gen. Sherman's army. Such a gathering of Freedmen's sons and daughters, that proud city had never seen before." By July, although the walls of the Bryan School were still draped in black cloth to mourn the death of President Lincoln, the determined students inside, ranging in ages from seven to seventeen, were already being taught grammar, history, writing geography, arithmetic, elocution, and singing.[27]

The American Missionary Association (AMA) enlisted two white ministers from the North, Reverend S. W. Magill and Reverend William T. Richardson, to assist the Savannah Education Association with the administration and operation of their schools. The men were therefore surprised and dismayed when the leaders of this local organization refused their offer of assistance and financial support. Reverend Lynch and his board were adamantly opposed to Magill's suggestion that white teachers be employed to teach black children and that the black teachers already hired be demoted to "assistant teachers." The group countered that they would accept white teachers only if they agreed to serve as assistants to the black teachers. Magill was livid. He informed his superiors that the blacks wanted AMA funding but were unwilling to relinquish any control over the affairs of the schools. Yet by February 1865 Magill had somehow managed to develop a working relationship with the black ministers, for white teachers were soon teaching several classes of black students, although the association still maintained substantial control over the operation of the school system. According to Freedmen's Bureau reports, white teachers gradually assumed leadership roles in several of the freedmen's schools. By the end of 1865, the Oglethorpe Colored School had an enrollment of 450 students in eight classes that were being taught by two white teachers from South Carolina and one from Georgia.[28]

Whether the teachers were white or black, their efforts were plagued by a critical shortage of equipment and supplies. One AMA teacher described her school as a "very crude" structure that was nothing more than a canvas stretched over a framework of pine poles. Despite the primitive conditions, black pupils demonstrated an unbridled determination to master the basic rudiments of reading and writing. After witnessing an end-of-term examination given to the students, the white school inspector Reverend Alford admitted that he was delighted and encouraged by the progress of the pupils. He also reported that the Savannah black community had donated more than two thousand dollars during the first six months of 1865 to pay teacher salaries and support the operations of their schools.[29]

By the end of the year, the Savannah Education Association, with support from the American Missionary Association, the New York Society of Friends, the National Freedmen's Aid Society, and the New England Freedmen's Aid Society, was operating eight schools in the city. And while historian Jacqueline Jones argues that the efforts of Savannah blacks were not typical throughout Georgia, self-help initiatives to raise money, establish schools, and hire teachers were also organized in Columbus, Athens, Sandersville, Albany, Calhoun, and Lexington. During the first twelve months of freedom, sixty-six freedmen's schools were established in the state that provided education and training to approximately 3,500 black children and adults. Hundreds of freedmen also benefited from instruction provided in smaller, less formal "schools" that were usually operated by a sole black or white teacher.

These self-help initiatives demonstrated a keen awareness among freedmen that education was essential to their progress in the postslavery South. White Georgians were also aware that access to educational opportunity would aid the former slaves as they struggled to build a free society. Georgia's white majority was adamantly opposed to any effort to give their former bondsmen access to the knowledge of books. Many feared that Northern missionaries who aided black educational efforts were laying the groundwork for a fully integrated society where blacks would possess equal rights with whites. They feared that educated blacks would inevitably seek the full complement of citizenship rights, such as desegregated public accommodations and the right to vote and hold office. The *Albany Patriot* carefully articulated the concerns and fears of all but a few white Georgians. According to the editor, the efforts of "Northern fanatics" to educate freed blacks was nothing more than "the unhallowed attempts at elevating the brutal seed of Ham to an equality with that of Japhet [and] is only surpassed in absurdity by the vaunters who thought they could climb to Heaven by the erection of the Tower of Babel." In the final analysis, Negro education was the "strongest quiver in the abolitionist bow, to render the Negro worthy of the elective franchise," which according to the editor, "we are, as a people, unanimously and utterly opposed to his every exercising." [30]

FORTY ACRES AND A MULE

Second only to the freedmen's desire to gain access to education was the conviction that the ownership of land was the key to economic self-sufficiency. A reporter for the *Nation* remarked: "The sole ambition of the freedmen at the present time appears to be to become the owner of a little piece of land [and] there to erect an humble home." The black cry for "forty acres and a mule" resounded across the war-torn countryside. Reverend J. W. Alvord commented on what he described as a "passion for land" among the black population. Although historians have ridiculed the notion of general confiscation and redistribution of Confederate land to freed slaves as far-fetched and fanciful, many influential Republican congressmen believed that the policy should serve as the cornerstone of federal Reconstruction legislation. This belief was based on the assumption that Southern white landholders would continue to exploit black laborers unless they were given the protection of land ownership.[31]

The initial effort toward land redistribution actually began in 1864 when Edwin M. Stanton, Lincoln's secretary of war, appointed the American Freedmen's Inquiry Commission to visit areas in the South under federal control and to examine the condition of former slaves and make policy recommendations. The commission concluded that, without general land reform, black Southerners would be trapped in a cycle of serfdom and poverty. One of the members wrote: "No such thing as a free, democratic society can exist in any country where all lands are owned by one class of men and cultivated by another." They unanimously endorsed a proposal recommending that the federal government implement programs to ensure that freed slaves would be made "owners in fee of the farms or gardens they occupy." [32]

From the earliest days of the war, white and black abolitionists argued that three primary strategies could be successfully employed to carry out general land reform in the South. Some believed that, after the war, freed slaves should be resettled on government-owned properties under the auspices of the federal Homestead Act; others suggested that the federal government should purchase Southern land and resell it to blacks on long-term payment plans. The most popular and controversial strategy involved the seizure and redistribution of land owned by former slaveholders. Although all three alternatives were thoroughly considered, the majority of those involved in the discussions favored confiscation. Supporters of redistribution argued that confiscation was just punishment for ex-Confederates who had committed treason against the United States and that it would serve as fair reparations for the unrequited labor of American slaves.

In January 1865, General Sherman had taken the first bold steps in this direction when he heeded the advice of twenty black leaders in Savannah who stated that the best way they could become self-supporting "is to have land, and . . . till it by our own labor." His Special Field Order Number 15, as noted earlier, established what became known as the Sherman Reservation, which included the Sea Islands along the coasts of South Carolina, Georgia, and Florida and the abandoned rice lands along the rivers for a distance of thirty miles inland. General Rufus Saxon was appointed Inspector of Settlements and Plantations and placed in charge of the freedmen colonization program. Black families who settled on the land were given "possessory titles" to forty acres of tillable land until Congress could develop a final plan for redistribution. Hundreds of horses, mules, and other livestock confiscated by Union soldiers during the march from Atlanta to Savannah were also turned over to the black settlers.[33]

Among the thousands of black colonists was Reverend Ulysses L. Houston, the pastor of the Third African Baptist Church in Savannah and a future member of the Georgia legislature. He led a thousand black Savannahians to Skidaway Island a few miles southeast of the city, where they controlled and tilled three thousand acres of land. They assigned farming plots, set aside land for a school and church, and laid out plans for an entire city. Houston vowed, "We shall build our cabins and organize our town government." By the end of the summer of 1865, he and his followers had several hundred acres planted in vegetables and cotton, and were confident of a prosperous future. They were among the forty thousand blacks who were established on farms and settlements on the Sherman Reservation. According to a report prepared by the congressional Committee on Reconstruction, this soon-to-end program was considered a success.[34]

Along with their efforts to create educational opportunities and acquire land, Georgia freedmen developed a growing interest in local, state, and national politics. On the first "free" Fourth of July, freedmen around the state participated in large and festive parades that featured speeches by white and black political leaders. In Augusta, Lieutenant Colonel Charles T. Trowbridge and members of the thirty-third United States Colored Troops led a procession of four thousand blacks through the streets of the city. A committee of black ladies presented Trowbridge with three banners that read: "Abraham Lincoln, the father of our liberties and savior of his country"; "Slavery and disunion—dead!"; and "Freedom and equality is our motto." At the conclusion of the procession, Reverend James Lynch, the prominent black Savannah minister, addressed a crowd of more than ten thousand people.

In Savannah, Reverend James Sims, another black minister, delivered an eloquent address to a gathering of blacks and white political organizers associated with the Republican Party. Augustus Longstreet Hull recalled that an Athens parade was "headed by a Negro on horseback with a sash and sword followed by a mixture of ignorant blacks and renegade whites." These early stirrings were little more than a tempest in a teapot compared to the violent and divisive political battles that would soon alter the complexion of Georgia's political landscape. During the more radical phases of

Reconstruction, black demands for the right to vote and hold elective office would intensify and bear fruit with the election of Georgia's first black legislators in 1868.[35]

Throughout 1865 black Georgians possessed only a passing interest in politics—their primary focus continued to revolve around acquiring food, clothing, shelter, education, and land. The freedmen became convinced that the establishment of the Sherman Reservation was the first phase of a much broader federal land redistribution plan that would be implemented during the 1865 Christmas season. Although agents of the Freedman's Bureau tried to dispel the widespread rumor, nothing could dissuade the expectant blacks. Some freedmen decided to take matters into their own hands by forcibly seizing the property of white Georgia landowners. A black man living near Macon presented a piece of paper to a white woman, believing that it gave him title to her farm. Freedmen Arnold Shugg and his followers were removed by federal troops from the Whitehall plantation owned by William Heyward Gibbons, a former Confederate military officer. Abalod Shigg and scores of freedmen also took control of two large plantations along the Savannah River.

One of the immediate outgrowths of this expectation of land redistribution was the refusal of freedmen to enter into work contracts with their former owners. In Washington, D.C., the next year, ex-Confederate Vice President Alexander Stephens would testify before the joint Committee on Reconstruction that the belief that property redistribution was to have occurred at Christmas 1865 severely restricted the signing of work contracts for 1866. He maintained that black Georgians chose not to bind themselves for the following year because they did not want commitments to white planters to interfere with the planting and harvesting of their own farms. Whites, who were accustomed to docile and obedient slaves, were now confronted with a much more assertive and demanding workforce, which in many instances simply refused to work in the cotton fields. An elderly black man expressed the feelings of many:

If ole massa want to grow cotton, let him plant it himself. I'se work for him dese twenty years; done got nothin' but food and clothes; and dem mighty mean; now
I'se Freedman, and I tell you I ain't going to work cotton
no how.[36]

Upper-income white females were especially distressed by their
loss of absolute control over household servants. The wife of General
Howell Cobb exclaimed that she was completely exasperated with
free black labor. In November 1865 Cobb confessed that she was
"hopeless" and "heartless in anything concerning freedmen, or freedmen's labor." She offered a halfhearted boast: "Let us wash our hands
of the eternal negro. The Yankee has taken upon himself the responsibility of ... his ebony idol—let him have it in full." She continued:

I am in purgatory all the week because I presume to
superintend my servants and have my work executed
according to my views. As to having it done in a given
time—that is impossible. Two strong washerwomen are
engaged all the week with my washing and ironing, and a
third one goes out on Saturday. Excepting the dresses,
which Angeline does up, the rest of the washing & iron'g
are not possible—though one woman had five years training as a washerwoman. Oh, the negro will not do for
work . . . —the negro only works by compulsion.[37]

On this issue Southern whites gained willing allies among
Freedmen's Bureau agents and Union military leaders. Although
they were generally sympathetic to the plight of the former slaves,
federal officers had little tolerance for what they considered to be
idle and irresponsible behavior. General Oliver O. Howard directed his agents throughout the South to "quicken the industry of the
Freedmen." In August 1865, Reverend Mansfield French empha-

sized to a gathering of blacks in Albany that "freedom allows you to work, allows you to play, and allows you to starve if you wish." Hoping to encourage blacks to go back to work and squelch the persistent land redistribution rumor in northeast Georgia, General Davis Tillson was summoned from Augusta early in December 1865 to tell a large group of freedmen gathered on the University of Georgia campus the disappointing truth that neither the acreage nor the mule would be forthcoming.[38]

"THERE SHALL HENCEFORTH BE . . . NEITHER SLAVERY NOR INVOLUNTARY SERVITUDE"

Early in June 1865 Confederate Governor Joseph Brown had naively attempted to reestablish civil government in Georgia by summoning the Civil War legislature back into session. He was prevented from doing so by military order, and was promptly placed under arrest by Union authorities, released, and forced to resign the governorship. On June 17 federal officials named James Johnson, a Columbus lawyer, the provisional governor of Georgia. Johnson had opposed secession in 1861 and refused to serve in the Confederate military during the Civil War. He moved quickly to dispel any lingering hopes among white Georgians that slavery could be modified instead of being abolished. Speaking at Macon, the governor declared that Southern secession had been an act of "stupendous folly." During a speech in Savannah Johnson stated that, "slavery . . . is gone and gone forever and I have no tears to shed or lamentations to make over its departure." On July 13 he issued a proclamation calling for the election of delegates to a state convention to be convened on October 4, 1865, that would have the responsibility of officially repealing the ordinance of secession and amending the Georgia Constitution to abolish slavery. All eligible voters and delegates were required to take an oath of loyalty to the United States of America prior to their participation in the election. In October nearly three hundred delegates assembled in Milledgeville at the state capitol. Without debate or dissent, the convention unanimously voted to repeal, but not nullify, the secession ordinance of January 18, 1861. The delegates attempted to acquiesce to the superior will of the federal government while still preserving the notion that the various states possessed the constitutional right to secede from the Union.[39]

The repeal of the secession ordinance took less than two minutes, while the motion to officially abolish slavery in Georgia took even less time. According to historian Alan Conway, "further resistance at this point was as feeble as the light from the flickering candle held in the hand of the clerk by which the clause was read and accepted." Article 1, Section 20 of the new constitution read:

> The government of the United States having, as a war measure, proclaimed all slaves held or owned in this State emancipated from slavery, and having carried that proclamation into full practical effect, there shall henceforth be, within the State of Georgia, neither slavery nor involuntary servitude, save as punishment for crime, after legal conviction thereof. Provided, this acquiescence in the action of the government of the United States is not intended to operate as a relinquishment, waiver or estoppel of such claim for compensation of loss sustained by reason of the emancipation of his slaves, as any citizen of Georgia may hereafter make upon the justice and magnanimity of that government.[40]

Conway noted that the lack of debate over this particular amendment did not reflect "any fundamental belief in the desirability of abolition" but rather a resignation that obedience to the federal mandate was nonnegotiable. The most instructive language in the article was the qualifying provision that expressed a hope that the federal government would provide some form of compensation to former slave owners, similar to the compensated emancipation adopted by Britain in 1833. This bit of recalcitrance on behalf of the delegates portended the racially divisive period that would follow during the more radical congressional Reconstruction period.[41]

The convention adjourned and Charles J. Jenkins, a lawyer from Richmond County, was elected governor in November 1865. The Georgia legislature convened on December 4 in Milledgeville and quickly elected a congressional delegation that included U.S. Senator-elect Alexander H. Stephens, the former vice president of the Confederacy. However, the primary responsibility of the legislature was to implement President Andrew Johnson's plan for Southern Reconstruction. The first requirement was ratification of the Thirteenth Amendment to the United States Constitution that abolished slavery. Although there was underlying resentment, Governor Jenkins warned the legislators that Georgia could not revive slavery even if the majority voted to do so. He optimistically declared that "the ratification of this amendment . . . will remove from among us that cause of bitterness and sectional strife which has wasted our property and deluged our land in blood." Blind allegiance to the principle of "states' rights" led a few legislators to offer an amendment stating that the state of Georgia, not Congress, possessed the power of emancipation. This ill-conceived effort was quickly voted down. Over December 5-6, 1865, the Georgia legislature adopted the Thirteenth Amendment that officially abolished slavery in the United States of America.[42]

Governor Jenkins was inaugurated on December 14, 1865, and he urged the legislators to enact legislation that would establish a limited set of rights for Georgia freedmen. Jenkins tried to assuage the collective conscience of the group by asserting that black slaves had actually benefited from bondage because they had been "raised immeasurably above the contemporary African by a system which lightly taxed his physical energies and supplied all his needs from cradle to grave." He argued, somewhat disingenuously, that Georgia slaves had remained loyal during the war and behaved extremely well since their emancipation. He urged the legislators to grant blacks the right to protect their person and property. The governor also declared that the General Assembly should do everything in its power to ensure that black Georgians would never adopt the "fatal delusion of social and political equality" and more importantly, "the necessity of subordination and dependence should be riveted on their convictions." [43]

Former Governor Brown also urged the legislators to grant the freedmen a limited set of civil rights. He reiterated his belief that God had not created whites and blacks equally, that blacks were inferior both intellectually and socially and "unless madness rules the hour...will never be placed upon a basis of political equality with us . . . [because] they are not competent to the task of self-government, much less to aid in governing a great nation of white people." Heeding the advice of Johnson and Brown, the legislature proceeded to pass a series of eleven laws that formed the basis of Georgia's Black Codes. The code contained a vagrancy law with heavy penalties, including prohibitions against "enticing" laborers. Limited civil rights were established, giving blacks the right to testify in court, but only in cases involving other blacks. Every black child born after the passage of the statute was declared to be the legitimate child of his mother and his black father, if the father acknowledged the child. Although Alexander Stephens suggested that the right to vote should be extended to blacks "after they had reached a certain cultural standard and acquired an amount of wealth," the legislators unanimously voted against extending the right to vote and hold public office to black Georgians. Relatively speaking, Georgia's black codes were not as draconian as similar

statutes passed in neighboring Southern states. However, the legislation banished black Georgians to "political oblivion, social inferiority, and superficial legal equality." As soon as this work was completed, the General Assembly adjourned *sine die* and the legislators
rushed back to their homes to protect their families and possessions
during what many predicted would be an all-out race war.[44]

As Christmas 1865 neared, black freedmen remained convinced that land owned by ex-Confederates would be redistributed
to them. White Georgians were concerned that once the blacks
realized that redistribution would not take place, the enraged
freedmen would resort to pillage and bloodshed. Throughout the
state, fearful whites increased internal security and prepared to
defend themselves. Lumpkin County residents established a "pat-
role company" to ensure that black residents were keep under
close scrutiny. This was also true in Macon, where white men conducted around-the-clock patrols on the roads leading to the city.
Columbus imposed a 9:30 P.M. curfew from December 24 through
January 2, 1866. In Athens, so-called "reliable" blacks confessed
that a rebellion was planned. This information was buttressed by
the fact that local freedmen were buying an unusual number of
pistols and revolvers. Local officials were warned to "keep a sharp
lookout" and the town council added twenty extra policemen to
the regular force of four men. Some blacks near Watkinsville were
arrested and jailed in Athens for allegedly helping to plan the rebellion. In Augusta, the local paper editorialized that local blacks
should be removed to rural areas because, if they were allowed to
remain inside the city limits during the Christmas season, it would
"be difficult to maintain Order." [45]

However, the much discussed slave insurrections failed to materialize, and Christmas 1865 was a quiet, uneventful season throughout Georgia. Holiday celebrations were marred only by the suspicions and prejudices that defined race relations between blacks and
whites. As the eventful year came to a close, the unbridled joy that

accompanied emancipation began to subside as freedmen faced the sobering realities of postslavery existence. Racked by disease, ravaged by poverty, and scorned by the great majority of white Georgians, the former slaves discovered that emancipation had not brought an end to their many troubles. They still faced the monumental task of having to build a free culture and society with the splintered blocks of American slavery. Tens of thousands of children and adults would have to be educated, scattered families reunited, churches organized, and the physical, emotional, and psychological wounds of bondage would somehow have to be healed. But regardless of the challenges and uncertainties that clouded their future, black Georgians were free—their long-prayed-for Jubilee had finally arrived.

EPILOGUE

In the summer of 1865, Susie King Taylor and her first husband, Sergeant Edward King, returned to Savannah. Although Taylor was born into slavery in 1849, her ambitious grandmother had arranged for her to receive a basic education at one of Savannah's clandestine schools for free and enslaved children. During the early stages of the Civil War, Taylor and several members of her family escaped to Union-occupied St. Simons Island. They were subsequently transported to Fort Saxon in Beaufort, South Carolina, where she served as nurse, teamster, laundress, and teacher to the First South Carolina Volunteers, America's first black military regiment. In 1862 Taylor married King, a member of that historic regiment, and after the war they returned to the city of her birth, where she opened a school for freed slaves in her home.

Taylor earned a modest living by charging the parents of her twenty pupils one dollar a month in tuition. This income was supplemented by fees generated by offering night classes to black adults who wanted to learn the rudiments of reading, writing, and arithmetic. In her memoirs, she recalled that her little school was located on a narrow tree-lined street in Savannah named Oglethorpe Avenue.

Taylor may or may not have known that this particular street had been renamed to honor General James Edward Oglethorpe, Georgia's founding father and a vocal critic of Negro slavery. Could she have been aware that Oglethorpe had waged a courageous battle to prohibit the importation of slaves into the colony? Did she know Oglethorpe repeatedly warned Georgia colonists that slavery would ultimately lead to their moral and economic ruin? Unfortunately, the historical record is silent on these points. Yet much can be gleaned from the fact that the disparate historical paths of Oglethorpe and Taylor intersected on this quiet street in Georgia's oldest city at a unique moment in American history.

By the summer of 1865, Oglethorpe had been resting in his crypt in Cranham, England, for approximately eight decades. One could easily imagine, however, that if he had been alive, the old general would have been pleased that slavery no longer blighted the Georgia landscape. No doubt he would have savored the sweet irony of knowing that former Georgia slaves were attending a school located on a street named in his honor. Still, the devastation that marked the path of Sherman's marauding army would have tempered his joy with a deep sense of loss and bitter disappointment. One can easily envision a heavy-hearted Oglethorpe surveying the ruins of Georgia cities and abandoned plantations, ruminating over the fact that his impassioned antislavery appeals had fallen on deaf ears.

By the summer of 1865, more than 130 years had passed since Oglethorpe first warned Georgia colonists that Negro slavery would inevitably lead to military defeat. Decades before Union soldiers and liberated blacks marched triumphantly through the state, this impassioned founding father declared that the presence of slaves would undermine and weaken the colony's military defenses. One hundred and thirty years before enslaved blacks cast down their hoes and shouldered Union rifles, Oglethorpe argued that black bondsmen would readily ally themselves with the enemies of their former masters. Long before poor, white, nonslaveholding Confederate soldiers complained that the Civil War was a "rich man's war and a poor man's fight," he had predicted that, in times of war, slave owners would avoid military service in order to protect their financial investment in slaves.

By the summer of 1865, Abraham Lincoln, the martyred commander in chief, had already become an American icon. In his second inaugural address, delivered only a few weeks before his assassination on April 15, he had professed that God had brought a "terrible war" to afflict the North and South as punishment for their complicity in prosecuting the "offence" of slavery. The president pledged that the Civil War would continue, even if it resulted in the destruction of all the wealth accumulated by "the bond-man's two hundred and fifty years of unrequited toil." His convictions were based on the belief that the "judgments of the Lord are true and righteous altogether."

Lincoln's words were reminiscent of the apocalyptic themes incorporated in a January 1739 antislavery petition that was endorsed, and possibly written, by Oglethorpe. The petition was "the first protest against the use of Africans as slaves, issued in the history of the New World." The petitioners asserted that sentencing "any race to perpetual Slavery was a sin shocking to human Nature." Oglethorpe and his antislavery supporters prophesied that slavery was the divinely inspired "Scourge" that would be used to punish the traffickers of human flesh.

By the summer of 1865, Oglethorpe's original vision of a slave-free Georgia had become a permanent reality. If he had been alive, he would probably have agreed with Lincoln's assessment that the Civil War had changed America in "fundamental and astounding" ways. No one appreciated this miraculous wartime transformation more than Susie King Taylor. She jubilantly proclaimed that the war had been "a wonderful revolution!" and observed that, "In 1860 the

Southern newspapers were full of advertisements for slaves, but now, despite all hindrances, my people are striving to attain the full standard of all other races born free in the sight of God."

Yet Taylor also realized that emancipation did not guarantee citizenship—the abolition of slavery heralded the beginning of another protracted struggle to achieve "the full standard" of civil and political rights. The succeeding post-slavery struggle would be led over the years by such people as Frederick Douglass, Booker T. Washington, W. E. B. Du Bois, Marcus Garvey, Mary Mcleod Bethune, A. Phillip Randolph, Malcolm X, and, during its climactic stages, by a charismatic young minister named Martin Luther King Jr. Susie King Taylor posed the question that would perplex these leaders and generations of black and white Americans: What do Negroes want? This not-yet-fully-answered question still haunts the descendants of those who made the fateful journey from slavery to freedom.

In the concluding paragraphs of her memoirs, Taylor weighed in on this question with an eloquent and concise explanation of the needs and dreams of her people. Forthrightly, with resolution, and without equivocation, she asserted that African Americans must be granted nothing less than equal "Justice." She added, "We ask—to be citizens of these United States, where so many of our people have shed their blood with their white comrades." And in conclusion, this brave woman, who had heard the celestial trumpets and witnessed the Dawning of the Jubilee, revealed that her most fervent desire for her country was "that the stars and stripes should never be polluted."

ENDNOTES

CHAPTER I
GEORGIA'S ANTISLAVERY HERITAGE

(1) Betty Wood, *Slavery in Colonial Georgia, 1730-1775* (Athens: University of Georgia Press, 1984), 5; Benjamin Martyn, *Reasons for Establishing the Colony of Georgia in America* (London: W. Meadows, 1733), 30; H. B. Fant, "The Labor Policy of the Trustees," *Georgia Historical Quarterly* 16 (1), 1-3; Phinizy Spalding, foreword to *The Publications of James Edward Oglethorpe,* Rodney M. Baine, ed. (Athens: University of Georgia Press, 1994).

(2) Phinizy Spalding and Harvey H. Jackson, eds., *Oglethorpe in Perspective: Georgia's Founder after Two Hundred Years* (Tuscaloosa: University of Alabama Press, 1989), 71.

(3) Milton Ready, "An Economic History of Colonial Georgia, 1732-1754" (Ph.D. diss., University of Georgia, 1970), 51; Wood, *Colonial Georgia*, 3; Mary Stroughton Locke, *Anti-Slavery in America* (Gloucester: Radcliffe College Monographs Noll, 1965), 11-12.

(4) Darold Duane Wax, "Georgia and the Negro before the American Revolution," *Georgia Historical Quarterly* 51 (1), 67 (March 1967).

(5) Wood, *Colonial Georgia*, 16; James Oglethorpe to the Trustees, August 12, 1733, Egmont Papers, 14200, pt. I, 37-39, University of Georgia Library.

(6) Henry Bruce, *The Life of Oglethorpe* (New York: Dodd, Meade & Company, 1890), 132-138.

(7) Ibid., 132-138; Donald L. Grant, *The Way It Was in the South: The Black Experience in Georgia* (New York: Carol Publishing Group, 1993), 85.

(8) Thomas Bluett, *Some Memoirs of the Life of Job, the Son of Solomon the High Priest of Boonda in Africa* (London, 1734), 32-33.

(9) Ibid.; Grant, *The Black Experience*, 105.

(10) Charles Lwanga Hoskins, *Black Episcopalians in Georgia: Strife, Struggle and Salvation* (Savannah, GA: Self-published, 1980), 61.

(11) Harold E. Davis, *The Fledgling Province: Social and Cultural Life in Colonial Georgia, 1733-1776* (Chapel Hill: University of North Carolina Press, 1976), 149.

(12) Ruth Scarborough, *The Opposition to Slavery in Georgia Prior to 1860* (Nashville: George Peabody College for Teachers, 1933), 69-70.

(13) Wood, *Colonial Georgia*, 66-67; David Taft Morgan Jr., "The Great Awakening in the Carolinas and Georgia, 1740-1775" (Ph.D. diss., University of North Carolina, 1969), 122-124.

(14) Scarborough, *Opposition to Slavery*, 69; Julia Floyd Smith, *Slavery and Rice Culture in Low Country Georgia, 1750-1860* (Knoxville: University of Tennessee Press, 1985), 53.

(15) Allen Candler, ed., *Colonial Records of the State of Georgia*, vol. 1 (Washington, D.C.: National Park Service, United States Department of the Interior, 1942), 50-51.

(16) Mills Lane, ed., *General Oglethorpe's Georgia*, vol. 2 (Savannah: Beehive Press, 1990), "A Petition to the Trustees," December 9, 1738, 371-375; Scarborough, *Opposition to Slavery*, 33.

(17) Oglethorpe to the Trustees, January 17, 1739, *Oglethorpe's Georgia*, ed. Lane, 389; Wood, *Colonial Georgia*, 31.

(18) Wood, *Colonial Georgia*, 30; Charles Spalding Wylly, *The Seed That Was Sown in the Colony of Georgia: The Harvest and the Aftermath* (New York: Neale Publishing Company, 1910), 28-29.

(19) Inhabitants of Ebenezer to James Edward Oglethorpe, March 13, 1739, *Oglethorpe's Georgia*, ed. Lane, 397.

(20) Scarborough, *Opposition to Slavery*, 28, 37; Wylly, *Seed That Was Sown*, 34.

(21) *Publications of Oglethorpe,* ed. Baine, 252.

(22) Ibid.

(23) Ibid.

(24) Kenneth Porter, *The Negro on the American Frontier* (New York: Arno Press, 1971), 168.

(25) *Publications of Oglethorpe,* ed. Baine, 254; Porter, *American Frontier,* 168.

(26) A. Leon Higginbotham Jr., *In the Matter of Color: Race and the American Legal Process: The Colonial Period* (New York: Oxford University Press, 1978), 230; From Hugh Anderson and others to the Trustees, December, 2, 1740, *Oglethorpe's Georgia,* ed. Lane, 491-496.

(27) *Oglethorpe's Georgia,* ed. Lane, 491-496; Edward J. Cashin, *The Story of Augusta* (Spartanburg, SC: Reprint Company, Publishers, 1991), 12.

(28) Ready, "Economic History," 267.

(29) Higginbottom, *Matter of Color,* 231-232.

(30) Ibid.

(31) *Publications of Oglethorpe,* ed. Baine, 253.

(32) Jane Landers, *Fort Mose: Gracia Real de Santa Teresa de Mose: A Free Black Town in Spanish Colonial Florida* (St. Augustine, FL: St. Augustine Historical Society, 1992), 15-16; Porter, *American Frontier,* 102.

(33) Landers, *Fort Mose,* 19.

(34) Buddy Sullivan, *Early Days on the Georgia Tidewater: The Story of McIntosh County & Sapelo* (Darien, GA: McIntosh County Board of Commissioners, 1990), 25.

(35) Sullivan, *Georgia Tidewater,* 25.

(36) Huge McCall, *The History of Georgia: Containing Brief Sketches of the Most Remarkable Events up to the Present Day* (Atlanta: A. B. Caldwell, reprint 1909), 104-105; Marion Ernestine Anthony, "The Unindexed Official Record of the Negro in Georgia, 1733-1766," (M.A. thesis, Atlanta University, 1937), 47.

(37) Anthony, "Negro in Georgia," 47.

(38) Porter, *American Frontier,* 170.

(39) Ibid., 172.

(40) Kenneth Coleman, gen. ed., *A History of Georgia* (Athens: University of Georgia Press, 1977), 33.

(41) Scarborough, *Opposition to Slavery*, 47.

(42) Wood, *Colonial Georgia*, 73.

(43) Lewis G. Jordan, *Negro Baptist History, U.S.A.* (Nashville: Sunday School Publishing Board, N.B.C., 1930), 2.

(44) Wood, *Colonial Georgia*, 143, 163.

(45) Ibid., 163.

(46) James B. Lawrence, "Religious Education of the Negro in the Colony of Georgia," *Georgia Historical Quarterly* 14 (1), 51 (March 1930); C. Duncan Rice, *The Rise and Fall of Black Slavery* (New York: Harper & Row, 1975), 143.

(47) Wood, *Colonial Georgia*, 160.

(48) Lawrence, "Religious Education," 54.

(49) Ibid., 44 –54.

(50) Wood, *Colonial Georgia*, 118.

(51) Ibid., 119.

(52) Ibid.

(53) Anthony, "Negro in Georgia," 48.

(54) *Georgia Gazette*, April 1763.

(55) Scarborough, *Opposition to Slavery*, 62.

(56) Ibid., 62-63.

(57) Ibid., 63.

(58) Phinizy Spalding, foreword to *Publications of Oglethorpe*, ed. Baine.

CHAPTER II
BLACK GEORGIA DURING
THE REVOLUTIONARY WAR ERA

(1) John Hope Franklin, *From Slavery to Freedom: A History of Negro Americans*, 5th ed. (New York: Alfred A. Knopf, 1980), 83.

(2) Benjamin Quarles, preface to *The Negro in the American Revolution* (New York: W. W. Norton & Company, 1961).

(3) W. E. Burghardt Du Bois, *The Suppression of the African Slave-Trade to the*

United States of America, 1638-1870 (New York: Social Science Press, 1954), 45.

(4) Ibid.

(5) Peter Force, *American Archives* (New York: Johnson Reprint Corporation, 1972), 6th ser., 279-281.

(6) Ibid.

(7) Du Bois, *Suppression of the Slave-Trade*, 46.

(8) Cornel Lengyel, *Four Days in July* (Garden City, NY: Doubleday Company, 1958), 174.

(9) Franklin, *Slavery to Freedom*, 84; Du Bois, *Suppression of the Slave-Trade*, 49; Lengyel, *Four Days*, 176.

(10) Candler, *Colonial Records of Georgia*, vol. 1, 50.

(11) Ibid.

(12) Sylvia Frey, *Water From the Rock: Black Resistance in a Revolutionary Age* (Princeton: Princeton University Press, 1991), 86-87; Joseph T. Wilson, *The Black Phalanx: African American Soldiers in the War of Independence, the War of 1812 and the Civil War* (New York: Da Capo Press, 1994), 22.

(13) U. B. Phillips, *American Negro Slavery: A Survey of the Supply, Employment and Control of Negro Labor as Determined by the Plantation Regime* (Baton Rouge: Louisiana State University Press, 1918), 123-125; James St. G. Walker, *The Black Loyalist: The Search for a Promised Land in Nova Scotia and Sierra Leone, 1783–1870* (New York: African Publishing Company, 1976), 5.

(14) Phillips, *American Negro Slavery*, 5.

(15) Carter G. Woodson, ed., "Letters Showing the Rise and Progress of the Early Negro Churches of Georgia and the West Indies," *Journal of Negro History* 1 (1916), 70-71.

(16) Mechal Sobel, *Trabelin' On: The Slave Journey to an Afro Baptist Faith* (Princeton: Princeton University Press, 1979), 105-106; Reverend Edward L. Ellis Jr., "Bicentennial Celebration: Historic First Bryan Baptist Church" (Savannah, 1988, church program); Reverend Thurmond Tillman, "The First African Baptist Church History" (Savannah, 1989, church program).

(17) Walter H. Brooks, *The Silver Bluff Church: A History of Negro Baptist Churches in America* (Washington, D.C.: Press of R. L. Pendleton, 1910), 7; Reverend Emmett T. Martin, "History Book: Springfield Baptist Church, 1787-1979" (Augusta, 1979, church program).

(18) Quarles, *American Revolution,* 154; Walker, *The Black Loyalists,* 5.

(19) George Livermore, *Opinions of the Founders of the Republic on Negroes as Slaves, as Citizens, and as Soldiers* (Boston: A. Williams & Company, 1863), 91.

(20) Jack D. Foner, *Blacks and the Military in American History* (New York: Praeger Publishers, 1974), 12.

(21) George H. Moore, *Historical Notes on the Employment of Negroes in the American Army of the Revolution* (New York: C. T. Evans, 1862), 11; Foner, *Blacks and the Military,* 12; Morris J. MacGregor and Barnard C. Nalty, eds., *Blacks in the United States Armed Forces: Basic Documents* (Wilmington, DE: Scholarly Resources, 1981), 49.

(22) Moore, *Historical Notes,* 8-9.

(23) Livermore, *Opinions of the Founders,* 139; Phillips, *American Negro Slavery,* 125.

(24) Moore, *Historical Notes,* 14.

(25) Herbert Aptheker, *To Be Free* (New York: First Carol Publishing Group, 1991), 38.

(26) George Gilmer, *Sketches of some of the First Settlers of Upper Georgia* (Americus, GA: Americus Book Company, 1926), 165.

(27) Alton Hornsby Jr., *The Negro In Revolutionary Georgia* (Atlanta: Georgia Commission for the National Bicentennial Celebration and Georgia Department of Education, 1977), 10.

(28) Candler, *Colonial Records of Georgia,* 1786 Statute.

(29) Hornsby, *Revolutionary Georgia,* 10.

(30) Acts of South Carolina Assembly, October 15, 1776; Force, *American Archives,* 5th Series, III, 68.

(31) Candler, *Colonial Records of Georgia,* 80-86.

(32) Melvin Drimmer, *Black History: A Reappraisal* (Garden City, NY: Doubleday & Company, 1968), 141; Kenneth Coleman, *The American Revolution in Georgia, 1763-1789* (Athens: University of Georgia Press,

1958), 145-146.

(33) Peter M. Bergman and Jean McCarroll, *Negro in the Congressional Record, 1789-1801* (New York: Bergman, 1969), 86-123.

(34) Cashin, *Story of Augusta,* 13-14.

(35) Aptheker, *To Be Free,* 13.

(36) Grant, *The Black Experience,* 19; Sidney Kaplan and Emma Nogrady Kaplan, *The Black Presence in the Era of the American Revolution* (Amherst: University of Massachusetts Press, 1989), 85.

(37) Kaplan and Kaplan, *Black Presence,* 85.

(38) Christopher Collier and James Collier, *Decision in Philadelphia: The Constitutional Convention of 1787* (New York: Ballantine Press, 1986), 185.

(39) Merton L. Dillon, *Slavery Attacked: Southern Slaves and Their Allies, 1619-1865* (Baton Rouge: Louisiana State University Press, 1990), 40.

(40) J. David Griffin, *Georgia and the United States Constitution, 1787-1789* (Atlanta: Georgia Commission for the National Bicentennial Celebration and the Georgia Department of Education, 1977), 10.

(41) Paul Finkelman, "A Covenant with Death," *American Visions* (May-June 1986), pt. 1, 25.

(42) Ibid.

(43) Collier and Collier, *Decision in Philadelphia*, 202.

(44) Ibid., 216.

(45) Ralph Ketcham, ed., *The Anti-Federalist Papers and the Constitutional Convention Debates* (New York: New American Library, A Mentor Book, 1986), 160.

(46) Catherine Drinker Bowen, *Miracle at Philadelphia: The Story of the Constitutional Convention: May to September 1787* (Boston: Little, Brown & Company, 1966), 201.

(47) Ibid., 202-204.

(48) Ketcham, *Anti-Federalist Papers*, 162; Bowen, *Miracle at Philadelphia*, 203.

(49) Du Bois, *Suppression of the Slave-Trade*, 56; Ketcham, *Anti-Federalists Papers*, 163.

(50) Ketcham, *Anti-Federalists Papers*, 163-164; Bowen, *Miracle at Philadelphia*, 203-204.

(51) Bowen, *Miracle at Philadelphia*, 204.

(52) Finkelman, "A Covenant with Death," 31.

(53) Drimmer, *A Reappraisal*, 128; Finkelman, "A Covenant with Death," 29.

(54) Finkelman, "A Covenant with Death," 29.

CHAPTER III
THE WAR OF 1812 AND THE
EMANCIPATION OF GEORGIA SLAVES

(1) Mary Bullard's *Black Liberation on Cumberland Island in 1815* (South Dartmouth, MA: M. R. Bullard, 1983) stands alone as the most comprehensive treatment of the British occupation of Cumberland Island and the evacuation of fugitive coastal Georgia slaves during the War of 1812.

(2) Ibid., 70-71.

(3) Ibid., 57, 71.

(4) Ibid., 69.

(5) Ibid.

(6) Caroline Couper Lovell, *The Golden Isles of Georgia* (Boston: Little, Brown & Company, 1932), 104; Wylly, *Seed That Was Sown,* 52.

(7) Bullard, *Black Liberation*, 76.

(8) Ibid., 122-123.

(9) Ibid., 92.

(10) Ibid., 102.

(11) Ibid., 113.

(12) Ibid., 115.

(13) Lucius Q. Lamar, *A Compilation of the Laws of the State of Georgia Passed by the Legislature since the year 1810 to the year 1819* (Augusta: T. S. Hannon, 1822), Act No. 508, December 19, 1816, 804.

(14) Ibid., 95.

(15) William Renwick Riddell, "Slavery in Canada," *Journal of Negro History* 5 (3), 373-375 (July 1920); John K. Mahon, *The War of 1812*

(Gainesville: University of Florida Press, 1972), 370-371.

CHAPTER IV
RED AND BLACK:
ALLIES ON THE GEORGIA FRONTIER

(1) Joseph A. Qpala, *A Brief History of the Seminole Freedmen* (Austin: African and Afro-American Studies and Research Center, University of Texas at Austin, 1980), 3; William G. McLoughlin, "Red Indians, Black Slavery and White Racism: America's Slaveholding Indians," *American Quarterly* 26 (October 1974), 370.

(2) Joshua R. Giddings, *The Exiles of Florida or The crimes committed by our government against the maroons, who fled from South Carolina and other slave states, seeking protection under Spanish laws* (Baltimore: Black Classic Press, 1997), 4.

(3) William Haynes Simmons, *Notices of East Florida* (Gainesville: University of Florida Press, 1973), 76; J. Leitch Wright, *The Only Land They Knew: American Indians in the Old South* (Lincoln: University of Nebraska Press, 1999), 12.

(4) Kevin Mulroy, *Freedom on the Border: Seminole Maroons in Florida, the Indian Territory, Coahuila, and Texas* (Lubbock, TX: Texas Tech University Press, 1993), 18.

(5) Giddings, *Exiles of Florida*, 29.

(6) Qpala, *Seminole Freedmen*, 6.

(7) Virginia Berman Peters, *The Florida Wars* (Hamden, CT: Archon Books, 1979), 40-41.

(8) Aptheker, *To Be Free*, 16; Qpala, *Seminole Freedmen*, 4.

(9) Kenneth Porter, *The Black Seminoles: History of a Freedom-Seeking People* (Gainesville: University Press of Florida, 1996), 191. Mr. Porter is without peer among those who have researched and written about the unique culture and history of the Negro-Seminoles.

(10) Ibid., 197-198.

(11) Peters, *Florida Wars,* 40.

(12) Porter, *Black Seminoles*, 198.

(13) Peters, *Florida Wars*, 22-23.

(14) Ibid., 25.

(15) Ibid., 26.

(16) Porter, *Black Seminoles*, 224.

(17) Ibid., 226.

(18) Giddings, *Exiles of Florida*, 53; Peters, *Florida Wars*, 53.

(19) Aptheker, *To Be Free*, 26; Porter, *Black Seminoles*, 238.

(20) Porter, *Black Seminoles*, 244; Peters, *Florida Wars*, 136.

(21) Porter, *Black Seminoles*, 238-245; Aptheker, *To Be Free*, 26.

(22) Qpala, *Seminole Freedmen*, 10; Porter, *Black Seminoles*, 248.

(23) Porter, *Black Seminoles*, 249.

(24) Ibid., 277.

(25) Qpala, *Seminole Freedmen*, 10; Porter, *Black Seminoles*, 256.

CHAPTER V
FREE BLACK GEORGIANS: BETWEEN SLAVERY AND CITIZENSHIP

(1) Scarborough, *Opposition to Slavery,* 192.

(2) Woodson, ed., "Rise and Progress of Early Negro Churches," 69-87; Aptheker, *To Be Free,* 31.

(3) Helen Ungar, "Free Negroes in Ante-Bellum Georgia," (M.A. thesis, University of Georgia, 1949), 2. Although Ungar's thesis is helpful, research concerning free black Georgians during the slavery era is limited and the topic is ripe for additional study by students and historians.

(4) Scarborough, *Opposition to Slavery*, 129.

(5) Ibid.

(6) Aptheker, *To Be Free*, 31.

(7) U. B. Phillips, ed., *Plantation and Frontier Documents* (Cleveland: A. H. Clark Company, 1909), 41. Letter Dated 1854.

(8) Ira Berlin, *Slaves without Masters: The Free Negro in the Antebellum South* (New York: Pantheon Books, 1974), 48.

(9) Scarborough, *Opposition to Slavery*, 138; Ralph B. Flanders, "The Free Negro in Antebellum Georgia," *North Carolina Historical Review* 9 (January-October 1932), 258.

(10) Flanders, "The Free Negro," 260.

(11) Ibid.

(12) Ibid.

(13) Ibid.

(14) Ibid., 254.

(15) Ibid., 255

(16) *Bryan v. Walton*, 14 GA 185, 202 (1853).

(17) *Cleland v. Waters*, 16 GA 496, 520 (1855).

(18) Ibid.

(19) Ibid.

(20) Flanders, "The Free Negro," 256.

(21) Woodson, "Rise and Progress of Early Negro Churches," 77-78.

(22) Ibid., 78.

(23) Carter G. Woodson, ed., "Free Negro Owners of Slaves in the United States in 1830," *Journal of Negro History* 9 (1924), 40-41.

(24) Aptheker, *To Be Free,* 38-39.

(25) Woodson, "Rise and Progress of Early Negro Churches," 86-87.

(26) Clarence M. Wagner, *Profiles of Black Georgia Baptists* (Gainesville, GA: Bennett Brothers Printing Company, 1980), 14-16.

(27) Whittington B. Johnson, "Free Blacks in Antebellum Savannah: An Economic Profile," *Georgia Historical Quarterly* 64 (4), 424-425 (Spring 1980).

(28) Whittington B. Johnson, "Free African-American Women in Savannah, 1880-1860: Affluence and Autonomy amid Adversity," *Georgia Historical Quarterly* 76 (2), 266-267 (Summer 1992).

(29) Ibid., 267, 270.

(30) Ibid., 265.

(31) Johnson, "Free Blacks in Savannah," 422.

(32) Flanders, "Free Negro in Ante-Bellum Georgia," 267.

(33) Donnie D. Bellamy, "The Legal Status of Black Georgians During the Colonial and Revolutionary Eras," *Journal of Negro History* 74 (Winter-Autumn 1989), 6.

(34) Susie King Taylor, *A Black Woman's Civil War Memoirs* (Princeton: Markus Wiener Publishers, 1994), 29-30.

(35) Johnson, "Free African-American Women," 278-279.

(36) Early Lee Fox, *The American Colonization Society, 1817-1840* (Baltimore: Johns Hopkins Press, 1919), 47.

(37) F. N. Boney, *A Pictorial History: The University of Georgia* (Athens: University of Georgia Press, 1984), 14. For a more in-depth analysis of Robert Finley's ideas regarding African colonization, see Robert Finley, *Thoughts on the Colonization of Free Blacks* (Washington, D.C.: s.n., 1816), I-8.

(38) Fox, *American Colonization Society*, 57-58.

(39) William C. Dawson, *A Compilation of the Laws of the State of Georgia* (Milledgeville, GA: Grantland & Orme, 1831), Resolutions, 84.

(40) Fox, *American Colonization Society*, 129.

(41) Scarborough, *Opposition to Slavery*, 198; American Colonization Society, *The African Repository and Georgia Journal* (New York: Kraus Reprint Corporation, 1967), vol. 3, 370.

(42) Scarborough, *Opposition to Slavery*, 207-208; 23 GA 448.

(43) James M. Gifford, "Emily Tubman and the African Colonization Movement in Georgia," Georgia Historical Quarterly 61 (1), 12 (Spring 1975).

(44) Ibid., 10.

(45) Ibid., 18-19.

(46) Ibid.

(47) Scarborough, *Opposition to Slavery*, 214; American Colonization Society, *African Repository*, vol. 9, 316.

CHAPTER VI
A WHITE MAN'S WAR

(1) James M. McPherson, *The Negro's Civil War: How American Negroes Felt and Acted During the War for the Union* (New York: Pantheon Books, 1965), 19-26; David W. Blight, *Frederick Douglass' Civil War: Keeping Faith in Jubilee* (Baton Rouge: Louisiana State University Press, 1989), 149.

(2) McPherson, *Negro's Civil War*, 23.

(3) Ibid., 161-162; Blight, *Douglass' Civil War*, 149.

(4) McPherson, *Negro's Civil War*, 61; Benjamin Quarles, *Lincoln and the Negro* (New York: Oxford University Press, 1962), 154.

(5) Edmund L. Drago, "How Sherman's March Through Georgia Affected the Slaves," *Georgia Historical Quarterly* 57 (3), 362 (1973).

(6) Taylor, *Civil War Memoirs,* 32.

(7) Clarence L. Mohr, *On the Threshold of Freedom: Masters and Slaves in Civil War Georgia* (Athens: University of Georgia Press, 1986), 75.

(8) Ibid.

(9) Ibid.

(10) Ibid., 74.

(11) Ibid.

(12) Ibid., 78.

(13) Ibid.,77.

(14) Ibid.

(15) Ibid.

(16) Ibid., 85.

(17) McPherson, *Negro's Civil War*, 163-164.

(18) Dudley Taylor Cornish, *The Sable Arm: Black Troops in the Union Army, 1861-1865* (Lawrence, KS: University of Kansas Press, 1956), 40-41.

(19) Ibid., 40-42.

(20) Ibid., 45.

(21) Ibid., 55.

(22) *The New South* (Port Royal, SC), September 13, 1862.

(23) Benjamin Quarles, *The Negro in the Civil War* (New York: Da Capo Press,

1953), 113.

(24) Spencer B. King Jr., *Darien: The Death and Rebirth of a Southern Town* (Macon, GA: Mercer University Press, 1981), 35.

(25) Quarles, *Negro in the Civil War*, 127.

(26) Ibid.,135.

CHAPTER VII
BLACK SOLDIERS AND THE DAWNING
OF THE JUBILEE

(1) King, *Darien,* 37.

(2) Cornish, *Sable Arm,* 86.

(3) Mohr, *Threshold of Freedom,* 79.

(4) Ibid.; Cornish, *Sable Arm,* 86; Quarles, *Negro in the Civil War*, 119.

(5) Cornish, *Sable Arm,* 35.

(6) Thomas Wentworth Higginson, *Army Life in a Black Regiment* (New York: W. W. Norton & Company, 1984), 97-98.

(7) Cornish, *Sable Arm,* 136.

(8) Charles Edmund Vetter, *Sherman: Merchant of Terror, Advocate of Peace* (Gretna, LA: Pelican Publishing Company, 1992). Vetter offers a detailed analysis of Sherman's controversial philosophy of "total warfare" and his desire to punish Southerners for their collective "war guilt."

(9) Quarles, *Negro in the Civil War*, 12.

(10) Ibid., 64.

(11) *Official Records of the Union and Confederate Navies in the War of the Rebellion,* vol. 14 (Washington, D.C.: U.S. Government Printing Office, 1894–1927), 462.

(12) Ibid., 466-467; Sullivan, *Georgia Tidewater,* footnote 12.

(13) King, *Darien,* 67.

(14) Ibid., 68; Cornish, *Sable Arm,* 149.

(15) Noah Andre Trudeau, *Like Men of War: Black Troops in the Civil War, 1862-1865* (Boston: Little, Brown & Company, 1998), 73; King, *Darien,* 69.

(16) *Savannah Daily Morning News*, June 16, 1863.

(17) Ibid.; Sullivan, *Georgia Tidewater*, footnote 27.

(18) E. Merton Coulter, *Thomas Spalding of Sapelo* (Baton Rouge: Louisiana State University Press, 1940), 371.

(19) Burke Davis, *Sherman's March* (New York: Vintage Books, 1980), 20.

(20) Ibid., 21.

(21) Ibid.

(22) William Tecumseh Sherman, *Memoirs of General W. T. Sherman* (New York: The Library of America, 1990), 656. General Sherman's *Memoirs* is a must-read for those interested in an eyewitness account of the liberation of Georgia slaves during the March to the Sea. B. Davis, *Sherman's March*, 23.

(23) B. Davis, *Sherman's March*, 28; Sherman, *Memoirs*, 656-657.

(24) Sherman, *Memoirs*, 32; Ibid., 657.

(25) Ibid.; Ibid.

(26) Ibid.; Ibid.

(27) Drago, "Sherman's March Through Georgia," 363.

(28) B. Davis, *Sherman's March*, 45-46.

(29) Drago, "Sherman's March Through Georgia," 363.

(30) Ibid.

(31) B. Davis, *Sherman's March*, 46.

(32) Ibid., 47; James Leggette Owens, "The Negro in Georgia During Reconstruction, 1864-1872: A Social History," (Ph.D. diss., University of Georgia, 1975), 14.

(33) Drago, "Sherman's March Through Georgia," 364-365.

(34) Ibid., 365.

(35) B. Davis, *Sherman's March*, 139.

(36) Ibid., 46.

(37) Ibid., 87.

(38) Drago, "Sherman's March Through Georgia," 366; Mohr, *Threshold of Freedom*, 90.

(39) B. Davis, *Sherman's March*, 46.

(40) Ibid., 49.

(41) Ibid.

(42) Sherman, *Memoirs*, 662.

(43) B. Davis, *Sherman's March*, 58.

(44) Ibid., 60.

(45) Sherman, *Memoirs*, 664.

(46) B. Davis, *Sherman's March*, 63.

(47) Ibid., 63-64.

(48) Ibid., 64-65.

(49) Ibid., 67.

(50) Webb Garrison, "Sudden Death at Ebenezer Creek," *Georgia Journal* (Spring 1995), 33.

(51) B. Davis, *Sherman's March*, 92.

(52) Ibid., 92-93.

(53) Drago, "Sherman's March Through Georgia," 370.

(54) B. Davis, *Sherman's March*, 93-94.

(55) Ibid.

(56) William A. Byrne, "'Uncle Billy' Sherman Comes to Town: The Free Winter of Black Savannah," *Georgia Historical Quarterly* 79 (1), 91 (Spring 1995).

(57) Ibid., 91-92, 97, 105.

(58) Ibid., 91-93.

(59) Sherman, *Memoirs*, 728; B. Davis, *Sherman's March*, 131.

(60) B. Davis, *Sherman's March*, 131-132.

(61) Ibid., 136.

(62) Josef C. James, "Sherman at Savannah," *Journal of Negro History* 39: 1/4 (January/October 1954), 127-128.

(63) Sherman, *Memoirs*, 725-726.

(64) Ibid., 726-727.

(65) Byrne, "'Uncle Billy' Sherman," 106; Sherman, *Memoirs*, 726.

(66) Sherman, *Memoirs*, 726.

(67) Ibid.

(68) B. Davis, *Sherman's March*, 136-137; Sherman, *Memoirs*, 727.

(69) Drago, "Sherman's March Through Georgia," 372.

(70) Byrne, "'Uncle Billy' Sherman," 112.

(71) Ibid.

(72) Ibid., 108-109.

CHAPTER VIII
BLACK MEN IN GRAY?

(1) Richard E. Beringer, et al., *Why the South Lost the Civil War* (Athens: University of Georgia Press, 1986), 370-371.

(2) Ibid., 370; Phillip D. Dillard, "The Confederate Debate over Arming Slaves: Views from Macon and Augusta Newspapers," *Georgia Historical Quarterly* 79 (1), 120 (Spring 1995).

(3) Dillard, "Confederate Debate," 121.

(4) Ibid., 122-123.

(5) Ibid., 124.

(6) Ibid., 129.

(7) Beringer, et al., *Why the South Lost*, 373; Lee to Andrew Hunter, January 11, 1865, *The War of Rebellion: A Compilation of the Official Records of the Union and Confederate Armies* (Washington, D.C.: U.S. Government Printing Office, 1880–1901), ser. 4, vol. 3, 1012-13.

(8) Carter G. Woodson, ed., "The Employment of Negroes as Soldiers in the Confederate Army," *Journal of Negro History* 4 (1919), 249.

(9) Mohr, *Threshold of Freedom,* 278-279; Dillard, "Confederate Debate," 145.

(10) Beringer, et al., *Why the South Lost*, 383-384.

(11) Cobb to James A. Seddon, January 8, 1865, *The War of Rebellion*, ser. 4, vol. 3, 1009.

(12) Beringer, et al., *Why the South Lost*, 372-373.

(13) William Oates, *The War Between the Union and the Confederacy* (New York: Neale Publishing Company, 1905), 501.

(14) Ibid.

(15) Ibid., 506.

(16) Mohr, *Threshold of Freedom*, 284. Additional details regarding the

Southern debate over black enlistment in the Confederate army can be garnered from two books that often lack historical objectivity but are helpful in documenting the participation of blacks in the Southern war effort. Robert F. Durden's *The Gray and the Black: The Confederate Debate on Emancipation* (Baton Rouge: Louisiana State University Press, 1972) and *Black Southerners in Gray*, edited by Richard Rollins (Redondo Beach, CA: Rank and File Publications, 1994), are limited by the distinctly "Southern bias" of the authors.

(17) Beringer, et al., *Why the South Lost*, 371.

(18) Michael L. Thurmond, *A Story Untold: Black Men and Women in Athens History,* 2nd ed. (Athens: Green Berry Press, 2001), 4; Ella Gertrude Clanton Thomas, May 7, 1865, *The Secret Eye: The Journal of Ella Gertrude Clanton Thomas, 1848-1889*, edited by Virginia Ingraham Burr (Chapel Hill: University of North Carolina Press, 1990).

(19) C. Mildred Thompson, *Reconstruction in Georgia* (Atlanta: Cherokee Publishing Company, 1971), 137; Alan Conway, *The Reconstruction of Georgia* (Minneapolis: University of Minnesota Press, 1966), 26.

(20) Thompson, *Reconstruction in Georgia*, 45-47; Thurmond, *A Story Untold*, 14; Owens, "Negro in Georgia," 25.

(21) Robert S. Gamble, "Athens: The Study of a Georgia Town During Reconstruction," (M.A. thesis, University of Georgia, 1965), 31; *Southern Watchman*, August 16, 1865.

(22) Thurmond, *A Story Untold*, 10.

(23) Owens, "Negro in Georgia," 89; Eliza Frances Andrews, *The War-Time Journal of a Georgia Girl, 1864-1865*, Spencer Bidwell King Jr., ed. (Macon, GA: Ardivan Press, 1960), 322.

(24) Thurmond, *A Story Untold*, 10, note 24a; Owens, "Negro in Georgia," 91.

(25) Conway, *Reconstruction of Georgia*, 76-77; Kenneth M. Stampp, *The Era of Reconstruction, 1865-1877* (New York: Alfred A. Knopf, 1972), 131.

(26) Jacqueline Jones, *Soldiers of Light and Love: Northern Teachers and Georgia Blacks, 1865-1873* (Athens: University of Georgia Press, 1992), 73-75; Conway, *Reconstruction of Georgia,* 86-87.

(27) Owens, "Negro in Georgia," 150; Conway, *Reconstruction of Georgia*, 86-

87; Jones, *Soldiers of Light*, 73-75; W. E. Burghardt Du Bois, *Black Reconstruction in America, 1860-1880* (New York: Macmillan Publishing Company, 1962), 644-645.

(28) Conway, *Reconstruction of Georgia*, 86-87; Jones, *Soldiers of Light*, 73-75.

(29) Jones, *Soldiers of Light*, 73-75.

(30) Owens, "Negro in Georgia," 151-153.

(31) Ibid., 38.

(32) Stampp, *Era of Reconstruction*, 125.

(33) Owens, "Negro in Georgia," 38-40.

(34) Byrne, "'Uncle Billy' Sherman," 113.

(35) Thurmond, *A Story Untold*, 18-19; Conway, *Reconstruction of Georgia*, 72.

(36) Owens, "Negro in Georgia," 24.

(37) Gamble, "Athens," 35; Howell Cobb Collection, September 15–November 21, 1865, University of Georgia Library.

(38) *Macon Daily Telegraph*, August 24, 1865.

(39) Conway, *Reconstruction of Georgia*, 40-48.

(40) Ibid.

(41) Ibid.

(42) Ibid., 52-54.

(43) Ibid., 54-55.

(44) Ibid., 56-59.

(45) Owens, "Negro in Georgia," 45-47.

BIBLIOGRAPHY

PRIMARY SOURCES

MANUSCRIPTS

Brown, Joseph E. Papers. Felix Hargrett Collection, University of Georgia Library.

Howell Cobb Collection, University of Georgia Library.

Egmont Papers. University of Georgia Library.

GOVERNMENT DOCUMENTS

Chatham County, Georgia. *Registry of Free Persons of Color*.

Georgia. *House Journal*.

Georgia. *Senate Journal*.

Georgia. *Journal of the Proceedings of the Convention of the People of*

Georgia. Milledgeville, October-November 1865.

Georgia General Assembly. *Acts.*

Georgia Supreme Court. *Reports.*

Official Records of the Union and Confederate Navies in the War of the Rebellion. 30 vols. Washington, D.C.: U.S. Government Printing Office, 1894–1927.

The War of Rebellion: A Compilation of the Official Records of the Union and Confederate Armies. 70 vols. in 128 parts. Washington, D.C.: U.S. Government Printing Office, 1880–1901.

U.S. Bureau of the Census. *Inhabitants of the United States.* Washington, D.C.: U.S. Government Printing Office, 1790–1860.

U.S. Congress. *The New American State Papers: Labor and Slavery.* 1st Session, 1st Congress to Session, 35th Congress, 2nd Series, vol. 5: Foreign Relations, 1858.

NEWSPAPERS

Augusta Chronicle and Sentinel
Augusta Constitutionalist
Boston Journal
Boston Evening Journal
Charleston Mercury
Chicago Tribune
Christian Recorder (Macon, GA)
Christian Index (Macon, GA)
Columbus Enquirer

Georgia Gazette

Louisiana Gazette

Macon Telegraph and Confederate

Massachusetts Gazette

Mobile Register

Nation

National Intelligencer

New Bedford Mercury

New Orleans Gazette

New South (Port Royal, SC)

New York Herald

New York Post

New York Tribune

New York Times

New York World

Savannah Daily Morning News

Savannah Republican

Southern Banner (Athens, GA)

Southern Watchman (Athens, GA)

SECONDARY SOURCES

BOOKS

American Colonization Society. *The African Repository and Georgia Journal*. New York: Kraus Reprint Corporation, 1967.

Andrews, Eliza Frances. *The War-Time Journal of a Georgia Girl, 1864–1865*. Edited by Spencer Bidwell King Jr. Macon, GA: Ardivan Press, 1960.

Aptheker, Herbert. *To Be Free*. New York: First Carol Publishing

Group, 1991.

Baine, Rodney, ed. *The Publications of James Edward Oglethorpe.* Athens: University of Georgia Press, 1994.

Barrow, Charles Kelly, J. W. Segars and R. B. Rosenburg. *Forgotten Confederates: An Anthology about Black Southerners.* Atlanta: Southern Heritage Press, 1995.

Bennett, Lerone, Jr. *Forced into Glory: Abraham Lincoln's White Dream.* Chicago: Johnson Publishing Company, 2000.

Bergman, Peter M. and Jean McCarroll. *Negro in the Congressional Record, 1789-1801.* New York: Bergman, 1969.

Beringer, Richard E., Herman Hattaway, Archer Jones, and William N. Still Jr. *Why the South Lost the Civil War.* Athens: University of Georgia Press, 1986.

Berlin, Ira and Ronald Hoffman, eds. *Slavery and Freedom in the Age of the American Revolution.* Charlottesville: University Press of Virginia, 1983.

Berlin, Ira. *Slaves without Masters: The Free Negro in the Antebellum South.* New York: Pantheon Books, 1974.

Black, Clinton V. *History of Jamaica.* Kingston: Longman Group UK, 1983.

Blight, David W. *Frederick Douglass' Civil War: Keeping Faith in Jubilee.* Baton Rouge: Louisiana State University Press, 1989.

Bluett, Thomas. *Some Memoirs of the Life of Job, the Son of Solomon the*

High Priest of Boonda in Africa. London, 1734.

Boney, F. N. *A Pictorial History: The University of Georgia*. Athens: University of Georgia Press, 1984.

————. *Slave Life in Georgia: A Narrative of the Life, Sufferings, and Escape of John Brown, A Fugitive Slave, Now in England*. Savannah: Beehive Press, 1991.

————. *Rebel Georgia*. Macon, GA: Mercer University Press, 1997.

Bowen, Catherine Drinker. *Miracle at Philadelphia: The Story of the Constitutional Convention: May to September 1787*. Boston: Little, Brown & Company, 1966.

Brooks, Walter H. *The Silver Bluff Church: A History of Negro Baptist Churches in America*. Washington, D.C.: Press of R. L. Pendleton, 1910.

Brown, Sterling A., Arthur P. Davis, and Ulysses Lee. *The Negro Caravan*. New York: Citadel Press, 1941.

Brown, William Welles. *The Negro in the American Rebellion: His Heroism and Fidelity*. Boston: Lee & Sheppard, 1867.

Bruce, Henry. *The Life of Oglethorpe*. New York: Dodd, Meade & Company, 1890.

Buckmaster, Henrietta. *The Seminole Wars*. New York: Macmillan Company, 1966.

Bullard, Mary. *Black Liberation on Cumberland Island in 1815*. South Dartmouth, MA: M. R. Bullard, 1983.

Candler, Allan, ed. *The Colonial Records of the State of Georgia.* Washington, D.C.: National Park Service, United States Department of the Interior, 1942.

Cashin, Edward J. *Old Springfield: Race and Religion in Augusta, Georgia.* Augusta: Springfield Village Park Foundation, 1995.

————. *The Story of Augusta.* Spartanburg, SC: Reprint Company, Publishers, 1991.

Coleman, Kenneth. *The American Revolution in Georgia, 1763-1789.* Athens: University of Georgia Press, 1958.

————, gen. ed. *A History of Georgia.* Athens: University of Georgia Press, 1977.

Collier, Christopher and James Collier. *Decision in Philadelphia: The Constitutional Convention of 1787.* New York: Ballantine Press, 1986.

Conway, Alan. *The Reconstruction of Georgia.* Minneapolis: University of Minnesota Press, 1966.

Cornish, Dudley Taylor. *The Sable Arm: Black Troops in the Union Army, 1861-1865.* Lawrence, KS: University of Kansas Press, 1956.

Coulter, E. Merton. *Thomas Spalding of Sapelo.* Baton Rouge: Louisiana State University Press, 1940.

Covington, James W. *The Seminoles of Florida.* Gainesville: University Press of Florida, 1993.

Davis, Burke. *Sherman's March.* New York: Vintage Books, 1980.

Davis, David Brion. *The Problem of Slavery in Western Culture*. Ithaca: Cornell University Press, 1988.

Davis, Harold E. *The Fledgling Province: Social and Cultural Life in Colonial Georgia, 1733-1776*. Chapel Hill: University of North Carolina Press, 1976.

Danson, William C. *A Compilation of the Laws of the State of Georgia*. Milledgeville, GA: Grantland & Orme, 1831.

Dillon, Merton L. *Slavery Attacked: Southern Slaves and Their Allies, 1619-1865*. Baton Rouge: Louisiana State University Press, 1990.

Drimmer, Melvin. *Black History: A Reappraisal*. Garden City, NY: Doubleday & Company, 1968.

Du Bois, W. E. Burghardt. *The Suppression of the African Slave-Trade to the United States of America, 1638-1870*. New York: Social Science Press, 1954.

———. *Black Reconstruction in America, 1860-1880*. New York: Macmillan Publishing Company, 1962.

———. *The Souls of Black Folks*. New York: New American Library, 1969.

Durden, Robert F. *The Gray and the Black: The Confederate Debate on Emancipation*. Baton Rouge: Louisiana State University Press, 1972.

Finley, Robert. *Thoughts on the Colonization of Free Blacks*. Washington, D.C., s. n.: 1816.

Foner, Jack D. *Blacks and the Military in American History*. New York:

Praeger Publishers, 1974.

Forbes, Jack D. *Africans and Native Americans: The Language of Race in the Evolution of Red-Black People*. Urbana: University of Illinois Press, 1988.

Force, Peter. *American Archives*. 6th ser. New York: Johnson Reprint Corporation, 1972.

Fox, Early Lee. *The American Colonization Society, 1817-1840*. Baltimore: Johns Hopkins Press, 1919.

Franklin, John Hope. *From Slavery to Freedom: A History of Negro Americans*. 5th ed. New York: Alfred A. Knopf, 1980.

Frey, Sylvia. *Water From the Rock: Black Resistance in a Revolutionary Age*. Princeton: Princeton University Press, 1991.

Giddings, Joshua R. *The Exiles of Florida or The crimes committed by our government against the maroons, who fled from South Carolina and other slave states, seeking protection under Spanish laws*. Baltimore: Black Classic Press, 1997.

Gilmer, George. *Sketches of Some of the First Settlers of Upper Georgia*. Americus, GA: Americus Book Company, 1926.

Goodwine, Marquetta L. *The Legacy of Ibo Landing: Gullah Roots of African-American Culture*. Atlanta: Clarity Press, 1998.

Grant, Donald L. *The Way It Was in the South: The Black Experience in Georgia*. New York: Carol Publishing Group, 1993.

Grant, Douglas. *The Fortunate Slave*. New York: Oxford University

Press, 1968.

Griffin, J. David. *Georgia and the United States Constitution, 1787-1789*. Atlanta: Georgia Commission for the National Bicentennial Celebration and the Georgia Department of Education, 1977.

Greenberg, Martin H. and Charles G. Waugh, eds. *The Price of Freedom: Slavery and the Civil War*. Nashville: Cumberland House, 2000.

Harding, Vincent. *There Is a River: The Black Struggle for Freedom in America*. San Diego: Harcourt Brace & Company, 1981.

Higginbotham, A. Leon, Jr. *In the Matter of Color: Race and the American Legal Process, the Colonial Period*. New York: Oxford University Press, 1978.

Higginson, Thomas Wentworth. *Army Life in a Black Regiment*. New York: W. W. Norton & Company, 1984.

Hornsby, Alton, Jr. *The Negro in Revolutionary Georgia*. Atlanta: Georgia Commission for the National Bicentennial Celebration and Georgia Department of Education, 1977.

Horton, James Oliver and Lois E. Horton. *A History of the African-American People*. London: Salamander Books, 1995.

Horton, James Oliver. *Free People of Color: Inside the African-American Community*. Washington: Smithsonian Institution Press, 1993.

Hoskins, Charles Lwanga. *Black Episcopalians in Georgia: Strife, Struggle and Salvation*. Savannah, GA: Self Published, 1980.

Hughes, Langston and Milton Meltzer. *A Pictorial History of the Negro in America*. New York: Crown Publishers, 1963.

Jackson, Harvey H. and Phinizy Spalding. *Forty Years of Diversity: Essays on Colonial Georgia*. Athens: University of Georgia Press, 1984.

Jones, Jacqueline. *Soldiers of Light and Love: Northern Teachers and Georgia Blacks, 1865-1875*. Athens: University of Georgia Press, 1992.

Jones, Maxine D. and Kevin M. McCarthy. *African Americans in Florida*. Sarasota: Pineapple Press, 1993.

Jordan, Lewis G. *Negro Baptist History, U.S.A.* Nashville: Sunday School Publishing Board, N.B.C., 1930.

Jordan, Winthrop D. *White over Black: American Attitudes Toward the Negro, 1550-1812*. Chapel Hill: University of North Carolina Press, 1968.

Kaplan, Sidney and Emma Nogrady Kaplan. *The Black Presence in the Era of the American Revolution*. Amherst: University of Massachusetts Press, 1989.

Katz, William Loren and Paula A. Franklin. *Proudly Red and Black: Stories of African and Native Americans*. New York: Macmillan Publishing Company, Atheneum, 1993.

Katz, William Loren. *Black Indians: A Hidden Heritage*. New York: Macmillan Publishing Company, Atheneum, 1986.

Ketcham, Ralph, ed. *The Anti-Federalist Papers and the Constitutional Convention Debates*. New York: New American Library, A Mentor

Book, 1986.

King, Spencer B., Jr. *Darien: The Death and Rebirth of a Southern Town*. Macon, GA: Mercer University Press, 1981.

Lamar, Lucius Q. *A Compilation of the Laws of the State of Georgia Passed by the Legislature since the Year 1810 to the Year 1819*. Augusta: T. S. Hannon, 1822.

Landers, Jane. *Fort Mose: Gracia Real de Santa Teresa de Mose: A Free Black Town in Spanish Colonial Florida*. St. Augustine, FL: St. Augustine Historical Society, 1992.

Lane, Mills. *General Oglethorpe's Georgia*. 2 vols. Savannah: Beehive Press, 1990.

Lengyel, Cornel. *Four Days in July*. Garden City, NY: Doubleday Company, 1958.

Littlefield, Daniel F., Jr. *Africans and Seminoles: From Removal to Emancipation*. Westport, CT: Greenwood Press, 1977.

Livermore, George. *Opinions of the Founders of the Republic on Negroes as Slaves, as Citizens, and as Soldiers*. Boston: A. Williams & Company, 1863.

Locke, Mary Stroughton. *Anti-Slavery in America*. Gloucester: Radcliffe College Monographs Noll, 1965.

Lovell, Caroline Couper. *The Golden Isles of Georgia*. Boston: Little, Brown & Company, 1932.

MacGregor, Morris J. and Bernard C. Nalty, eds. *Blacks in the United*

States Armed Forces: Basic Documents. Wilmington, DE: Scholarly Resources, 1981.

Magdol, Edward. *A Right to Land, Essays on the Freedmen's Community.* Westport, CT: Greenwood Press, 1977.

Mahon, John K. *History of the Second Seminole War, 1835-1842.* Rev. ed. Gainesville: University of Florida Press, 1967.

———. *The War of 1812.* Gainesville: University of Florida Press, 1972.

Martyn, Benjamin. *Reasons for Establishing the Colony of Georgia in America.* London: W. Meadows, 1733.

McCall, Hugh. *The History of Georgia: Containing Brief Sketches of the Most Remarkable Events up to the Present Day.* Atlanta: A. B. Caldwell, 1909.

McPherson, James M. *The Negro's Civil War: How American Negroes Felt and Acted During the War for the Union.* New York: Pantheon Books, 1965.

———. *Marching Toward Freedom: Blacks in the Civil War, 1861-1865.* New York: Facts On File, 1991.

Miller, Randal M. and John Davis Smith. *Dictionary of Afro-American Slavery.* New York: Greenwood Press, 1988.

Miller, Stephen F. *Bench and Bar of Georgia: Memoirs and Sketches.* Philadelphia: J. B. Lippincott & Co., 1858.

Mohr, Clarence L. *On the Threshold of Freedom: Masters and Slaves in*

Civil War Georgia. Athens: University of Georgia Press, 1986.

Moore, George H. *Historical Notes on the Employment of Negroes in the American Army of the Revolution*. New York: C. T. Evans, 1862.

Moseley, J. Edward. *Disciples of Christ in Christ*. St. Louis: Bethany Press, 1954.

Mulroy, Kevin. *Freedom on the Border: Seminole Maroons in Florida, the Indian Territory, Coahuila, and Texas*. Lubbock, TX: Texas Tech University Press, 1993.

Oates, William. *The War Between the Union and the Confederacy*. New York: Neale Publishing Company, 1905.

Oubre, Claude F. *Forty Acres and a Mule: The Freedmen's Bureau and Black Land Ownership*. Baton Rouge: Louisiana State University Press, 1978.

Patrick, Rembert W. *Florida Fiasco: Rampant Rebels on the Georgia-Florida Border, 1810-1815*. Athens: University of Georgia Press, 1954.

Peters, Virginia Berman. *The Florida Wars*. Hamden, CT: Archon Books, 1979.

Phillips, U. B., ed. *Plantation and Frontier Documents*. Cleveland: A. H. Clark Company, 1909.

———. *American Negro Slavery: A Survey of the Supply, Employment and Control of Negro Labor as Determined by the Plantation Regime*. Baton Rouge: Louisiana University Press, 1918.

Porter, Kenneth. *The Black Seminoles: History of a Freedom-Seeking*

People. Gainesville: University Press of Florida, 1996.

———. *The Negro on the American Frontier.* New York: Arno Press, 1971. Qpala, Joseph A. *A Brief History of the Seminole Freedmen.* Austin: African and Afro-American Studies and Research Center, University of Texas at Austin, 1980.

Quarles, Benjamin. *Lincoln and the Negro.* New York: Oxford University Press, 1962.

———. *The Negro in the American Revolution.* New York: W. W. Norton & Company, 1961.

———. *The Negro in the Civil War.* New York: Da Capo Press, 1953.

Rice, C. Duncan. *The Rise and Fall of Black Slavery.* New York: Harper Row, 1975.

Rollins, Richard, ed. *Black Southerners in Gray.* Redondo Beach, CA: Rank and File Publications, 1994.

Scarborough, Ruth. *The Opposition to Slavery in Georgia Prior to 1860.* Nashville: George Peabody College for Teachers, 1933.

Sherman, William Tecumseh. *Memoirs of General W. T. Sherman.* New York: Library of America, 1990.

Simmons, William Haynes. *Notices of East Florida.* Gainesville: University of Florida Press, 1973.

Sims, James M. *The First Colored Baptist Church in North America.* New York: Negro Universities Press, 1969.

Smith, Julia Floyd. *Slavery and Rice Culture in Low-Country Georgia, 1750-1860.* Knoxville: University of Tennessee Press, 1985.

Sobel, Mechal. *Trabelin' On: The Slave Journey to an Afro Baptist Faith.* Princeton: Princeton University Press, 1979.

Spalding, Phinizy and Edwin L. Jackson. *James Edward Oglethorpe: A New Look at Georgia's Founder.* Athens: Carl Vinson Institute of Government, University of Georgia, 1988.

Spalding, Phinizy and Harvey H. Jackson, eds. *Oglethorpe in Perspective: Georgia's Founder after Two Hundred Years.* Tuscaloosa: University of Alabama Press, 1989.

Stampp, Kenneth M. *The Era of Reconstruction, 1865-1877.* New York: Alfred A. Knopf, 1972.

Sullivan, Buddy. *Early Days on the Georgia Tidewater: The Story of McIntosh County & Sapelo.* Darien, GA: McIntosh County Board of Commissioners, 1990.

Taylor, Susie King. *A Black Woman's Civil War Memoirs.* Princeton: Markus Wiener Publishers, 1994.

Thomas, Ella Gertrude Clanton. *The Secret Eye: The Journal of Ella Gertrude Clanton Thomas, 1848-1889.* Edited by Virginia Ingraham Burr. Chapel Hill: University of North Carolina Press, 1990.

Thompson, C. Mildred. *Reconstruction in Georgia.* Atlanta: Cherokee Publishing Company, 1971.

Thurmond, Michael L. *A Story Untold: Black Men and Women in Athens History.* 2nd ed. Athens: Green Berry Press, 2001.

Trudeau, Noah Andre. *Like Men of War: Black Troops in the Civil War, 1862-1865*. Boston: Little, Brown & Company, 1998.

Vetter, Charles Edmund. *Sherman: Merchant Terror, Advocate of Peace*. Gretna, LA: Pelican Publishing Company, 1992.

Wagner, Clarence M. *Profiles of Black Georgia Baptists*. Gainesville, GA: Bennett Brothers Printing Company, 1980.

Walker, James St. G. *The Black Loyalists: The Search for a Promised Land in Nova Scotia and Sierra Leone, 1783–1870*. New York: African Publishing Company, 1976.

White, Ronald C. *Lincoln's Greatest Speech: The Second Inaugural*. New York: Simon & Schuster, 2002.

Wilson, Joseph T. *The Black Phalanx: African American Soldiers in the War of Independence, the War of 1812 and the Civil War*. New York: Da Capo Press, 1994.

Wood, Betty. *Slavery in Colonial Georgia, 1730-1775*. Athens: University of Georgia Press, 1984.

Wright, J. Leitch. *The Only Land They Knew: American Indians in the Old South*. Lincoln: University of Nebraska Press, 1999.

Wylly, Charles Spalding. *The Seed That Was Sown in the Colony of Georgia: The Harvest and the Aftermath*. New York: Neale Publishing Company, 1910.

ARTICLES

Bellamy, Donnie D. "The Legal Status of Black Georgians During the Colonial and Revolutionary Eras." *Journal of Negro History* 74 (Winter-Autumn, 1989): 1-10.

Byrne, William A. "'Uncle Billy' Sherman Comes to Town: The Free Winter of Black Savannah." *Georgia Historical Quarterly* 79 (1): 91-116 (Spring 1995).

Dillard, Phillip D. "The Confederate Debate Over Arming Slaves: Views from Macon and Augusta Newspapers." *Georgia Historical Quarterly* 79 (1): 117-146 (Spring 1995).

Drago, Edmund L. "How Sherman's March Through Georgia Affected the Slaves." *Georgia Historical Quarterly* 57 (3): 361-375 (1973).

Fant, H. B. "The Labor Policy of the Trustees." *Georgia Historical Quarterly* 16 (1): 1-3.

Farley, Foster M. "The South Carolina Negro in the American Revolution, 1775-1783." *South Carolina Historical Magazine* 79 (April 1978): 75-86.

Finkelman, Paul. "A Covenant with Death." *American Visions* (May-June 1986): Pts. 1 and 2, 21-27.

Flanders, Ralph B. "The Free Negro in Ante-Bellum Georgia." *North Carolina Historical Review* 9 (January-October 1932): 250-272.

Garrison, Webb. "Sudden Death at Ebenezer Creek." *Georgia Journal* (Spring 1995): 31-34.

Gifford, James M. "Emily Tubman and the African Colonization Movement in Georgia." *Georgia Historical Quarterly* 61 (1), 12 (Spring 1975).

James, Josef C. "Sherman at Savannah." *Journal of Negro History* 39: 1/4 (January/October 1954): 127-137.

Johnson, Whittington B. "Free African-American Women in Savannah, 1800-1860: Affluence and Autonomy Amid Adversity." *Georgia Historical Quarterly* 76 (2): 260-283 (Summer 1992).

———. "Free Blacks in Antebellum Savannah: An Economic Profile." *Georgia Historical Quarterly* 64 (4): 418-431 (Spring 1980).

Lawrence, James B. "Religious Education of the Negro in the Colony of Georgia." *Georgia Historical Quarterly* 14 (1): 41-57 (March 1930).

McLoughlin, William G. "Red Indians, Black Slavery and White Racism: America's Slaveholding Indians." *American Quarterly* 26 (October 1974): 567.

Marshall, Thurgood. "Reflections on the Bicentennial of the Constitution." *American Visions* (August 1987): 26-27.

Porter, Kenneth Wiggins. "Florida Slaves and Free Negroes in the Seminole War, 1835-1842." *Journal of Negro History* 28 (October 1943): 390.

Riddell, William Renwick. "Slavery in Canada." *Journal of Negro History* 5 (3): 375 (July 1920).

Tucker, Phillip Thomas. "John Horse: Forgotten African-American

Leader of the Second Seminole War." *Journal of Negro History* 77 (Spring 1992): 74-84.

Wax, Darold Duane. "Georgia and the Negro before the American Revolution." *Georgia Historical Quarterly* 51 (1): 63-77 (March 1967).

Woodson, Carter G., ed. "Free Negro Owners of Slaves in the United States in 1830." *Journal of Negro History* 9 (1924): 41-47.
———, ed. "Dispatches of Spanish Officials Bearing on the Free Negro Settlement of Garcia Real de Santa Teresa de Mose, Florida." *Journal of Negro History* 9 (1924): 144 –195.

———, ed. "Letters Showing the Rise and Progress of the Early Negro Churches of Georgia and the West Indies." *Journal of Negro History* 1 (1916): 69-92.

———, ed. "The Employment of Negroes as Soldiers in the Confederate Army." *Journal of Negro History* 4 (1919): 239-253.

THESES, DISSERTATIONS, AND OTHER MATERIALS

Anthony, Marion Ernestine. "The Unindexed Official Record of the Negro in Georgia, 1733-1766." M.A. thesis, Atlanta University, 1937.

Ellis, Reverend Edward L. Jr. "Bicentennial Celebration: Historic First Bryan Baptist Church." Church program, Savannah, 1988.

Gamble, Robert S. "Athens: The Study of a Georgia Town During Reconstruction." M.A. thesis, University of Georgia, 1965.

Gifford, James M. "The African Colonization Movement in

Georgia, 1817-1860." Ph.D. diss., University of Georgia, 1977.

Hendricks, George. "Union Army Occupation of the Southern Seaboard, 1861-1865." Ph.D. diss., Columbia University, 1954.

Martin, Reverend Emmett T. "Historical Book: Springfield Baptist Church, 1787-1979." Church program, Augusta, 1979.

Morgan, David Taft, Jr. "The Great Awakening in the Carolinas and Georgia, 1740-1775." Ph.D. diss., University of North Carolina, 1969.

Owens, James Leggette. "The Negro in Georgia During Reconstruction, 1864-1872: A Social History." Ph.D. diss., University of Georgia, 1975.

Ready, Milton L. "An Economic History of Colonial Georgia, 1732-1754." Ph.D. diss., University of Georgia, 1970.

Tillman, Reverend Thurmond. "The First African Baptist Church History." Church program, Savannah, 1989.

Ungar, Helen. "Free Negroes in Ante-Bellum Georgia." M.A. thesis, University of Georgia, 1949.

INDEX

Page numbers in italics refer to illustrations.